POPULAR RADICALISM IN NINETEENTH-CENTURY BRITAIN

D1354017

Social History in Perspective

General Editor: Jeremy Black

Social History in Perspective is a series of in-depth studies of the many topics in social, cultural and religious history.

PUBLISHED

John Belchem *Popular Radicalism in Nineteenth-Century Britain*
Sue Bruley *Women in Britain Since 1900*
Anthony Brundage *The English Poor Laws, 1700–1930*
Simon Dentith *Society and Cultural Forms in Nineteenth-Century England*
Joyce M. Ellis *The Georgian Town, 1680–1840*
Peter Fleming *Family and Household in Medieval England*
Kathryn Gleadle *British Women in the Nineteenth Century*
Harry Goulbourne *Race Relations in Britain since 1945*
Anne Hardy *Health and Medicine in Britain since 1860*
Tim Hitchcock *English Sexualities, 1700–1800*
Sybil M. Jack *Towns in Tudor and Stuart Britain*
Helen M. Jewell *Education in Early Modern England*
Alan Kidd *State, Society and the Poor in Nineteenth-Century England*
Arthur J. McIvor *A History of Work in Britain, 1880–1950*
Hugh McLeod *Religion and Society in England, 1850–1914*
Donald M. MacRaild *Irish Migrants in Modern Britain, 1750–1922*
Donald M. MacRaild and David E. Martin *Labour in Britain, 1830–1914*
Christopher Marsh *Popular Religion in the Sixteenth Century*
Michael A. Mullett *Catholics in Britain and Ireland, 1558–1829*
Richard Rex *The Lollards*
George Robb *British Culture and the First World War*
R.Malcolm Smuts *Culture and Power in England, 1585–1685*
John Spurr *English Puritanism, 1603–1689*
W.B. Stephens *Education in Britain, 1750–1914*
Heather Swanson *Medieval British Towns*
David Taylor *Crime, Policing and Punishment in England, 1750–1914*
N.L. Tranter *British Population in the Twentieth Century*
Ian D. Whyte *Migration and Society in Britain, 1550–1830*
Ian D. Whyte *Scotland's Society and Economy in Transition, c.1500–c.1760*
Andy Wood *Riot, Rebellion and Popular Politics in Early Modern England*

Please note that a sister series, *British History in Perspective*, is available, covering key topics in British political history.

Social History in Perspective
Series Standing Order
ISBN 0–333–71694–9 hardcover
ISBN 0–333–69336–1 paperback
(outside North America only)

You can receive future titles in this series as they are published by placing a standing order. Please contact your bookseller or, in case of difficulty, write to us at the address below with your name and address, the title of the series and the ISBN quoted above.

Customer Services Department, Palgrave Ltd
Houndmills, Basingstoke, Hampshire RG21 6XS, England

POPULAR RADICALISM IN NINETEENTH-CENTURY BRITAIN

JOHN BELCHEM

Published by
PALGRAVE
Houndmills, Basingstoke, Hampshire RG21 6XS and
175 Fifth Avenue, New York, N. Y. 10010
Companies and representatives throughout the world

PALGRAVE is the new global academic imprint of
St. Martin's Press LLC Scholarly and Reference Division and
Palgrave Publishers Ltd (formerly Macmillan Press Ltd).

Outside North America
ISBN 0–333–56574–6 hardcover
ISBN 0–333–56575–4 paperback

Inside North America
ISBN 0–312–15799–1 hardcover
ISBN 0–312–15806–8 paperback

This book is printed on paper suitable for recycling and
made from fully managed and sustained forest sources.

A catalogue record for this book is available
from the British Library.

Cataloging-in-Publication Data is available
from the Library of Congress.

Transferred to digital printing 2002
Printed and bound in Great Britain by
Antony Rowe Ltd, Chippenham and Eastbourne

CONTENTS

WITHDRAWN

ACKNOWLEDGEMENTS

As much has been compressed in this brief study of radicalism in the 'long' nineteenth century, I must apologize to those scholars whose work I have misrepresented, overlooked or acknowledged inadequately. In the notes and the Guide to Further Reading I endeavour to clear some of my vast burden of intellectual debt. An old friend, Richard Price, and a new colleague, Jon Lawrence, have put me straight on a number of key issues, helping me to retain some semblance of balance and historical sanity, the 'linguistic turn' notwithstanding. Mary-Rose, my partner in radicalism, has done much to improve the quality of the argument.

Liverpool   J. B.

INTRODUCTION

Radicalism in nineteenth-century Britain was a political project with a number of programmes, differing for the most part only in detail, presentation and appeal. Important as these differences were, there was an underlying commitment to the essential features of British political culture. Whether they wished to go back to the roots (the literal meaning of radicalism) or to return to first principles (which might suggest a complete rejection of the past), radicals sought almost without exception to extend and redefine, not to challenge and subvert, the proud political heritage of constitutional rights and parliamentary government. Throughout the period under study, this 'constitutionalist idiom' – and the particular history it embodied – served to identify and distinguish competing political groups.[1] Conservatives imbued the constitution with the force of established law and divine providence: as upheld in the Glorious Revolution and the Act of Settlement, it had delivered England from popery, poverty and disorder. Radicals were inspired by a different reading, a history of recovery and resistance in which the constitution confirmed the sovereignty of the people and the contingent authority of parliament. The liberal version of constitutional history grew steadily in influence: a chronicle of progressive improvements founded on the concepts of liberty and tolerance, it justified continued but moderate reform.

Although essentially political in language and values, nineteenth-century radicalism has generally been interpreted by historians in socio-economic terms, as the means by which the expanding middle and working classes of urban-industrial Britain sought to attain their respective 'class' interests. United in radical opposition to aristocratic privilege and 'Old Corruption', the 'useful classes' pursued (whether consciously or not) conflicting 'ideological' aims. The middle class advocated parliamentary reform to hasten the free-market 'entrepreneurial ideal', while the working class looked to a reformed parliament to protect their living standards against economic deregulation and laissez-faire. Seen in these socio-economic terms, radicalism thus served to mediate either class harmony and/or class conflict, controversial issues of debate which dominated and enlivened traditional historiography.[2] Class, however, has now fallen from favour. Dubious of the priority traditionally accorded to socio-economic factors, and increasingly aware of the fluidity of social identities (whether class, gender, ethnic, national, sectarian or whatever), historians are exploring a new political and cultural agenda. The purpose of this short study is to provide a critical introduction to these latest approaches.

Of the various factors which have contributed to the demise of socio-economic interpretation and class-based narratives of radicalism, two require brief mention here. First, the recent (or 'fourth-generation') reassessment of the 'industrial revolution', reduced in some revisionist calculations and perspectives almost to myth.[3] A diverse range of manufacturing structures coexisted across and within industries as proto-industrialization led to industrial growth in some regions and to deindustrialization in others. The transition to 'machinofacture', to highly mechanized, factory-based mass-production industry, was cautious and protracted, far from complete by the 1840s when over 75 per cent of manufacturing remained in unmodernized industries, small in scale, little affected by the use of steam power and characterized neither by high productivity nor by comparative advantage.[4] In the absence of a sudden and dramatic 'take-off', the first industrial revolution no longer serves as the paradigm of modernization, the historical guide to economic development. A slow-moving and multi-dimensional process of combined and uneven development, industrialization in Britain was accompanied by such a diversity of material experience that a united or 'class' response by workers was seemingly precluded. In the absence of common experience, appeals to working-class solidarity – however much they might impress historians – lacked resonance and purchase.

The questioning of class, however, is by no means a peculiarity of British economic historiography. It is symptomatic of a wider *fin de siècle* political revisionism. 'Across the "developed" industrial world', Robbie Gray has noted, 'class as an organizing and legitimizing political identity no longer has the assured place it once (and quite recently) seemed to occupy; while observers of all persuasions have been disoriented by the swift and remorseless collapse of regimes of avowedly Marxist inspiration, and the fragmentation of both liberalism and social democracy in the absence of the communist "other"'.[5] In its most strident and iconoclastic form, however, the decentring of class derives less from empirical revisionism and political disorientation than from the embrace of post-modernist theory, the second factor which requires some brief introductory (but alas jargon-ridden) comment.

Where revisionist historians have increasingly recognized the diffuse and plural nature of social relations and identities, post-modernists have privileged such notions as complexity, diversity, fragmentation, relativity, multiplicity and discontinuity. Dismissing class-based (and other) grand historical narratives – along with the allegedly totalizing, system-building, intellectual theories of modernism – post-modernist historians insist on the primacy of language and discourse. As post-structuralists, their interest is in the 'representational', in the construction of identity and social reality through language and discourse.[6] Fortunately, however, most practitioners of the 'linguistic turn' stop short of linguistic determinism or its semiotic deconstruction into arbitrariness and aporia, into 'an anti-system

3

challenging the very possibility of objective knowledge'.[7] Shorn of post-structuralist fervour, the engagement with critical theory has led historians to appreciate the complex interaction of language and social structure, to examine more thoroughly the link between structure and action, the medium between material conditions and consciousness. As a constitutive and organizing framework, language could empower broad-based radical movements, uniting workers whose material experience of industrialization diverged considerably. Attention has thus shifted away from the structural foundations of collective action to examine the ways in which radical political formations deployed rhetoric, narrative and other discursive practices to construct identities, to create constituencies of support, to forge alliances among heterogeneous social groups.

While offering important insights into the construction of a large radical audience in the unpropitious material conditions of combined and uneven economic development in industrializing Britain, the new linguistic approach is disabled by a number of inconsistencies and anachronisms. These are most notable in the denial of class and the insistence on radical–liberal continuity. While all other meanings, identities and formations are seen as constantly in the making within the constitutive role of language, class is unaccountably excluded from discourse analysis. Instead, Patrick Joyce has constructed an unattainable criterion, an ideal form of class-consciousness, static and immutable. Rather in the old cold-war spirit, Joyce looks for an idealist Marxist–Leninist view of class, finds it missing and duly proclaims the complete absence of class.[8] By failing to deconstruct class in historical action, to interrogate its potential for change, continuity and cultural adaptability, Joyce and his acolytes subvert their own theoretical mission. As a constantly shifting cultural and discursive product, class (as this short study will argue) served to inform, if not define, the promotion and reception of the various radical programmes and campaigns throughout the nineteenth century.

4

Its theoretical pretensions aside, the new linguistic approach (as pioneered by Gareth Stedman Jones[9] and even as practised by Joyce and Vernon) is not really concerned with semiotics, but with the history of ideas and beliefs as expressed in public political language. Here, it has served, somewhat ironically, to reinforce a well-established narrative of radical continuity extending from the late eighteenth century through Chartism and mid-Victorian liberalism to the revival of socialism and beyond. Within this radical tradition, the dominance of liberal values is taken as natural and unproblematic.[10] This study will argue otherwise, stressing the shifting tensions – organizational and tactical as much as rhetorical and ideological – between liberalism and radicalism. In particular, it draws attention to the various *contextual* factors which often divided liberals from radicals – and indeed radicals themselves – along what are best described as 'class' lines.

Leaving theory aside, this study applies the linguistic approach to reconstruct the nature of radical thought and the manner of its transmission, while taking due account of the material influences in the production and reception of radical language. Unfortunately, space precludes adequate attention to local differences and variations, to the local dialects and accents, as it were, of radical politics. The localist emphasis on a disaggregated approach to politics as recently practised by Duncan Tanner has highlighted important nuances and distinctions, stressing the specificity of structural, organizational and other factors. Such disaggregation, however, runs the risk of perplexing and confusing the inattentive reader as it may tend to obscure a wider sense of national developments.[11] Radical movements, like other political formations, were unstable coalitions, but the image and identity of the national whole was always more important than the sum of the local parts. The capacity for collective action was doubtless influenced, as Michael Savage has shown, by the particular local configuration of skill, gender relations and community bonding.[12] Whatever form it took, however,

5

collective action was initiated, encouraged and legitimized by a language of a wider resonance and appeal.

While contesting the current orthodoxy, this study does not deny the proximity of radicalism and liberalism. Radicals and liberals developed their programmes within the same 'mental furniture' or intellectual paradigms. Radicalism, however, needs to be located not only within the history of ideas but also within the framework of popular culture. As a popularizing influence, radicalism deployed populist (and nationalist) idioms to broadcast its programme. In the battle for the popular mind, rhetorical strategy could take precedence over theory and principle.

Radical rhetoric must be read as language in action. Hence the attention accorded in this study to (national) context as well as content, to the changing codes and conventions of political behaviour and public space interposed between utterance and representation, intention and perception. Here the mid-nineteenth-century remains an important watershed as the old open-access procedures – the ritual and street theatre of open elections, the carnival of the radical mass platform – finally gave way to more organized, disciplined and 'respectable' indoor forms.[13] Much of the boisterous interaction between platform and crowd was unrecorded, but historians have begun to recover and decode the rich repertoire of rituals, symbols and iconography which characterized the great radical mass meetings of the early nineteenth century, a language of class without words.[14] After the demise of this mass platform (and the dominance of print over oral culture), there was a 'closure' in context and style, and hence in the message and its reception, factors ignored by those who insist – simply on the narrow and literal reading of 'texts' – on the continuity of radical public language.

Throughout the nineteenth century, radical movements faced a more difficult task than other political formations since they sought not merely to construct an audience – to find a language which resonated with people's material and other needs and grievances – but to mobilize for change. Here options were limited as radicals had to conform to the rhetorical, organizational and agitational norms of constitutional culture in order to attract popular legitimacy and support. This is where the relationship with liberalism was particularly problematic. At critical points, radicals found it difficult to establish a distinct identity, to secure a political space which whigs and liberals, traditional constitutional guardians of liberty, retrenchment and reform, could not re-occupy. Whether on the working-class platform or in middle-class pressure groups, radicals faced marginalization should whigs and liberals chose to place themselves at the head of 'respectable' public opinion – above social classes, divisive politics and irresponsible agitation – to assume control of the discussion of reform.[15]

Radicalism and liberalism appeared to converge in the mid-Victorian period as Chartist veterans finally conformed to the new political culture of disciplined and organized respectability, in which ticketing, direct mailing, door-to-door canvassing and other mechanisms excluded the unruly crowd. These were the methods pioneered by middle-class single-issue pressure groups – middle-class radicalism, it has recently been argued, is best conceived not as an idealized tradition based on abstract political principles, but rather in terms of a number of specific issues.[16] In the 1840s, the Anti-Corn Law League (ACLL) pointed the way further forward, extricating itself from pressure from without – the old 'brickbat argument' of the Reform Bill days, agitation which required 'something in our *rear* to frighten the aristocracy'[17] – to concentrate on the more efficient politics of electoral pressure. Party politics were transformed when other pressure groups followed this course, bringing the Liberal Party into being as a union of progressive sentiment in the constituencies.[18] Liberal Party organization came to rely on the commitment and resources of middle-class radicals, 'entryists', as it were, who looked to the party to prioritize their particular 'fad' or single issue.[19] The party leadership, however, chose not to project the party in such narrow programmatic terms. As party politics became the absorbing national passion in the age of Gladstone and Disraeli, each formation deployed 'populist' rhetoric to maximize its constituency, avoiding specific class or policy appeals which would lead to closure. Gladstone, the People's William, articulated a radicalism of moral entitlement, promising inclusion to all who displayed respectability and worth. Workers in trade unions and other new model forms of collective mutuality were incorporated in the rhetoric, but they were denied a significant presence either on the parliamentary benches or in party organization, where the middle class monopolized the new caucus system. By the end of the century, various factors, including the extension of trade unionism into the ranks of the less skilled, exposed tensions in Lib-Labism, allowing space for other political formations to gain a popular audience. Popular Toryism made considerable advance. Upholding the interests of nation rather than party, Tories defended traditional ways of life – not least, good old-fashioned (working-class) fun – and the rights of the freeborn Englishman against the moral coercion of (middle-class) caucus liberalism.[20] As the new socialist groupings failed to engage a popular audience there is much debate among historians as to whether the formation of the Labour Party represented a decisive new departure, a final break with radical-Liberal tradition, or merely its 'dynamic recomposition' in the new political circumstances.[21] One point is clear, however: in its rhetoric, organization and strategy, Labour was committed to the dominant British values of fair play, free speech and toleration. Holding firmly to parliamentary ways and means, Labour did not question the rules of the game. The constitutionalism of popular radicalism was to be recast into the parliamentarism of Labour.

1

THE EIGHTEENTH-CENTURY CONTEXT: CIVIC HUMANISM, COMMERCIAL LIBERALISM AND THE CROWD

The political crises of the early years of George III's reign, from the 'Wilkes and Liberty' campaigns to the loss of the American colonies, are generally considered as a watershed in politics and radicalism. Cumulative in impact, the issues raised by Wilkes – general warrants, the rights of electors, publication of parliamentary debates – comprised a frontal assault on the politics of oligarchy and its legitimizing notion of virtual representation (also under critical attack in the American colonies). The self-proclaimed champion of 'the middling and inferior class of people', Wilkes appears a crucial figure in extending the programme, constituency and organizational basis of reform. 'Wilkes and Liberty' shifted reform debate from 'country party' concern for the purity and independence of parliament to consider reform of representation and the extension of the suffrage. However, the extent of innovation should not be exaggerated.

In distinguishing itself from continental absolutism, the British constitutional settlement was forced to concede space to ambitious out-groups and the fickle crowd. As

Edward Thompson observed, the licence of the crowd was the price which aristocracy and gentry paid for the limited monarchy and a weak state.[1] Here was the point of entry for a succession of 'high-class rabble rousers'. One of this number, the rakish Wilkes, was more radical in methods than in programme, skilfully exploiting a new enterprise culture to package and promote his personal appeal beyond conventional local political boundaries. Wilkes's popularity, however, proved brief and tenuous, dependent less on the favour of the volatile crowd than on the sanction accorded by the 'unofficial opposition', disaffected out-groups opposed to established control of court, city and commercial empire. While outlawed from the political centre between 1714 and 1760, the Tories were tempted into a number of opportunistic sorties into extra-parliamentary 'radical' politics.[2] Wilkes was allowed similar licence by the Whigs, displaced (and aggrieved) by George III's accession to power and the prerogative. The Whigs, however, soon revised their tactics, withdrawing from such 'collusion and convergence' to develop (and legitimize) a new discipline of party opposition at Westminster. Conducted in a context of new commercialism and conventional partisan opportunism, Wilkite campaigns (which ran side by side with a number of independent and unrelated industrial disputes) left little legacy of political education and organization at the popular level. Fêted on the streets as a 'lord of misrule', Wilkes briefly enabled the crowd to remind the established authorities of the limits beyond which free-born Englishmen were not prepared to be pushed around.[3]

The absence of any popular political advance was graphically demonstrated by the Gordon Riots of 1780, an ugly display of religious intolerance. 'No Popery', an expression of xenophobia and gut patriotism, belonged to the same vocabulary of English libertarianism that Wilkes had evoked, celebrating the glorious struggles against continental absolutism, papistry and poverty. Articulated in the context of riot, it merged with other 'sub-political' attitudes, most notably the rough social justice favoured by the crowd, the desire to settle accounts with the rich, if only for the day. The riots were no indiscriminate Catholic 'pogrom'. Poor Catholics were left alone as the crowd ravaged the property of wealthy Catholics, rich supporters of the Catholic Relief Act, and then assailed various symbols of authority from prisons and toll-gates to the Bank of England, at which point they encountered the armed opposition of the formerly compliant city authorities, including the musket-bearing John Wilkes.[4]

The new organizations of the period, gentlemanly associations far above the fickle saturnalian crowd, sought to unite the various out-groups and unrepresented propertied interests, rural and urban, bourgeois and landed, Old Tory and True Whig Commonwealthmen. Here the Wilkites introduced system and method to the expression of extra-parliamentary opinion. Coordinated by the Society of the Supporters of the Bill of Rights (established in 1769 with the immediate purpose of settling Wilkes's debts), local political groups were encouraged to send petitions to parliament to be presented by sympathetic MPs, a device subsequently adopted by a gamut of reforming movements. As formulated by Horne Tooke and other ideologues, however, much of the debate within the Society and its successor organizations was backward-looking, conducted within what historians have described as the paradigm of civic humanism. This 'neo-Harringtonian' ideology accorded political priority to independent landowners: as in classical republicanism, it was their duty to resist imbalance and corruption in the polity through civic virtue, by active participation in political affairs. Articulated in this manner, radicalism served to amplify country party condemnation of government corruption, standing armies and placemen. Mediated through the classical republican frame of mind, eighteenth-century radicalism was also characterized by hostility to credit and commerce. Indeed, the new monied interest, the joint stock companies and holders of the burgeoning national debt were increasingly identified as the main threat to virtue.[5]

The disavowal of commerce, cities and luxury, however, became contentious as debate widened to include the urban 'middling sorts'. The English 'urban renaissance' stimulated a new culture of organized recreation and public display, establishing an infrastructure of improved communications and transport together with the facilities for voluntary association. Within this public sphere (to use Habermas's terminology), an increasingly self-conscious bourgeoisie sought to recast the political system in its own image.[6] In demanding representation for merchants, manufacturers and Dissenters, the ideologues of urban radicalism tended to eschew the 'republican' Harrington in favour of the 'whig' John Locke, seeking to extend his concern with rights and their preservation to secure all property (not just landed property) against corruption and arbitrary power. Some went further, carried forward by events across the Atlantic to a democratic exposition of natural rights.[7] In advance of Paine's *Rights of Man*, a number of radical ideologues acknowledged the superiority of republican government based on equal laws, common consent, manhood suffrage and the abolition of hereditary privilege. However, in advocating the case to the public, they adjusted the theory to suit the context, displaying an intellectual eclecticism, characteristic of reform debate in Britain, in which natural-rights arguments were subsumed, often concealed, within an appeal to history and precedent. Reform ideologues portrayed themselves as 'renovators' – the term radical was not to be applied until the early nineteenth century – restoring balance to the constitution with its hallowed mixture of monarchy, aristocracy and democracy in King, Lords and Commons. Condemning the onset of oligarchic factionalism since 1688-9, they looked back, far beyond the whig touchstone of the 'Glorious Revolution', to Saxon principles and practices of popular sovereignty, an original purity defiled by the 'Norman Yoke'.[8] Major Cartwright was particularly inventive in uncovering Saxon or other ancient precedent to legitimize radical innovation within the constitution. Most notably, he called for the *restoration* of a uniform and universal franchise, insisting that personality, not property, was the sole foundation of the right of representation. In *Take Your Choice!* (1776), he established the radical platform which was to persist into the age of the Chartists and beyond: manhood suffrage, annual parliaments, equal electoral districts, secret ballot and payment of MPs. Men of property and education, Cartwright and other ideologues would probably have been satisfied, however, with a householder or direct tax-payer suffrage.

In the absence of theoretical or programmatic rigour, country gentry, Commonwealthmen and the urban middling sorts were able to unite in concerted campaign for parliamentary reform. Justifying their stance in terms of history and precedent, they adopted the tactics first proposed in James Burgh's *Political Disquisitions* (1764): the calling of a national association of men of property to test opinion, petition and press for reform. Independent landowners, appalled by the cost and corrupt incompetence of the American wars, moved beyond the old country platform of economical reform of the 'fiscal-military' state (reductions in placemen, pensioners and expenditure) to join the Reverend Christopher Wyvill's Association to petition for parliamentary reform by the addition of 100 extra seats for independent county MPs. As the petitioning campaign developed, other groups sought to redefine the agenda. Some London radicals, impressed by American parallels, hoped to transform the organizational structure of the Association into an anti-parliament, a constituent convention committed to a broad extension of the franchise. The Westminster Committee even advocated manhood suffrage, the radical programme subsequently promoted by the new Society for Constitutional Information (SCI), which distributed vast numbers of free tracts in the hope of reviving in 'the COMMONALTY AT LARGE a knowledge of their lost rights'. Internal disagreement and doubt over the role and competence of the Association were much in evidence, but this pioneer exercise in pressure from without was hindered most of all by the opportunistic manoeuvrings of aristocratic parliamentary factions whom Wyvill was unable to exclude.[9]

Radicalism, then, was subject to a number of constraints as it began to broaden its constituency during the reform campaigns associated with Wilkes and the American crisis. Symbolic issues, flamboyant leadership and the opportunist compliance of opposition groups were required to engage public interest, while the battle for the mind had to be phrased in the 'ethno-historical ideology of English cultural nationalism'.[10] The urban crowd had responded to the call of 'liberty', but in a xenophobic, chauvinistic manner, at odds with the frenchified cosmopolitan culture of the corrupt and treacherous aristocracy. A volatile force, this nationalism could take either a radical or a loyalist inflexion according to circumstance and the perceived threat to British freedom. As yet, formal political representation mattered little to the freeborn Englishman, whose political identity and enjoyment were secured on the streets, through rough and ready exclusion of the alien and disloyal 'other'.

There were incipient indications of class consciousness among the urban 'middling sorts', some of whom, most notably the rational Dissenters, took their stand on universal natural rights in campaigning for repeal of the Test and Corporation Acts.[11] Richard Price was the most celebrated of these natural rights ideologues, the radical who drew Burke's wrath. However, he was by no means enthusiastic about further expansion of commerce. In terms of political economy, indeed, the language of the Whig aristocratic establishment was more modern, pointing towards a commercial liberalism built upon the genteel and polite motifs of Dugald Stewart, Adam Smith and the Scottish Enlightenment.[12] Traditional aristocratic concerns for virtue, balance and the progress of civilization were gradually recast in commercial mould as the emphasis shifted from *civic* virtue to *civil* liberty – the freedom to engage in private affairs, the enjoyment and accumulation of property, the cultivation of moral and intellectual faculties. Here was the basis of a commercial political economy upon which Whig grandee and urban bourgeois could agree, but the Whig attitude to reform displayed no such forward development. Convinced by the events of the first decades of George III's reign that all ills stemmed from the corrupting influence of the crown, the Whigs continued to look first and foremost to party at Westminster to redress the balance, supplemented, if necessary, by no more than temperate parliamentary reform, a programme which fell short of middle-class demands.

2

RADICALISM, REVOLUTION AND WAR, 1790–1815

According to most accounts, reform debate shed its eighteenth-century constraints in the 1790s as the French Revolution offered a new political vocabulary, a new style, a new universalism. Although restricted at first to radical Dissenters, enthusiasm for revolution in France – otherwise regarded as a tardy continental version of 1688 – was dramatically accentuated by the publication and widespread diffusion of Tom Paine's *Rights of Man* (1791–2) which, on the most conservative estimate, probably sold between 100,000 and 200,000 copies in the first three years after its publication. Repudiating the exclusive conventions of previous debate, Paine's 'intellectual vernacular prose' rendered natural rights and rational republicanism accessible, all-embracing and uncompromising.[1] In language, programme and organization, radicalism was extended to 'members unlimited'. The symbolic gestures associated with French and thus universal liberty – planting liberty trees, wearing tricolour cockades, singing the 'Marseillaise' and 'Ça Ira', toasting victories of the French republic over its enemies, addressing fellow democrats as 'citizen' – became common practice in London, Nottingham, Norwich, Manchester, Sheffield, Edinburgh and other radical centres. However, this Jacobin tenor was not to persist. Furthermore, such 'ideological' radicalism did not attract the labouring poor. The most famous of the new democratic societies inspired by Paine, the London Corresponding Society (LCS), had an active membership of less than 1000 for most of its existence, composed in the main of artisans, tradesmen and various members of the 'uneasy' middle class – booksellers, printers, publishers, authors and insecure members of the legal and medical professions.

In the political confrontation and experimentation which accompanied the Burke–Paine debate, the reaction provoked by Paine proved stronger than the radicalism he excited. Compelled to answer the democratic Jacobin challenge, opponents of reform developed a convincing defence of the existing order. Here Burke had already set the tone, recapturing the language of nationalism for the conservative cause in his *Reflections on the Revolution in France* (1790). A trenchant critic of the universalist idioms (and millenarian predictions) of Price, Priestley and the radical Dissenters who immediately enthused over revolution, Burke upheld the historical integrity of the Englishman's particular legacy of rights and duties. Vindicated by the subsequent course of events in France, Burke's prescient pronouncements duly confirmed the supremacy of the accumulated wisdom of precedent and prescription over the wild fanaticism of abstract reason. Natural rights arguments, already challenged by the socio-economic relativism of the Scottish Enlightenment, lost intellectual purchase against this organic or 'romantic' frame of mind.[2]

At the vernacular level, however, in the unprecedented battle for the popular mind in the 1790s, rhetorical strategy and propaganda device took precedence over ideology and intellectual argument.[3] In this political confrontation, the charge of 'levelling', or economic equality, emerged as the crucial factor in the loyalist triumph over the Paineites, although, as Gregory Claeys has shown, it was neither central to Burke's case nor really implied by Paine

in his famous welfare proposals in Part Two of *The Rights
of Man*, published in February 1792.[4] Where Burke looked
back to gothic feudalism and past glories, loyalist popular propagandists celebrated Britain's commercial progress,
the contemporary wealth of the nation threatened by the
spoliation and anarchy of republican egalitarianism. In
defending inequality and hierarchy, loyalists stood forward
to save Britain from the pre-commercial 'primitivism' of
natural-rights republicanism.

As they endeavoured to refute the charge and assert
their economic modernity, radical ideologues were carried forward into a social radicalism in which the labouring poor, systematically disadvantaged in the course of
commercial progress, were entitled to additional rights.
Previously a staunch advocate of commerce and minimal
government, Paine drew upon natural jurisprudence to
establish a positive right to assistance: the rich were to
pay into a fund to support the poor so that all would
benefit from increasing affluence.[5] John Thelwall took
Jacobinism to the borders of socialism, insisting that the
poor, through their property in labour, had a natural right
to the increased wealth of society. Natural right, he opined,
was determined not by some aboriginal state of nature,
but by human capacities, by changing and enlarging wants.[6]
Amid the 'Painophobia' of the time, however, such important theoretical advances counted for little. They failed
either to attract the labouring poor or to reverse the
general rejection of natural-rights argument.

Paine's inopportune avowal of deism in his *Age of Reason*
(1794–5) enabled loyalists to add infidelism to the charges
of primitivism and levelling. However, the propaganda victory of the loyalists over the godless republican levellers
should not be attributed to superior argument. Much of
the loyalist case, as John Dinwiddy demonstrated, relied
on evasiveness, misrepresentation and transparent special
pleading.[7] Where loyalists triumphed was in quantity not
quality, through their supremacy in what sociologists call
'resource mobilization'. Untroubled by the authorities or

by lack of funds, loyalists deployed every medium and resource from parish pulpit to national organization – Reeves Association for the Preservation of Liberty and Property against Republicans and Levellers was the largest political organization in the country – to spread the patriotic conservative message in popular and homiletic form among the lower orders. Many of the new 'corresponding' societies fell victim to this conservative onslaught: only those which were well-rooted in old artisan centres like Norwich and Sheffield were able to withstand the charge of levelling, primitivism and infidelism. The surviving societies judiciously excised the offending Paineite vocabulary of rational republicanism with its alien and revolutionary stigma.

Before this prudent shift in register, a number of Scottish radicals, moderates not revolutionaries, had fallen foul of the none too tender mercies of the Scottish legal system. The use of French idioms, symbols and oaths at the Scottish Convention of 1792–3 caused the authorities serious alarm. Muir and Palmer were the first victims of a ruthless 'legal' purge, sentenced on the charge of sedition to fourteen and seven years' transportation respectively. There was little suggestion, however, of any revolutionary intent. Most members of the Scottish Convention favoured moderate reform and looked back to the practice of earlier gentlemanly associations. The intervention of the authorities served to polarize positions, carrying some radicals closer to the French example and Paineite prescription – in his *Letter Addressed to the Addressers of the Late Proclamation* (1792), Paine had called for a national convention to elicit the general will and establish a republican revolution. In defiance of Scottish law, delegates representing the LCS, SCI, Norwich and Sheffield attended the reconvened Edinburgh convention, which in emulation of the French, proclaimed itself the 'First Year of the British Convention'. For this heroic act of self-sacrifice, Margarot, Gerrald and Skirving were promptly convicted of sedition in the Scottish courts and transported

19

to Botany Bay. Haunted by fears of a French invasion, the government in Westminster began to contemplate treason trials and repressive legislation after the Report of the Committee of Secrecy of 1794 noted that the convention 'in almost every Particular, assumed the Stile and Mode of Proceedings adopted by the National Convention of France'.[8]

Appalled by the tenor of conservative propaganda and the fate of the 'Scottish martyrs', radicals abandoned French idioms and sought to appropriate the establishment vocabulary of patriotism. Having been stigmatized as revolutionary, alien and traitorous Jacobins, radicals trusted to rehabilitate themselves as true loyalists and defenders of the constitution. Henceforth radicalism was legitimized through the people's history: radicals proudly claimed descent from 'that patriotic band who broke the ruffian arm of arbitrary power, and dyed the field and scaffold with their pure and precious blood, for the liberties of the country, – Hampden, Russell, Sidney'.[9] In the unequal politics of public space, however, radicals could not match the loyalists in 'patriotic' display. While radicals struggled to gain a public hearing – 186 publicans in Manchester, for example, signed a declaration banning Jacobins from their rooms – loyalists chose to treat the crowds to an increasing number of patriotic demonstrations to celebrate royal anniversaries and victories over the French. The success of these free holidays and licensed street festivals was not without irony. In combatting democracy through such popular nationalist participation, loyalists had established what the radicals had failed to achieve, the extension of national politics to a mass public. As subsequent events were to show, this public expressed its loyalty to the nation, not necessarily to the status quo.[10]

As need arose, propaganda and patriotic participation were reinforced by repression. The first measures of the 'Terror' – the Royal Proclamation against Seditious Publications and the Suspension of Habeas Corpus – have been seen by historians mainly as exercises in 'high politics', designed to embarrass and divide the Whigs by enticing Portland into the ranks of government.[11] The Two Acts of 1795, however, were a straightforward attack on incipient politics from below, in particular the ominous new tactic of the radical mass meeting.

The *crise de subsistence* of 1795 produced a wave of traditional, non-political food-rioting throughout the country, but in London the radicals stood forward to organize and coordinate popular protest. Until this point, the London crowd had displayed its usual fickleness. War with France was greeted with great enthusiasm. Radicals who refused to illuminate their windows to celebrate military and naval victories incurred popular wrath – the pregnant wife of Thomas Hardy, secretary of the LCS, died shortly after a jubilant crowd rampaged through their house in the course of celebrating the Glorious First of June. A few months later, however, the London crowd championed Hardy as the victim of persecution when he was tried and triumphantly acquitted of High Treason in November 1794. As the first signs of war-weariness appeared in 1795, the LCS stood forward on a radical patriotic platform. Vast crowds were attracted to St George's Fields and Copenhagen Fields where the radical programme was addressed to the economic plight of the freeborn Englishman, victim of the 'dreadful scarcity and high price of provisions' caused by the 'cruel, unjust and unnecessary war'. 'Why, when we incessantly toil and labour, must we pine in misery and want?', the Remonstrance adopted at Copenhagen Fields demanded: '*Parliamentary Corruption*... like a foaming whirlpool, swallows the fruit of all our labours'.[12] Three days later, when the king drove to open parliament, huge crowds carrying tiny loaves in black crepe and shouting for peace, hooted at him, and someone threw a stone at his coach, thereby providing the government with the requisite pretext for the introduction of the 'Gagging Acts', banning all meetings of more than forty people and licensing lecture halls.

The introduction of repression was a clear signal of the

government's unwillingness to negotiate with the extra-parliamentary movement. Having already abandoned Jacobinism for popular constitutionalism, radicals were compelled to undertake a more thorough reassessment of their project. The 'utopians' were among the first to withdraw. William Godwin abandoned activist radicalism after the treason trials of 1794, convinced that true political reform required rational conviction and an austere morality, principles obscured by the beer, tobacco and rhetoric of working men's democratic societies.[13] Averse to populist bonhomie and political confrontation, Godwin sought to preserve the intellectual purity of Enlightenment radicalism. Godwin relied on the 'multiplication of reason', the spread of knowledge, to implement his utopian agenda through intellectual conviction and rational consensus. Equality and liberty of the individual were to be achieved by the elimination of private property and government in a world-wide system of small communities of producer-run farms and democratic councils. There was even the suggestion of some gender equality as Godwin, husband of Mary Wollstonecraft, advocated the 'Pantisocratic' rearrangement of domestic life on communal lines.

Thomas Spence also withdrew from radical agitation, but in promoting his utopia, he recognized the need for a populist approach to education together with active preparation for the seizure of power. Spence's ideas, although influenced by the Enlightenment, were formed in the indigenous Harringtonian tradition of classical republicanism with its profound suspicion of wealth, commerce and luxury. His famous 'plan', the blueprint for 'Spensonia', was based on the purchase and expropriation of private land to facilitate a parish-administered, rent-based popular utopia of political and gender equality. Formulated in the 1770s in the artisan milieu of Newcastle upon Tyne, the plan acquired an apocalyptic tone at the time of the French Revolution when Spence moved to London. In this heady millenarian atmosphere, he subscribed to a post-millennialist theology in which

Levitican jubilee and political revolution became synony-
mous: prior to the second coming, the millennium would
be effected by human agency, by revolution secured
through land redistribution. He was increasingly prepared
to advocate violence, recognizing the need for physical
force to undermine the economic base of landed political power, hence his reputation as the inspirational force
of the 'revolutionary party'. After the imposition of repression
in the mid-1790s, however, Spence was not prepared to
lead the challenge himself. His role was that of popular
educator, using a variety of innovatory techniques – coins,
chapbooks, broadsides, songs, allegorical maps, chalk graffiti
and a 'genuine, scientific, phonetic alphabet' – to popu-
larize the 'Plan'. More conscious than Paine of the politics of language, it was Spence who did most to extend
debate to members unlimited, using the linguistic and
literary genres of the vulgar, poor and semi-literate. In
1801 he opened the first 'Spensonian' society at a tavern
free-and-easy, where the revolutionary underground merged
with the criminal underworld.[14]

Other responses to repression were more pragmatic.
Some radicals, mainly self-respecting tradesmen, retreated
into educational gradualism. While political education was
to continue among working men, extra-parliamentary
agitation was to be held in reserve as auxiliary support
for parliamentary initiatives by the groups most likely to
gain concessions. Prepared to wait upon events, the next
political crisis or financial collapse, pragmatists like Francis
Place, the radical tailor of Charing Cross, sought an understanding with aristocratic and middle-class reformers.
Repression, Place appreciated, had altered the context.
Cooperation between parliamentary and extra-parliamentary forces had been ruptured in the early 1790s when
Paine's uncompromising tone had divided democratic
radicals from moderate reformers, the plebeian 'Friends
of Liberty' from the refined 'Friends of the People'. United
in opposition to repression, however, Whigs and radicals
could rediscover some common ground.[15]

Foxite and other gentlemanly 'liberals' continued in legal opposition to the war and repression after 1795, but there was no realignment of radical forces. The Whigs charted an independent middle course. Moderate reform, legitimized in eclectic terms of constitutionalism, utilitarianism and political economy, was tentatively proffered as a necessary corrective to both democratic and reactionary excess. Household suffrage, as defined in Grey's 1797 motion, acquired emblematic significance. The requisite compromise between liberty and property, it came to represent the modern urban equivalent, as it were, of the old county independence. In seeking to incorporate the town-based direct tax-payer and property-holder, the Whigs moved closer towards a middle-class language of reform, an important stage in the transformation of Whiggism into liberalism. But the Foxite Whigs remained resolutely aristocratic in preoccupations, methods and cultural style. As a party (present or not at Westminster), their functions remained first, to curb the influence of the crown, when unnecessary war with France threatened to increase its powers, and second, to act as the people's trustees. Here, of course, they exercised discretion in deciding how and when to act on the people's behalf, standing aloof from agitation which seemed to be aimed against parliament, but stepping forward when civil liberties were under threat.[16]

While repression prompted some radicals towards utopian withdrawal or gradualist alliance, it carried others forward into underground insurrectionary politics. In ways and means, as in language and programme, radicals were swept along in the 1790s less by ideological prescription than by the force of events and the dynamics of confrontation. Attitudes hardened after the Scottish trials as radicals continued to place their hopes in some form of national convention, Paineite or otherwise, but there was little evidence of any revolutionary intent as the verdicts at the treason trials of Hardy and others confirmed. After the repression of the late 1790s, however, insurrectionary conspiracy moved, *faute de mieux*, to the top of the tactical agenda. Recent research has confirmed E. P. Thompson's insights into this opaque area of activity: the efficiency of the government intelligence services, the international dimensions of revolutionary strategy, and the remarkable continuity of the revolutionary tradition at local level, all attest to the importance of the wartime radical underground.[17]

Spies and informers were generally carefully recruited, vetted and protected, although some unsavoury characters were perforce employed after 1795 to infiltrate the increasingly secret radical societies.[18] The intelligence obtained revealed plans for an oath-bound conspiracy of international dimensions, a union of revolutionary forces in Ireland, France and Britain. The naval mutinies of 1797 at the Nore and Spithead highlighted the danger as a politically conscious minority, dominated by cells of United Irishmen, tried to persuade their exploited shipmates – driven to mutiny by poor pay and appalling conditions of service – to desert to the enemy and thereby assist a French invasion of Ireland.

These Irish and French links continued to dominate underground strategy. Modelled on the United Irishmen, the oath-bound United Englishmen enrolled the increasingly impoverished weavers, spinners and labourers of the north-west, groups unattracted to earlier Jacobin societies. Militant sections of the LCS established the Society of United Britons, whose central committee – of which Colonel Despard was the most famous member – prepared plans for English and Irish risings to accompany a French invasion. The government, fully informed of the details discussed in Lancashire and London with Irish delegates *en route* to France, pre-empted the conspiracy by arresting most of the leaders. Prosecutions were not secured, however, since the government decided not to reveal its most useful and reliable informers in open court. Through these protected channels of information, ministers learnt of new insurrectionary plans – elaborated after the failure of the

Irish rebellion of 1798 – in which the capture of London was to be the first priority after the essential French invasion. Habeas corpus was suspended again (a convenient means of locking up the leaders without any embarrassing courtroom defeats), followed by new laws curbing the press, banning the United Societies and the LCS by name, and outlawing workers' combinations.[19]

This tightening of repression in 1799 failed to crush the radical threat, serving instead to politicize the increasingly war-wearied masses, to clinch the industrial control, John Foster observes, 'of those who were themselves outlaws, the working-class radicals. In south-west Lancashire almost every labour organization seems to have passed into their hands. "The republicans", reported one agent, "are drinking Mr Pitt's health".'[20] Certainly, there were important changes in the pattern of collective behaviour. Previously, the north- west had witnessed considerable Church and King rioting, for the most part spontaneous effusions of popular loyalty, triggered by the excitement of a public gathering or holiday (Boxing Day, Easter Monday, wakes week, royal birthdays, military victories, etc.). As wages fell and prices rose – by 1799 wartime inflation had reduced weavers' wages to half their real value in 1792 – textile workers rallied behind a new set of slogans: 'No War', 'Damn Pitt' and 'A Free Constitution'. Organized by 'underground' radical and trade union groups, the food riots of 1799–1801 were characterized by careful planning and an extended demonology: alongside the speculators, factors and middlemen, the magistrates, clergy and local paternalists stood condemned as members of the repressive propertied class.[21]

Such developments suggest that conspiracy, previously an elitist affair, had potential mass support, at least in the north-west. Had Despard effected a successful *coup d'état* in London, the Lancashire workers might well have responded. Once again, however, the government moved early: Despard was arrested in November 1802 as there was sufficient evidence to secure his conviction. His execution, followed by the failure of Robert Emmet's rising in Ireland, was a severe reverse.[22] Thereafter the underground was in decline, but local studies have uncovered some remarkable continuities. Many of 'Despard's men' were to the fore in Luddism and the risings of 1817 and 1820, proud veterans who bequeathed a commitment to physical force to the Chartist movement.[23] Apart from a handful of mainly Spencean conspirators, however, insurrectionary ways and means were held in reserve, pending the conversion of the masses to the radical cause. As the millenarian enthusiasm of the 1790s evaporated, the time-scale for such conversion was necessarily extended. Now recognized as a long-term task, political education was to be accomplished through the language of populist nationalism, in which constitutionalism, not French-inspired international republicanism, was the dominant motif.

This adjustment was part of a wider process of political and cultural appraisal. After the polarization of political rhetoric in the 1790s, the opening decade of the nineteenth century was a time of considerable flux and confusion as war, patriotism and reform were all reassessed and redefined. Once Napoleon's imperial ambitions became apparent, the character of the war effort changed. Having previously opposed the war – an aggressive conflict against a neighbouring country which simply wanted to reform its internal system of government – radicals now came forward as ardent patriots at the head of recruiting and volunteering drives. As supporters of the war – the cause of liberty against military despotism – radicals were enabled to shed their Jacobin stigma and re-enter 'legitimate' political debate among freeholders, electors and ratepayers. In so doing, Peter Spence claims, radicals underwent a fundamental shift, adopting a 'romantic' or organic framework.[24] Certainly there were a number of discursive (and tactical) adjustments, but it is debatable whether they constitute a new paradigm, a fundamental ideological realignment or simply a set of *ad hoc* tactical positions around which radicals, having been battered by conservative propaganda and repression, could regather. In supporting the war as a patriotic and ideological conflict, radicals adopted and adapted the dominant Burkean ideology of an historically-formed organic community. Corruption, the internal threat to the nation's liberty and defence, was no longer traced to the crown, but to avaricious boroughmongers. The monarchy, the great symbol of patriotism, was placed in potential alliance with the plundered and unrepresented people.

Having redefined their role as guardians of national virtue, radicals began to attract a wide audience as a series of scandals – the Melville affair, the Convention of Cintra, the Duke of York affair, the charges against Perceval and Castlereagh, the Walcheren campaign – suggested a connection between military incompetence and parliamentary corruption. Public indignation at such malversation and misconduct produced what one historian has described as 'a middle-class revolt against patrician society'.[25] Protest was expressed in the new terminology of class, but there was little reference to radicalism. As articulated by provincial manufacturers, merchants, Dissenters and other 'friends of peace', the new language of class was a register of social dissidence, an assertion of cultural superiority.[26] Defining themselves against the corruption, immorality and incompetence exposed in high places, anti-war liberals addressed themselves to the 'middle class', the particular victims of the financial demands, economic uncertainties and social consequences of the 'war system'. Liberal opinion and economic interests were aligned in a campaign for peace, an end to a conflict unduly prolonged by the ruling oligarchy and its privileged coterie of contractors, financiers and placemen. A 'symbolic' protest, the middle-class peace campaign stopped short of political commitment to radical reform, but it succeeded in mobilizing considerable resources. Trade organizations, chapel communities and other 'interests' were enlisted to liberate commerce and enterprise from war-inflated monopoly, oligarchy and corruption. The Whigs lent parliamentary assistance, most notably in the person of Henry

Brougham, architect of the successful new tactics of 'petition and debate' by which the various mechanisms of the extra-parliamentary platform – meetings, petitions, press reports – were closely coordinated and linked to the efforts of the opposition in the Commons. Subjected to such cumulative pressure, the government was compelled to revoke the Orders-in-Council in 1812 and the Property Tax in 1816, remarkable victories for middle-class opinion in the unreformed system.[27]

Opposition to corruption and incompetence brought commercial interests and aristocratic whigs closer together. At the same time, disaffected loyalists joined the radicals in condemnation of the depredations of the fiscal-military state. Among such converts were William Cobbett, the most prolific and influential radical journalist of the early nineteenth century, and Henry Hunt, the Wiltshire gentleman farmer turned radical orator. Defiantly independent, these former loyalists injected a mood of impatience and intransigence at odds with the accommodating pragmatism of older radicals. Major Cartwright, one of the pre-Jacobin veterans who returned to prominence, was prepared to moderate traditional radical demands to construct alliances and associations which would place reform on the agenda of 'legitimate' opposition politics.[28] Cobbett and Hunt, however, refused to compromise their new radical principles in subservience either to the Whigs, damned by their profligacy and apostasy during the brief Ministry of All the Talents in 1806–7, or to commercial interests, castigated in Cobbett's famous 'Perish Commerce' articles of 1807.

As independent radicals, Cobbett and Hunt looked to the leadership of the wealthy patrician Sir Francis Burdett whose previous Jacobin reputation, acquired through links with the Irish and the Horne Tooke circle, was cast aside by careful adjustment to patriotic radicalism. An independent English landed gentleman, Burdett stood forward to expose corruption, condemn oligarchy and restore 'purity' to the Commons. Country party nostalgia merged with

more modern methods and concerns when Burdett secured a sensational election victory in 1807 in Foxite
Westminster, the most urban of constituencies. Victory was
achieved not through his purse (exhausted by early contests in Middlesex) but by the organizational efficiency of
the new Westminster Committee, composed of small shopkeepers and tradesmen, several of whom (including Francis
Place) were former members of the LCS. Burdett's gentlemanly lifestyle, however, precluded close attention to
parliamentary duties, frustrating hopes that he would
galvanize and lead a radical group in the Commons. He
preserved his credentials as 'Westminster's Pride and
England's Glory', however, by identifying his name with
the most advanced programme discussed in 'legitimate'
political circles: direct-taxation (or household) suffrage,
equal electoral districts and annual parliaments.[29]

It was around this programme that Cartwright sought
to effect union, hoping that Whitbread and the popular
Whigs, the so-called 'Mountain', would join Burdett to
head a Wyvill-like national 'association'. The response was
disappointing. Despite the feelings aroused by wartime
incompetence, failure and corruption, the Friends of Peace
were slow to adopt the cause, although a number of newly
established provincial newspapers expressed interest in
parliamentary reform. London was more fertile territory,
thanks to the efforts of Robert Waithman, the patriotic
linen draper, who fought long and hard in the ratepayers'
democracy of the Common Hall to transform the City from
a bastion of Pittite loyalism into a stronghold of peace,
retrenchment and reform. Out of deference to the Whigs,
however, Waithman stopped short of radical prescriptions.[30]

The Whigs shunned Cartwright's overtures, seeking
thereby to distance themselves from Burdett and demagogic Westminster radicalism. Ill at ease with developments
in popular Westminster, where radical involvement in the
tumultuous 'Old Price' riots at Covent Garden confirmed
their fears of uncontrollable activity out of doors, the Whigs
reaffirmed their commitment to the principle of party,

the programme of economical reform and the practice of aristocratic exclusiveness. Some popular whigs questioned this aloofness, as did new liberal journals, such as the *Edinburgh Review* and *The Examiner*, although they were no less critical than the party leadership of irresponsible demagogic radicalism. Francis Jeffrey, editor of the *Edinburgh Review*, called on the Whigs to regain the initiative through a moderate reform of the electoral system, extending the suffrage to the respectable classes. In 1810, in the midst of further Burdettite agitation on the streets, Brand promoted a suitably modest programme, stopping short of annual parliaments, equal electoral districts and a uniform household suffrage. Not dissimilar from Grey's proposals of 1797, it secured 115 votes in the Commons, the largest vote for reform since Pitt's motion of 1785.

Although well-intentioned, Cartwright's unity efforts served to polarize positions, to emphasize the gulf which divided Burdettite radical or 'real' reform from the moderate or 'mock' reform proffered by Brand and the popular Whigs. At this point, however, Burdett gave the first indication of retraction. A past master of Wilkite popular political theatre, he was reluctant to commit himself further to the politics of the street. True to past form, he championed the cause of John Gale Jones, a former leading member of the LCS, who was called before the bar of the House and committed to Newgate when he proposed to use the British Forum, one of the newly-revived debating clubs, to discuss the exclusion of strangers from the Commons during the damaging committee of inquiry into the failure of the Walcheren expedition. Having condemned the committal as unconstitutional, Burdett repeated his protest in Cobbett's *Political Register*. For this, he was charged with a breach of privilege and ordered to be detained in the Tower until the end of the parliamentary session. He refused to surrender to the Commons' warrant, and barricaded himself in his house in Piccadilly, protected by large and riotous crowds, until finally apprehended, in a superbly stage-managed scene, reading

Magna Carta to his young son. It was during these riots, and a flood of petitions calling for Burdett's release, that Brand introduced his reform motion. On his release, Burdett unexpectedly abandoned the ways and means which Brand and the Whigs condemned. Leaving the Tower by the back exit, Sir Francis 'Sly-go' took to the river, thereby avoiding the colossal crowds who waited to fête him on the streets.

From this point on, radical prospects declined. Having served to rehabilitate the radicals, the switch to romantic or organic arguments ultimately proved self-defeating. Radicals were hoist by their own petard. Predicated on corruption and incompetence, the case for reform lost much of its salience as political and military fortunes revived, boosted by the new efficiency of Perceval's administration and judicious use of the libel laws against the troublesome press. Tables were turned – and reputations ruined – as the moral pretensions of the 'virtuous' radicals came under critical and sensational scrutiny to expose an embarrassing network of sexual liaison, linking the most vociferous critics of corruption. As mutual distrust widened between radical and moderate reformers, Cartwright's efforts at unity ended in the formation of two distinct societies. With its £300 property qualification, Thomas Northmore's Hampden Club was strictly for those with a substantial stake in the country: it studiously avoided commitment to any specific programme. Cartwright's Union for Parliamentary Reform, by contrast, was more broadly based and identified with the Burdettite programme. Although it attracted Cobbett and Hunt, it was soon to languish, unable to enlist the necessary one hundred sponsors.[31]

It was this adverse change of context – the marginalization of radicalism in the legitimate arenas of opposition politics – which prompted a further shift in language and presentation. Turning to the wider audience beyond the bounds of conventional political debate, radicals addressed the harsh economic realities of wartime living.

More populist (and unrestrained) than the commercial arguments of the middle-class friends of peace, the economic thrust of popular radicalism began to engage a 'working-class' audience. Assuming the role of the poor man's friend, Cobbett used the columns of his *Register* to explain how the war had consolidated 'the Thing', the system of political corruption and financial plunder – now known to historians as the 'fiscal-military state' – which had been tightening its hold since the late seventeenth century at the expense of the unrepresented and heavily-taxed poor. Paper money and inflation were but the latest horrors of this funding system, which, being built upon the monstrous national debt, produced lucrative profits for political peculators and financial speculators, but imposed an intolerable, demand-stifling tax burden on the poor. What separated the parasitic plunderers from the hard-working plundered, the rich from the poor, was the monopolistic possession of political power.[32] Cartwright took the same political message direct to the workers, in a series of pioneering missionary tours through the manufacturing districts, lately the scene of Luddite disturbance. While encouraging workers to break through the constraints of Hampden Club and Union Society organization, he enrolled their support in a printed petition campaign which retained the Burdettite programme of household suffrage.

Addressed to workers, radical propaganda contributed to what sociologists call the modernization of protest, or 'politicization of discontent', the transition from direct-action protest to political agitation.[33] The extent and pace of change in collective behaviour, already apparent in some districts in the 1799–1801 food riots and subsequent 'Black Lamp' disturbances, varied according to 'community ecology'. As John Bohstedt has shown, traditional forms of popular protest – conducted within a shared discourse of custom, tradition and the unity of interests – proved increasingly dysfunctional outside the 'organic ecology' of medium-size stable towns, where patricians and plebeians continued to respect the protocol of riot. Rebellious in defence of custom, the riotous crowd in old-established towns in the south and west still sought to recall local authorities and employers to their paternalist duties, to uphold the hallowed (doubtless mythologized) customs of the past, a 'moral economy' of fair prices, just wages, honest measures and decent, unadulterated quality. In big industrial boom towns, by contrast, the structural mechanisms of effective community politics were unable to operate as vertical ties and horizontal groupings were overwhelmed by economic change.[34]

The disciplined and ritualized violence of traditional collective bargaining by riot was ultimately legitimized by old paternalist legislation governing work practices, apprenticeship and payment. Obsolete as this legislation was, its final repeal during the Napoleonic Wars was a devastating blow for the trades, a far more serious reverse than the new legislation of 1799 prohibiting workers' combinations. The Wiltshire shearmen, the skilled elite of the west country woollen trade, were the first to encounter the strident spirit of laissez-faire when parliament, having rejected their legal and constitutional efforts to enforce a complete ban on gig mills in accordance with 5 and 6 Edward VI c. 22, decided to repeal all statutes regulating the trade. Shearmen were left defenceless against gig mills, shearing frames and cheap, unskilled, unapprenticed labour.[35] Soon afterwards, textile workers in other districts – the east midlands hosiery districts, the Yorkshire wool and worsted areas, the Lancashire cotton belt – deployed a variety of complementary forms, from parliamentary petitions to Luddite machine-breaking, in a concerted effort to defend traditional labour practices and living standards.

A complex phenomenon of pronounced regional variation, Luddism is perhaps best understood as the crucial episode in wartime politicization.[36] It was neither strictly industrial nor politically revolutionary, although in some areas there was coordination between machine-breaking gangs, underground radical groups and/or organized crime. In Lancashire, the most advanced or 'modern' area, it was subsumed in general protest against the hated 'war system'. Here, there was no clear-cut division between political protest and industrial pressure, between partici- pation in constitutional reform movements and involve- ment in underground activity: the constitutionalism of the Manchester Committee for Peace and Reform, formed after the failure of the handloom-weavers' minimum wages cam- paign in 1811, was a useful cover behind which money and support could be raised for other purposes. Elsewhere, workers were quick to draw a political lesson from Lud- dism as parliament responded to their protest, first by abandoning protective legislation and paternalist responsi- bility, and then by despatching large numbers of troops – a greater military force than Wellington had under his command in the Iberian campaign – to defend the em- ployers' factories. Defeated and disabused, workers in Luddite counties turned to radicalism, to the forward-look- ing struggle for democratic control of the state and the economy.

London workers underwent a similar political educa- tion. Craft workers, 'artisans' as they started to call them- selves, were forced into new levels of militancy during the war simply to maintain their customary standard of living, to ensure that wage rates remained just and fair, determined by custom and status differentials, not by supply and demand. Unhindered by the Combination Acts, inter- trade links were forged in a sustained campaign to en- force and extend the Elizabethan code, including the appointment of a lawyer to prosecute offending masters. Parliament's decision to repeal the crucial apprenticeship clauses of the Statute of Artificers in 1814 served both to radicalize the trades and restrict their influence to the diminishing 'honourable' or bespoke sector. Lacking se- curity, they adopted radical reform, reading into its pro- gramme an alternative 'artisan' political economy of regulation, control and compensation for change.[37] By minimal linguistic shift, the simple substitution of manhood for household suffrage, the post-war radical platform offered recognition, representation and protection for workers' property in labour and skill.

By the end of the war, it was becoming clear that radicalism meant different things to different audiences. In popular understanding, it implied artisan protectionism; to middle-class adherents, steadily increasing in number, it was the guarantee of continued progress towards commercial freedom. These rival interpretations, with their fundamentally opposed political economies, were to harden into 'class' positions. Unity, however, was not necessarily precluded. Audience expectations may have differed, and there were differences of detail in specific proposals, but radicalism retained a common core: the constitutional language of historicist restoration and national regeneration. Bentham's alternative epistemology and vocabulary, his utilitarian *Plan of Parliamentary Reform* was in private circulation in 1809, but was not published until 1817.[38]

As it emerged much amended by a generation of war, the rhetoric of popular radicalism was not class-exclusive. Located in the 'master narrative' of providential constitutional freedom, its language was shared with middle-class reformers, aristocratic Whigs and residual civic humanists. The programme of the people, the radical mass platform which emerged at the end of the war – the eventual point of breakthrough to 'members unlimited' – looked to the leadership of 'independent' gentlemen, patriots above faction, interest or class.

3

THE RADICAL MASS PLATFORM, 1815–20

Shall Englishmen o'ercome each foe
and now at home those rights forgo
Enjoy'd by none beside?
Degenerate race! ah! then in vain
Your birthrights sacred to maintain
HAMPDEN and SYDNEY died!

('Ode', *Manchester Observer*, 9 January 1819)

The transition to peace without plenty gave added resonance to the radical economic message. Demobilization, deflation and distress were compounded by adverse climatic factors: the spring and summer of 1816 were the worst in recorded history, the result of unprecedented volcanic eruptions in the Pacific which obscured the sky for months on end. Henceforth, the old demand for 'economical reform', a programme to reduce the influence of the executive, gave way to the new slogan of 'cheap government', promoted as the means to economic relief and recovery. Whether to facilitate commercial liberalism or artisan protectionism, parliamentary reform was increasingly recognized as the necessary first step to economic amelioration.

Encouraged by the successful coordination of parliamentary and external pressure mobilized by the anti-slave trade and 'petition and debate' campaigns, moderate reformers redoubled their efforts, seeking to galvanize concern at economic distress into support for direct-taxation household suffrage. Their methods and approach, however, failed to satisfy the more ardent 'patriotic' radicals, most notably the former loyalists who reacted with anger as postwar deflation redistributed wealth from productive labourers to unproductive (and upstart) financiers and rentiers, undermining the vestigial bonds of duty, respect and mutual obligation. The champion of the unrepresented and overtaxed people, 'Orator' Hunt broke through the constraints of conventional extra-parliamentary politics to establish the radical mass platform, the format which was to dominate popular protest until the final collapse of Chartism.[1]

Encouraged by Cobbett, Hunt acquired notoriety as he stood forward to expose the machinations of the Westminster Committee or 'Rump' as it was now known. The old LCS members had been purged as the constituency had become more prosperous, leaving the Committee securely in the hands of those who sought moderate reform through alliance with the Whigs. Their intention was to promote Henry Brougham, successful strategist of 'petition and debate' campaigns, as Burdett's running-mate. Dismayed by Burdett's compliance, Hunt used every public opportunity to condemn the caucus of '*petty shop-keepers, and little tradesmen,* who under the denomination of *taxpaying housekeepers,* enlisted themselves under the banner of Sir Francis Burdett, in order to set themselves up as a sort of privileged class, above the *operative* manufacturer, the artizan, the mechanic and the labourer'.[2]

At the same time, Hunt lost patience with the restrictive premises of extra-parliamentary politics, where the veteran Major Cartwright still set the agenda. The Hampden Club campaign of 1816–17, the continuation of Cartwright's pioneering petitioning tours of the Luddite counties, was a mixture of old and new. While it drew upon the success recently achieved by the small central committee which had led the campaign against the Slave Trade, it was structured and informed by older attitudes and procedures. Having enlisted Burdett's name and prestige, Cartwright promoted a national petition campaign in the name of the Hampden Club, relying on an image – far removed from reality – of strong central leadership by wealthy independent gentlemen. There were no restrictions on who could sign, but the petitions were intended to support direct-taxation household suffrage. Cartwright and Burdett were to draw up a bill to this effect to present to the 'persons who may be deputed from petitioning Cities, Towns, or other Communities, to confer together in the Metropolis, on the best means of effectuating a constitutional Reform'. As understood by Cartwright and Burdett, this convention was a revival of Wyvill's 'association' movement of 1780–81 in which the landed classes would assume their rightful role as leaders. Cartwright, indeed, tried to arrange an assembly of dignitaries at the Mansion House ready to take the lead once the humble provincial delegates arrived in London with their petitions. The Hampden Club campaign, however, was to be totally transformed when Hunt, in working alliance with the 'revolutionary party', found a platform at Spa Fields from which to propound inclusive and uncompromising democratic radicalism.[3] Heirs of the Despard *putsch* tradition, the revolutionary party (to use Terry Parssinen's useful terminology) were busy recruiting in metropolitan taverns, hoping for an uprising led by the physically intimidating – canal navvies, soldiers, sailors, dockworkers, the rough, unemployed and other masculine groups fond of their beer. As post-war distress intensified, they looked to a well-attended public meeting as the best springboard for insurrection, and hence invited all the reform celebrities of the day to address a meeting of 'Distressed Manufacturers, Mariners, Artisans, and others' at Spa Fields.[4] Hunt alone accepted after he had satisfied himself that he was not being drawn into a revolutionary plan to abolish private property in land. In a private interview with Dr Watson, the impecunious apothecary and leading ultra-radical strategist, Hunt insisted there must be no reference to Spencean principles, and no incitement to riot. The meeting, a legitimate extension of political activity, would be strictly 'constitutional', a forum at which the distressed masses would enrol in an extra-parliamentary campaign of petitions and memorials to 'save the wreck of the constitution' by the instauration of universal suffrage, annual parliaments and the ballot.

Keen to exploit Hunt's notoriety as a crowd-puller, Watson readily accepted these stipulations. Others were less willing to do so. Spa Fields divided strategists from ideologists, a recurring characteristic of 'revolutionary' radical groups. Thomas Evans, the leading ideologue, refused to compromise Spencean principles for the sake of mass agitation. Rejecting the platform posturing of Hunt and Watson, Evans confined himself to tavern debating clubs where he propounded his systematic Christian restatement of the Spencean plan. In his *Christian Policy, the Salvation of the Empire* (1816), however, Evans made some concessions to popular taste. A compound of economic prescription, populist idioms and nostalgia, it incorporated fierce condemnation of the war-inflated financial elite who conspired to enmesh the people in debt and dependence. Projected in this way, Spenceanism broadened its appeal among 'ragged radicals', urban artisans and lesser professionals. Evans, however, demanded the highest standards of new recruits: applicants for membership of his Society of Spencean Philanthropists had to undergo a formal test in the master's principles, affirming that the land was the people's farm. Evans, indeed, carried ideological pedantry and dispute to fissiparous extreme, steadily isolating himself from the populist conviviality of tavern clubs where audiences relaxed in anti-intellectual, blasphemous enjoyment of the ritual 'hullabaloo' of satirical toasts, patriotic songs and didactic debate, a burlesque 'counter-theatre' which mocked and demystified the establishment and its public ceremonial.[5]

By embracing plebeian cultural idioms in radical 'counter-theatre', post-war tavern radicals reached further towards a popular audience than their Jacobin forebears. Satirical debunking of the establishment helped to eradicate instinctive or unthinking loyalism, to sever automatic links with the *status quo*, but much more was required to mobilize the masses, to engage the active participation of 'members unlimited' in radical agitation. Radicals had both to ridicule establishment pageantry and to out-match it, to offer more attractive forms of public ceremonial. At Spa Fields Hunt pointed towards a new form of disciplined and defiant public display, a people's ceremonial which, having quickly invented its own ritual and tradition, enabled the radicals to challenge the establishment for control of public space.

Thanks to Hunt's commanding presence, the Spa Fields meetings were not sullied by criminal opportunism (at a time when the crime rate was soaring precipitously), by rioting (except for a breakaway group of demobilized seamen, awaiting arrears in pay and prize money) or by revolutionary *putsch*. Where Watson was prepared to postpone the *coup*, pending further mass mobilization, other revolutionaries, most notably Arthur Thistlewood and Watson's own son, were less patient. They made sure that a second meeting was called so that they could implement the original plan – every detail of which was well known to government informers – to inflame the assembled crowd and storm the Bank and the Tower. It was not until the disastrous failure of precipitate insurrectionism on 2 December 1816 that the more recalcitrant members of the 'revolutionary party' came to accept the utility of Hunt's constitutional mass platform.[6]

With their fruit-sellers, gingerbread stalls and fairground atmosphere, the Spa Fields meetings of 1816-17 established the popular context and tone of democratic radical endeavour. Identities merged in a wider solidarity. Having assembled behind banners and bands in trade, locality, family, ethnic and other groups, the crowd joined together in proud display as the sovereign, but unrepresented, people. Those without the political nation stood forward to demand universal suffrage, annual parliaments and the ballot, in open constitutional manner and in Sunday best clothes, relying on the proud and disciplined display of numbers (marshalled by demobilized ex-servicemen) to coerce the otherwise inexorable government, 'peaceably if we may, forcibly if we must'. Open and inclusive in procedure and programme, the mass platform deliberately exploited ambiguities in the law and constitution, drawing upon the emotive rhetoric of popular constitutionalism and 'people's history'. The popular format which Hunt introduced at Spa Fields – constitutional mass pressure from without for the constitutional democratic rights of all – continued to inform radical agitation throughout the age of the Chartists.[7]

In the provinces, news of Spa Fields instantly transformed the Hampden Club petitioning campaign. Before setting off for London, a group of northern working-class delegates, elected at mass meetings held in the wake of Spa Fields, met at Middleton. Having repudiated any 'doctrine of exclusion', they pledged support for the Spa Fields programme, justified in working-class terms of under-consumption and a labour theory of value:

They must seek a Power in the Constitution . . . a Power that will curtail luxury – by diminishing Taxation, and will enable the people to buy shoes, stockings, shirts, coats, hats, etc. and then there will be a demand for labour . . . suffrage commensurate with *direct* Taxation, seems to grant, that property only ought to be represented; whereas, labour makes property, and therefore in the name of common sense ought to be represented.[8]

The Convention itself confirmed the decisive change in mood and style. Burdett absented himself, leaving old Major Cartwright to defend the official programme of household suffrage against the blunt criticism of the 'country cousins'.

When the petitions were eventually presented to the Commons, calling for universal suffrage, Brougham, the great hope of moderate radicals, regained Whig party favour by leading the attack on radical extremists.

The mass platform was crushed by the 'dungeon parliament' of 1817. The spectre of Spencean revolution haunted the 'blue bags' of the parliamentary committees of secrecy, providing ample pretext for the suspension of habeas corpus, a new Seditious Meeting Prevention Act, and a general clampdown on radical societies and the radical press, which prompted William Cobbett, a belated convert to universal suffrage, to flee the country. 'Alarm' proved self-fulfilling, forcing radicals underground into the milieu of the *agent-provocateur*. The provincial risings of 1817 cannot be explained, however, solely in terms of the culpability of government and the nefarious spy-system. Plans were first mooted during the Hampden Club convention when William Benbow, Joseph Mitchell and other northern delegates were befriended by members of the 'revolutionary party' at the evening drinking and discussion sessions at the Cock, Grafton Street. Provincial radicals wanted to be sure of mass support and popular legitimacy before taking physical action. The March of the Blanketeers, their first response to repression, combined all the advantages of legality with all the opportunities of development into something else. In strict conformity with legislation against tumultuous petitioning, they decided to petition in groups of twenty, ten of which number, bearing blankets on their backs, were to march to London to present the petitions. Fearing a mass invasion of the capital, the authorities took swift and decisive action to curtail this pioneer hunger march, although a few poor weavers got as far as Ashbourne. Anger at the detention of Bagguley, Drummond, Johnston and other Blanketeer leaders prompted some indiscreet radicals to talk of making a 'Moscow of Manchester', upon which grounds the Ardwick Bridge secret committee and others (including Samuel Bamford and 'Dr' Healey) were

arrested. Most were soon discharged because of insufficient evidence. Meanwhile, plans for the general rising
first discussed at the Cock were taking shape. Central
coordination was entrusted to delegate meetings at
Wakefield, where it was agreed that there should be simultaneous uprisings in the towns of the midlands and
the north, a concentration of forces round Nottingham,
and then a march on London. To ascertain the support
which was likely to be forthcoming, Joseph Mitchell was
deputed to tour the country and report back to Wakefield.
As is well known, he soon acquired a travelling companion,
the infamous Oliver the spy.

Postponed to 9 June, the rising was a limited affair.
Several district delegate meetings had already been raided
and there were considerable suspicions about Oliver, but
even so, some radicals braved the hopelessly uneven odds
on the night. Clothing workers advanced upon Huddersfield in their hundreds in the Folley Hall rising, but wisely
dispersed before military reinforcements arrived. At
Pentrich, home base of Thomas Bacon, the veteran Jacobin
who had represented the east midlands radicals at the
Hampden Club convention, the discussions at the Cock,
and the central delegate meetings at Wakefield, Jeremiah
Brandreth led a contingent of men through the pouring
rain on the fourteen-mile march to Nottingham, stopping
at houses *en route* to demand arms and support: on one
occasion, a farm labourer was accidentally shot. When they
finally reached Nottingham, wet and demoralized, they
were immediately overpowered by a force of hussars ready
in waiting.[9]

There was a distinct working-class emphasis in the return
of persons arrested, committed or detained on treason-
able charges in 1817. Thistlewood was the solitary 'gentleman'; Drs Watson and Healey were entered as surgeons;
all the rest, some 90-odd names, were artisans, labourers
and factory workers.[10] This class identity was immediately
confirmed when radicals started to mobilize again. Links
with the trades were forged during the strikes of 1818,

when Manchester spinners and other workers took advantage of the brief economic recovery to seek restoration of former rates of pay through general unionism and intertrades assistance. At a mass meeting in Palace Yard, arranged by the Watsonites once the Seditious Meetings Prevention Act had run its course, Hunt was joined on the platform by John Gast, the shipwrights' leader, who implored the 'mechanical classes' to 'go forth' with the radicals 'as the Barons of old with a Sword in one hand and the Bill of Rights in the other and demand your birthrights'. A strident Remonstrance was adopted, reminding the Regent of the lessons of history and of the workers' right to protection – 'every industrious labourer, manufacturer and mechanic, has a right to reap the ample and substantial fruits of his virtuous and USEFUL TOIL'. To enlist northern workers in the new campaign, Hunt set off for Manchester in January 1819, taking the Remonstrance – and his radical reputation – with him.[11]

An advocate of 'the cause of truth', Hunt was hailed in the north as 'the intrepid champion of the people's rights'. 'The good old character of an independent country Gentleman was surely there in him', a correspondent wrote to the *Manchester Observer*:

I had almost compared him to an English Baron in the time of Magna Charta, but that Mr Hunt's motives were so much more praiseworthy; he was not there as they met that worthless King at Runnimede, to advocate the rights of a few, but of all.[12]

'Meaney who was Lukewarm jacks before', one of Colonel Fletcher's semi-literate informers reported, 'now Comes forward and Idlese hunt'.[13] After the champion's departure, momentum was maintained by a number of new societies. Through educational and cultural provision, these open organizations, based on the Wesleyan class-system, attracted community involvement in the radical cause, reinforcing the structural foundations for collective action.

When rejection of the Remonstrance coincided with economic downturn, this network of local societies provided the coordinating machinery for an unprecedented national campaign of mass pressure from without.

During the early summer of 1819, Union Societies and Political Protestants spread from their respective bases in Lancashire and Yorkshire to other manufacturing districts, Birmingham and the west midlands, Newcastle and the north-east. Trades which had earlier eschewed politics turned enthusiastically to radicalism, led by the most distressed of all, the handloom weavers of Carlisle, whose only hope previously had been government-assisted emigration to Canada. Particular efforts were made to enlist the growing number of Irish immigrants 'in the cause of Universal Civil and Religious Liberty'. To overcome the problem of size and communication in London and large cities, a system of parochial unions was introduced. Women were enrolled in special female reform societies, entering the public arena to pledge support for universal manhood suffrage through the rhetoric of manhood and domestic responsibility, the invocation of a 'natural' order threatened by economic change and adversity.[14]

The great mass meetings of 1819 were outings for whole families, trades and communities. Excitement was generated through the lively interaction between orators and the crowd, a complex mutual relationship of expectation, performance and response. The middle class were quite welcome to participate in this democratic arena of those *without* the political nation – phrased in the language of the people, radicalism was addressed to all the useful and unrepresented classes in society – but they chose to absent themselves. Class pride developed as the working class realized they were perforce on their own, save of course for the presence of their champion, the gentlemanly Hunt, flamboyant and independent in his famous white hat.

Working-class carnivals, mass meetings displayed a rich repertoire of symbols, ritual and iconography, a language of class without words, part appropriation, part parody of dominant motifs. The highlight was the arrival of the local female reform society, dressed in best white attire, to present the chairman, as at Blackburn on 5 July, with an elaborate cap of liberty 'made of scarlet silk or satin, lined with green, with a serpentine gold lace, terminating with a rich gold tassel'. The cap of liberty was well chosen as the rallying symbol of the 1819 campaign. The Roman badge of freedom, it was an ancient and revered emblem which had adorned Britannia's spear and the coinage of the realm until the 1790s when it acquired revolutionary connotations as the livery of French anarchy and Jacobin terror. By presenting such an audacious symbol with its multivocal constitutionalist and republican meanings, the women, otherwise apologetic and demure, added much to the drama and tension of the mass meetings, testing the resolve of the authorities. The ability to display the cap became the measure of the shifting balance of power as radicals and the authorities engaged in the politics of modern collective violence. Each side hoped the other would be the first to overstep the mark, transgress the constitution and lose public sanction.[15]

Community and class pride, reinforced by strict marshalling by demobilized ex-servicemen, ensured the discipline and good order of the mass meetings, each of which contributed to the 'national union'. This cumulative display of irresistible strength proceeded through local meetings to a series of huge regional demonstrations, of which that planned for St Peter's Field, Manchester, in August, under Hunt's chairmanship, was to be the largest yet, 'rather a meeting of the County of *Lancashire* etc. than of Manchester alone'. Convinced that Whitehall was being unduly circumspect – Sidmouth was confounded by the 'unprecedented Artifice with which the Demagogues of the present day contrive without transgressing the Law, to produce on the Public Mind the same effect which used only to be created by means unquestionably unlawful' – the Manchester magistrates decided to 'bring the matter to issue'. 'If the agitators of the country determine to persevere in their meeting', the stipendiary magistrate announced, 'it will necessarily prove a trial of strength and there must be a conflict.' On 16 August, the magistrates gained their bloody victory. At least eleven people were killed and many hundreds injured when the magistrates sent in the inebriated publicans, butchers and shopkeepers of the local yeomanry to arrest Hunt and other leaders on the platform, and then ordered in the 15th Hussars to disperse the peaceable crowd.[16]

The Peterloo massacre inflamed radical spirits, aroused middle-class public opinion and unnerved the government. The failure of the radicals to advance beyond this vantage ground pinpoints a recurrent critical flaw in popular constitutional radical strategy. At some point leaders had to decide whether or not the social compact had been violated, whether the time had come when the oppressed people should exercise their sovereign right of physical resistance as sanctioned by history, Blackstone and other authorities. It was this question of timing, this issue of judgement, rather than any absolute commitment to 'moral force' or 'physical force' which divided radicals at critical moments like the post-Peterloo crisis. Legitimacy proved self-defeating. As radicals agonized over constitutional right, they lost their physical might. While they hesitated and deliberated, mass support dwindled, excitement was squandered and the initiative passed back to the relieved authorities.

At the crucial point Hunt refused to sanction the Watsonite plans for a full-scale confrontation through simultaneous mass meetings. Indeed, he decided to forgo the platform altogether, resting the radical case on Peterloo itself. In the forum of public opinion, however, it was the established opposition, not the democratic radicals, who benefitted from the sense of outrage, while in the courts the authorities were exonerated without question, Hunt's unremitting efforts to bring them to justice notwithstanding. The moral and propaganda triumph of Peterloo proved a pyrrhic victory. Back in control, the government asserted its power. Parliament was specially convened to pass the Six Acts, an attempt to return to the narrow political participation of the eighteenth century: 'taxes on knowledge' were imposed on the press, and the right of public meeting was limited by a series of measures, prohibiting banners and flags, and restricting attendance to those actually resident in the parish.

Angered by the collapse of mass support and the imposition of repression, the aggrieved Watsonites, now under Thistlewood's leadership, reverted to conspiracy to be promptly entrapped by George Edwards, the government *agent-provocateur* in the Cato Street affair. This futile plan to assassinate the cabinet at dinner confirmed the government in its new powers and cut across wider moves in the provinces, where the initiative passed from Lancashire to the West Riding as the centre of insurrectionary planning. Links with other areas proved tenuous, unreliable or positively dangerous, but they extended across the Scottish border where the rising of 1820 took the form of a popular but short-lived general strike. The numbers involved in the English risings at Huddersfield on the night of 31 March–1 April and at Grange Moor on 11 April were less impressive, but significantly, this defiant last act of the post-war mobilization followed immediately on news of Hunt's conviction at York for his part in the Peterloo meeting. West Riding insurrectionists marched behind banners proclaiming 'Hunt the Intrepid Champion of the Rights and Liberties of the People'. The mass platform had failed, but with Hunt elevated to martyrdom, critics of the populist radicalism he personified so well were to find it impossible to dislodge him and redirect radical endeavour.[17]

The resonance of populist motifs was immediately confirmed when George IV, an unpopular symbol of repression and profligacy, endeavoured to divorce his estranged wife Caroline, on his ascent to the throne in 1820. Writers, publicists and *philosophes manqués*, impoverished by their radical stock-in-trade, discovered a lucrative new line in anti-establishment satire and pornography, while the press prospered from the 'aestheticization' of the affair. Incorporated in the conventions of melodrama and farce, Caroline's history and grievances were compulsive reading. Sexual morality became a political issue in a symbolic clash of aristocratic libertinism, conservative evangelicalism and plebeian flexibility. In melodramatic and romantic portrayal, Caroline was an emblem of purity and victimization, a wronged queen who would be rescued and protected by the moral virtue of the productive classes, chivalry which enshrined male dominance. Satirical accounts drew upon the rougher culture of the taverns, a lively brew of republicanism, infidelism and sexual freedom, which celebrated Caroline as a lusty, defiant wife, a queen of misrule who legitimized defiance of established order and conventional morality as well as women's participation in politics. As a multivocal symbol of opposition, Caroline attracted national support, reaching into small market and historic towns untouched by the post-war radical platform.[18] However, much of her appeal depended on 'collusion and convergence', on old-style political manipulation by Whigs, Burdettites, city reformers and other influential out-groups. Patronized by the opposition, public processions in support of the Queen were expensive and impressive spectacles, allowing the people, as Hazlitt shrewdly observed, to enjoy 'the mock equality with sovereign rank, the acting in a farce of state'.[19] The Queen's affair restored the freedom of political agitation, nullifying much of the Six Acts, but it failed to reactivate the radical platform. Once the high political drama had dissipated, radicals were unable to reach a popular audience.

4

IDEOLOGY, PUBLIC OPINION AND REFORM, 1820–35

The popular mobilization of the post-war years was followed by a period of critical self-analysis and internal dissension – a sequence subsequently familiar to the Chartists – as conflicting conclusions were drawn from the failure and decline of mass agitation. Other factors contributed to the revisionist mood of the 1820s, a time when a new pattern of economic fluctuation and distress was beginning to assert itself. Confronted by the industrial trade cycle, popular radicals rethought their ideology in conflict with the advanced guard of middle-class 'philosophic radicals', Utilitarian and didactic popularizers of Ricardian political economy. Popular radicals, however, failed to regain the initiative as 'public opinion', a middle-class construction, became increasingly 'liberal' and influential.

Disillusioned by vacillating crowds, some radicals abandoned popular agitation to strengthen their own individual commitment to the cause, subjecting themselves to an ascetic regime of mental and bodily self-improvement. Richard Carlile, the incorruptible Paineite ideologue, pursued this project of ideological purification and physical puritanism with exemplary counter-cultural rigour. A trenchant critic of the empty bluster and personalized style of Hunt's 'charismatic' leadership, Carlile displayed the

51

worst faults of an 'ideological' leader, provoking innu-
merable schisms among the votaries with his dictatorial
pronouncements on matters of doctrine, so different in
tone from the eclectic and undogmatic nature of popular radical argument. On the platform, distinctions between arguments based on historical precedent and those
based on natural rights, or between popular constitutionalism and republicanism, were rarely sharply drawn. Carlile,
by contrast, insisted on strict conformity to the infidel-
republican Paineite formulary, the exegesis of which (at
different times deist, atheist and spiritualist) he reserved
for himself alone. In this intensely sectarian and ideological form, rational republicanism failed to engage with
the general gut republicanism – the irreverence, scepti-
cism and anti-authoritarianism – which often ran deep in
working-class culture.

Like Godwin and the 'utopian' radicals of the 1790s,
Carlile withdrew from collective organization and its populist delusions to concentrate on the 'multiplication of
reason'. The language of science, James Epstein observes,
was to prevail in 'reason's republic', where Carlile 'privileged written texts over ritualized public display and ra-
tionalist discourse over meanings structured around the
workings of either metaphor or metonymy'. The 'march
of infidelity', the progress of scientific materialism against
superstition, myth and ignorance, placed him at the fore-
front of the struggle for the freedom of the press, the
rational agency which would 'work the great necessary
moral and political change among mankind – The Printing Press may be strictly denominated a Multiplication
Table, as applicable to the mind of man.' Through his
determination to expand the public domain of the printed
word, Carlile found himself in unwelcome alliance with
commercial pornographers, as private prosecuting societies
tried to ban the publication and distribution of obscene
and freethought literature. A martyr to the cause, the
imprisoned Carlile inspired an heroic campaign of resistance as his inexhaustible 'corps' of volunteers, male and

female, forced the societies to withdraw from the courts thwarted and defeated.[1]

Unlike the pornographers, Carlile and his supporters were libertarians, not libertines. In the sanctuary of their 'temples of reason', these votaries of Paineite republicanism, 'zetetics' as they were called, advocated contraception, female equality and free love, a programme of sexual radicalism articulated in the language of the liberal Enlightenment, of individual freedom and moral responsibility.[2] Infidel, republican and sexual radical, Carlile, the doctrinaire individualist, was also the proselyte of orthodox political economy, 'the science of the welfare of mankind'. His pioneer advocacy of birth control was motivated by Malthusianism as much as by feminism, by his conviction that distress was caused by the people themselves through bad and improvident habits and the 'excess of their numbers in relation to the supply of labour that can employ them': '*You cannot be free, you can find no reform, until you begin it with yourselves* . . . abstain from gin and the gin-shop, from gospel and the gospel-shop, from sin and silly salvation.' By the end of the 1820s, Carlile stood widely divorced from popular radicalism, culture and experience, a lone opponent of collective endeavour of 'any sect, party, or society . . . I carry the principle even to trade societies, and think them injurious to the general interests of the trades'.[3]

Other advocates of individualism, most notably the popularizers of Ricardian political economy, were less extreme. In pursuit of a progressive union of capital and labour in a free market society, Francis Place and the 'philosophic' radicals assumed the leadership of the campaign to repeal the Combination Laws. Repeal would remove an unnecessary antagonism between employers and employees, a grievance which diverted attention from the real factors governing labour, demographic and market forces beyond the control of legislation or trade unionism. Such laissez-faire prescriptions, however, encountered vigorous opposition.[4]

Established in the wake of legislation confirming the legal status of trade unions, the *Trades Newspaper* reprinted lengthy extracts from Thomas Hodgskin's *Labour Defended*, a foundation text of the new anti-capitalist political economy. Seizing upon Ricardo's use of labour as the measure of value, Hodgskin insisted that labour was the sole creator of value. Workers, however, were denied the whole produce of their labour by inequalities of exchange which, in incorporating 'unearned' rent and profit, distorted the natural economic laws and labour-embodied values upheld by Adam Smith. According to Hodgskin and other Ricardian or rather Smithian socialists, it was not taxation and political corruption which caused impoverishment but the inequitable operation of the economic system. Unproductive middlemen and capitalists were able both to add to the labour value of commodities and to purchase labour itself at less than its intrinsic value. Based on the labour theory of value, this 'new ideology' marked a decisive advance. The traditional agrarian analysis of Spence, Ogilvie, Paine and Hall had explained poverty and exploitation in terms of physical shortage and the primal theft of land, and was thus unable to account for cyclical depression, for distress in the midst of unparalleled abundance and glutted overstocked markets.

The new anti-capitalist economics was conducted in a discourse of 'natural' economic laws and values, in which attention was focused not on the relations of production (the later preoccupation of Marx) but on inequalities of distribution and exchange. Above all, it condemned the disproportionate market power which enabled unproductive capitalists and middlemen to buy labour cheaply and sell it dear. These inequalities were accentuated by the 'mysticism of money': currency, the medium used to effect exchange, obscured the true value of labour and commodities. Hence, exploitation and distress were to be eliminated through the independent creation of the necessary conditions for equitable exchange, beginning with labour exchanges and labour notes, a natural standard of value and medium of exchange. In the 'people's science' of labour economics there was no suggestion of forcible appropriation or redistribution.[5]

Here the Owenites set the example. Eschewing the need for class or political struggle, they provided the facilities – often at extravagant expense – wherein all classes could cooperate in practical implementation of the labour theory of value, the essential economic foundation for a new moral world of communitarian socialism. Owenism, however, was much more than an economic alternative to capitalism. It offered the vision of a society without competition, oppression, superstition or inequality, a cooperative community free from the selfishness engendered by the market, private property, religion and marriage, a new moral and technological world where housework would be shared and mechanized. A liberating influence on many women, Owenism laid the foundation of feminist-socialism, extending the programme of sexual equality and marriage reform advocated within the individualist confines of Carlile's ultra-radicalism.[6]

Owenites condemned the market altogether, repudiating its corrosive social and psychological influences. Other anti-capitalist economists sought merely to eradicate its inequalities – the corrupt institutions, self-interested legislation and monopoly power – which privileged the unproductive at the expense of the worker. Here the 'new ideology' of the 1820s, for all its stress on endogenous economic exploitation, proved compatible with traditional radical analysis. At the popular level, indeed, where eclecticism prevailed, the new ideology did not displace the old political attitudes, concepts and aims. It reinforced them. It was political monopoly, after all, which enabled idle and unproductive middlemen to control and manipulate the systems of currency, distribution and exchange, a point repeatedly stressed in the unstamped press. 'The process is this', the *Poor Man's Guardian* explained:

The landlords and capitalists make the law, – the law makes the institutions, – the institutions place the producers in such a position that they must either starve or sell their produce for a fraction of its value, that is to say, give up the major portion of it to the landlords and capitalists. Thus are the producers robbed, and thus do the rich acquire their riches.[7]

Thus the radicals persisted in explaining inequality and exploitation in political terms. Just as the war-inflated 'funding system' had been built on the base of political monopoly so it was political power that underpinned the capitalist system and denied the worker the right to the whole produce of his labour. The new ideology simply extended the ranks of radical demonology: alongside fundholders, sinecurists, pensioners and other tax-gorgers, there now sat the cotton lords, millocrats (note the significant political terminology) and other capitalists, parasitic middlemen whose privileged and tyrannical position of unequal exchange stemmed from their monopoly of political and legal power. Whether directed against tax-eaters and/or capitalists, the radical demand was always the same: an end to the system which left labour alone unprotected and at the mercy of those who monopolized the state and the law.

Previously swamped by mass agitation, middle-class radicals gained a hearing in the 1820s, when liberalism – imported into British politics from the Spanish 'Liberales' of the revolutions of 1812 and 1820 – became a fashionable addition to political vocabulary. A number of factors – economic, ideological and agitational – accounted for this increased assertiveness and confidence, the first signs of which were already apparent in the aftermath of Peterloo. J. E. Taylor, a Manchester cotton merchant and Unitarian, led the campaign against the 'murderous' conduct of the local authorities before becoming the first editor of the *Manchester Guardian* in 1821, one of several papers which gave voice to provincial middle-class radicalism and its growing demand for direct parliamentary representation. An expression of middle-class 'moral power', public opinion acquired a new influence in the 1820s, questioning the traditional practices of the *'ancien régime'*. Although dependent on close boroughs for support, and hostile to any suggestion of parliamentary reform, Canningite 'liberal Toryism' sought to enlist middle-class values of firmness, economy and morality.[8]

Canning's popularity notwithstanding, an increasing number of previously apolitical or Tory businessmen came to join liberal Dissenters in demanding direct representation for new and expanding manufacturing and commercial centres. This was the inevitable consequence of the advance of industrialism: uneven as it was, economic development brought with it a complex array of technical issues for parliamentary consideration. The popularization of Ricardian political economy added an ideological edge. Highlighting the conflict between landowners and other classes, popular expositions of the otherwise dismal science championed the capitalists as generators of economic progress, imbuing the middle classes, as John Dinwiddy noted, with a sense of collective identity and confidence and a willingness to question aristocratic political monopoly. Utilitarianism, once rendered accessible by James Mill and the *Westminster Review* (established 1824), acted in similar manner. A forceful critique of privilege, corruption and protection, its language of functional efficiency contributed substantially to the growth of reform sentiment within the middle classes.[9]

At the agitational level, middle-class radicals rejected the politics of 'interest', the old lobbying model of the General Chamber of Manufacturers, in favour of 'pressure from without', drawing upon the remarkable success of Daniel O'Connell's Catholic Association and the innovative tactics of the 'faddists' or 'anti-everythingarians'.

Among these 'crotcheteers' or 'moral radicals', the abolitionists set the pace, boosted by their successful campaign against the slave trade in 1807. Having taken advice from O'Connell, a group of anti-slavery militants established an Agency Committee with an independent fund and a team of paid lecturers who were sent round the country to win over the unconverted and to coordinate activity (including a consumer boycott of slave-produced sugar) in support of immediate abolition. Once parliamentary reform was secured in 1832, abolitionists introduced the pledge – the first step towards the politics of electoral pressure – calling upon parliamentary candidates to declare their position on immediate abolition, publishing the results for the guidance of voters.[10]

Although they had enhanced their profile in condemnation of Peterloo and in support of Caroline, the Whigs failed to keep pace with the increased commitment to reform among the middle classes. In the agricultural depression of 1821–3, many Whigs joined country gentlemen at county meetings to demand concessions for the landed interest and a moderate reform of parliament, a 'countryman' programme in which Cobbett, recently returned from America, sought to incorporate the labourers' politics of bread, bacon and beer.[11] There was less enthusiasm, however, for Lord John Russell's radical proposals to transfer seats from disfranchised corrupt boroughs to unrepresented towns. Boosted by prosperity, 'liberal Toryism', with its commitment to efficient cheap government and moral reform, continued to engage with public opinion. Canning's skilful flattery of the middle classes served to marginalize the Whigs – and reform. All this was to change, however, with Canning's sudden death. Toryism collapsed in the confusion of parties, torn asunder by Catholic Emancipation, severe economic distress and a general crisis of authority. At the end of the 1820s, reform was suddenly at the top of the agenda.

The disenchanted ultra-Tories, outraged by party treachery over 'corn, cash and catholics', were first in the field.

Drawing upon the old country party programme, Blandford and his colleagues called for the abolition of rotten boroughs and other reforms to curb the corrupt and traitorous executive. Following on their heels came Whig reformers: with the Catholic question settled, parliamentary reform could now be recognized as the party's defining issue. Schemes abandoned in the prosperity of the mid-1820s were picked up again, with Russell and others advocating the incorporation of new commercial and manufacturing interests to make parliament more representative. As party alignments fractured and economic depression intensified, parliamentary reform became practical politics.[12]

The Reform Bill agitation demonstrated the complex interaction between parliamentary and extra-parliamentary politics. Westminster politicians, as Wellington discovered, could not ignore outside support for reform, but it was the particular configuration of 'high politics', the confusion of parties, which determined the timing and format of the first Reform Bill. Appointed to office with a reform-pledged ministry on Wellington's departure in November 1830, Grey decided on a bold course, introducing proposals which gained enthusiastic popular support but encountered the obdurate resistance of Tories and 'Old Corruption'. As orchestrated by the middle-class leadership of the new Political Unions, extra-parliamentary agitation in favour of the Bill served a number of purposes. While keeping the otherwise irresolute Whigs firm to their proposals, pressure from without projected an image of class harmony among the industrious people and suggested a process of on-going liberal reform. Most popular radicals were swept along by the enthusiasm, convinced by their (mis)reading of Whig intentions and liberal propaganda that democratic reform would swiftly follow. Soon disabused, their radicalism acquired an independent working-class

edge. Conducted within the populist rhetoric of constitutional reform, the Reform Bill agitation thus exemplified
the complex mechanisms – linguistic, political, economic
and social – by which radicalism could give near simultaneous expression to both class harmony and class conflict. Grey's ministry comprised Whigs, liberals, moderates
and liberal Tories, united only by commitment to parliamentary reform. Historians have focused on moderates
and liberals to expose the conflicting sociological premises
of 'Whig' reform. For moderates, reform was an updated
'country'-style readjustment, a grudging but necessary
concession which, by removing the worst abuses, would
cure the discredited system, restoring the confidence the
governing classes had lost in their own institutions. Liberal reform was altogether more progressive, premised on
a realignment of the landed and commercial classes within
an enlarged political nation, reformed to incorporate middle-class ability, respectability and enterprise. As it was,
neither moderates nor liberals were represented in the
small committee which drafted the Bill. Shrewdly chosen
by Grey to ensure a thorough, once and for all, measure
of reform which would make parliament truly representative
of the key national interests, the committee comprised a
handful of radicals and old Whigs, aristocrats determined
to demonstrate their political usefulness and responsive-
ness, after lengthy absence from power. Averse to piece-
meal tinkering, the committee proposed a wholesale
reconstruction of the constitution, prescribing minimum
standards for the size of constituencies and uniform standards for enfranchisement.[13]

These core proposals – the disfranchisement of rotten
boroughs, the enfranchisement of new towns, and a uniform £10 household franchise – captured the public im-
agination. Although some of their own number disliked
the reform cry, the Whigs were reinvigorated as the party
of the people, constitutional liberty and reform. Whatever their intentions, the Whigs took repossession of the
traditional language of constitutional reform, attracting

a broad-based constituency of support which extended beyond the commercial classes specifically addressed by the liberals. Having expected so much less from the 'apostate' Whigs, popular radicals became ardent proselytes of the Bill, convinced that it left the full radical programme no more than an easy instalment away. True to the spirit of post-war radicalism, Hunt tried to dispel this pervasive popular delusion. Confronted by liberal propaganda, reformist sentiment and popular prejudice, he was unable to establish a platform of fundamentalist democratic opposition to the Bill.

Public space was at the disposal of the Bill's promoters and supporters, enabling the Political Unions to deploy the middle-class version of collective bargaining by riot in demanding 'the Bill, the whole Bill and nothing but the Bill'. By summoning up the spectre of uncontrollable popular fury should the Bill be dropped or diluted, they kept the Whigs committed to reform despite die-hard parliamentary opposition. In this 'art of revolution' in which the crowd was allowed considerable licence on the streets, rioting reached serious proportions at Derby, Nottingham and Bristol, dangerously exposing the thin line between 'order' and 'disorder' before the introduction of professional policing. At these moments of constitutional crisis, when crowds rioted on the streets and the political unions adopted a militant, almost para-military 'national guard' posture, working-class ultra-radicals joined their gradualist colleagues in fervent support of the Bill, anticipating the prospect of a real revolutionary confrontation.[14]

At other times, however, ultra-radicals displayed much less interest. Pupils of the new 'economic' ideologies of the 1820s, they dismissed as inadequate and/or irrelevant both the Bill and Hunt's radical opposition. Throughout most of the Reform Bill agitation, the metropolitan ultra-radicals of the National Union of the Working Classes (NUWC) 'stood at ease', concentrating their attention on other developments. The NUWC had emerged out of the Metropolitan Trades Union, formed to embrace the new

ideology of the British Association for Promoting Co-operative Knowledge and the general unionism of the northern-based National Association for the Protection of Labour.
Radical politics were not ignored: the new union believed
that 'the Working Classes of Great Britain and Ireland
must obtain their rights *as men*, before they can possess
their rights *as workmen*, or enjoy the produce of their own
labour'.[15] Radicalism of this order, with its class exclusive
language and anti-capitalist ideology, shocked the liberals
and popularizers of orthodox political economy, who established the rival National Political Union during the
autumn of 1831, 'as a step towards leading the two classes
to a better understanding and diminishing the animosity
which prevailed among the working people against those
who were not compelled to work with their hands for
wages'. Through this timely cross-class endeavour, Place
hoped to retain the initiative, to prevent a popular swing
towards the NUWC and its 'absurd notions' at a critical
point in the Reform Bill agitation.[16]

Cross-class initiatives, however, enjoyed greater success
in the provinces and in less ideological form. Birmingham, a city renowned for small workshops and friendly
contact between masters and men, projected a compel-
ling image (enshrined in prints of demonstrations on New
Hall Hill) of overwhelming class unity in support of reform. Harmony, however, did not endure as the Reform
Bill agitation ran its course. Political excitement briefly
concealed the divisive impact of structural change. None
of the powerful capitalists who dominated the ruling council
of the Birmingham Political Union (BPU) had risen from
the workshops, but the local myth of 'organic growth'
provided these leaders of the 'productive classes' with a
legitimizing language of economic opportunity and social
cohesion, virtues imbued with regional pride and popular appeal during the Reform Bill agitation. Once the Bill
was passed, however, the BPU (in line with practice elsewhere) withdrew from agitation for further reform to set
to work on the new electoral register. Disaffected working-

class groups – non-electors, united trades and unemployed artisans – promptly established the rival Midland Union of the Working Classes to demand continued progress towards democratic reform, the necessity of which was underlined in a lecture by Hunt to the new society. A self-righteous rehearsal of his unheeded criticisms and forewarnings, Hunt's lecture exposed the purpose of the Bill, which 'by bringing in the middle classes, was intended to enable the Whigs to carry on the Government as nearly in the old way as possible'. Thereafter, political discord in Birmingham was compounded by economic conflict: increasing competitive pressures compelled the once in-dependent small masters to adopt the methods and values of the large capitalists on whom they depended for credit and marketing facilities. The new structure of municipal government, which followed in the wake of parliamentary reform, confirmed the new alignment, leaving the workers excluded, disillusioned and embittered.[17]

As popular enthusiasm gave way to disillusionment, Hunt's stock rose dramatically. During the Reform Bill agitation, he was generally reviled and denigrated as a Tory. The *Poor Man's Guardian*, the most radical of the new unstamped press, offered him qualified support, en-dorsing his opposition of the Bill, while repudiating his old-fashioned unreconstructed radicalism. Hunt's basic democratic fundamentalism, his unsophisticated but un-compromising opposition to 'a *liberal* measure; it certainly was all very good, very *liberal*; but *would it get the people something to eat?*', struck home only where radical tradi-tion and economic distress were already mutually rein-forcing. This applied to Lancashire towns with a proud Peterloo connection, textile communities where handloom weavers were in irreversible decline following the heavy investment in powerlooms in the early 1820s and the riots of 1826. As the 'finality' of the Bill became appar-ent, however, Hunt was restored to former national glory, revered as the democratic champion, 'Who boldly said in thirty two / The Bill was a cheat and vain / Have we not found his judgement true / We shall never see his likes again.'[18]

True to Hunt's memory, Chartism was independent and class exclusive, drawing upon the object lessons – or rather the quickly-established mythology – of 1831–2. The most potent of the myths stressed how the people had been deluded and manipulated, mobilized by duplicitous middle-class reformers as a 'reserve army' to ensure the Bill's safe passage. While determined never to be hoodwinked again, the Chartists were empowered by another of the myths to keep up the pressure from without. In the popular mind (as opposed to current 'high political' historiographical judgement), it was the sovereign force of public opinion which had finally carried the Bill, overpowering the Lords and Tories during the 'Days of May'. Wise after the event, working-class radicals looked back on the Reform Bill agitation as inspiration for subsequent success.

In the immediate aftermath, however, working-class radicals displayed little enthusiasm for agitation against the reformed and much strengthened establishment. Dissatisfaction with the Reform Act led to a temporary disillusionment with politics. There was one final act of defiance when the NUWC, enraged by the Irish Coercion Act, stood forward to confront the 'base, bloody and brutal Whigs'. Plans for a national convention, the traditional revolutionary expedient, were brought to an abrupt and bloody end when the police dispersed the crowds at the preparatory meeting at Cold Bath Fields in May 1833.[19] By this time, however, attention was turning away from politics to other arenas, most notably the general extension of trade unionism. In his last public statement before his untimely death, Hunt, the implacable opponent of liberal reform and orthodox political economy, noted the change in emphasis as he re-stated the essential goal, the political and economic protection of labour:

There are seven millions of men in the United Kingdom, who are rendered so many *political outlaws* by the

Reform Bill: by the provisions of that act, they are to all intents and purposes so many political slaves. Therefore the Unionists say, you have deprived us of all share in the making the laws, and we will make laws for ourselves, as far as regulating the hours of our labour and the amount of our wages. Consequently, one of two things must happen, either the workmen must have *more wages* and *less work*, or an *equal share* in making the *laws* that are to regulate the measure of labour, wages, and profit.[20]

Trade union attempts at vertical and horizontal integration, stimulated first by the textile and mining disputes of 1829–31 and then by disputes in artisan trades in the economic upturn of 1833–4, exposed internal tensions and contradictions. At the same time, they encountered fierce opposition from employers and the government. Rigorous use of the 'document' was supplemented by recourse to the courts in an effort to curb workers' combinations whether in urban Derby or rural Dorset. The trade union struggles of the 1830s thus marked a further deterioration in class relations.

Tactical considerations were probably to the fore as workers sought to extend the framework of unionism, but there was considerable disagreement about how best to proceed. When the London tailors put themselves forward as the test case against the competitive downward slide into sweated piece-rate poverty, their strike action was condemned as sectional and irresponsible by an array of 'friendly' critics, including Robert Owen, who sought to incorporate sympathetic employers in a Grand National Moral Union of the Productive Classes; Owen's own syndicalist critics, who advocated a militant general strike to abolish wage-slavery and establish a 'House of Trades'; and other trades who disputed the tailors' priority. These disagreements and jealousies, however, did not prohibit the development of a wider trade or 'working-class' consciousness as conflict over the productive process brought workers into confrontation with employers and the newly-reformed state. This is not to suggest any advance towards a socialist trade union ideology. The labour movement of the 1830s, Robert Sykes has observed, may have been ideologically underdeveloped, but in terms of actual class conflict it was by no means backward, as illustrated by the National Regeneration Society. In advocating an eight-hour day, this northern-based general union drew upon a range of ideological positions, from Owenite socialism to an updated version of Cobbettite anti-commercialism. As modernized by John Fielden, a leading cotton manu-facturer and enthusiast of the industrial system, Cobbett's currency nostrums were recast as an alternative political economy of shorter hours, wage regulation and restricted competition. Acutely aware of the dangers of overproduc-tion and dependence upon fickle and precarious overseas markets, Fielden looked to regulation and control to curb competition and restrict production, to redirect industry to the security and stability of a prosperous home market. In the absence of support from other employers, how-ever, the National Regeneration Society was forced towards militant class confrontation until its proposed general strike fell victim to the collapse of unionism in 1834.[21]

Economic conflict generated very visible class antagonism, hostility which was soon to infuse political relationships. As the 1830s progressed, workers attributed their various defeats to a single cause, the reformed parliament which denied them the very right of combination. The prosecu-tion of the Glasgow spinners in 1837, the latest to join the Tolpuddle martyrs and other 'victims of Whiggery', completed this politicization. The campaign on their behalf, the struggle to defend union rights, carried many workers into Chartism.

Legal and other moves against trade unions ruptured what remained of the 'reform alliance', the joint efforts of working-class and middle-class radicals to pressure the Whigs into further reforms. Campaigns for common causes were increasingly conducted in different ways and for conflicting purposes. Through lobbying, petitioning and pressure from without, middle-class radicals campaigned for the repeal of the newspaper stamp duty, looking to a cheap press to instruct and elevate the masses, to inculcate the virtues of popularized political economy. By contrast, working-class radicals openly defied the law, engaging in the 'war of the unstamped' to promote a rather different political education. 'The only knowledge which is of any service to the working people', O'Brien declared in the aptly-named *Destructive*, 'is that which makes them more dissatisfied, and makes them worse slaves. This is the knowledge we shall give them.'[22] In 1836, by which time nearly 750 people had been brought before the London courts for selling and distributing unstamped papers, the government decided to reduce the stamp duty from 4d to 1d, a measure endorsed by the parliamentary Radicals. Viewed from the working-class perspective, however, the compromise was a further act of betrayal, a political bargain which 'made the rich man's paper cheaper, and the poor man's paper dearer'.[23]

Similar tensions were revealed in 'organic' reform, as parliamentary Radicals (who adopted the capital letter to suggest a separate party status) concentrated on the single issue of the ballot. The Reform Act failed to fulfil their expectations. There was minimal disruption and little change in the composition, conduct and culture of either parliamentary or electoral politics, enabling the traditional ruling class, the largely landed elite, to retain control. In socio-electoral terms, as recent research has confirmed, there was remarkable continuity: artisans, skilled craftsmen and shopkeepers dominated the electorate numerically both before and after 1832.[24] Similarly with the social composition of parliament: over one-third of all MPs sitting between the Reform Acts of 1832 and 1867 had blood ties with the aristocracy – at least 71 per cent of those sitting in the parliament of 1841–7 were direct descendants of peers, baronets or gentry families.[25] In this depressing context, the score or so Philosophic Radicals in the reformed parliament concentrated their energies on the ballot. Encouraged by their mentor John Stuart Mill, they looked to the ballot as the surest means to reduce aristocratic influence, exercised most forcibly by intimidation in open voting. Furthermore, it was an issue which would debunk the reform credentials of the Whigs and thereby hasten the required political realignment to guarantee the progress of improvement and reform. Whig opposition to the measure would expose their true character as crypto-Tories, unworthy of genuine radical support.

For all the apparent advantages of the ballot question, the Philosophic Radicals seriously miscalculated the political realities of the day. The aristocratic Whigs displayed considerable survival skills. Strengthened against Radical pressure by the Lichfield House compact with O'Connell and his tail of Irish MPs, Russell and the 'Foxite' Whigs seized the initiative, reasserting their closeness to the people by opposing the ballot. While insisting on the 'finality' of the 1832 settlement, Russell championed the interests of the non-elected against the narrow self-interest of middle-class Radicals. Open voting, Russell insisted, enshrined the principle of responsibility to public opinion: just as the MP was responsible to his constituents and the public generally, so the elector had a responsibility to non-electors and the entire community. Furthermore, the ballot was unEnglish, at odds with the openness, frankness, honesty and manliness which characterized the freeborn Englishman. For all their intellectual brilliance, the Philosophic Radicals were unable to counter such populist rhetoric. Nor could they deny the logic of Chartist opposition. For working-class radicals, the ballot was inseparable from universal manhood suffrage. On its own, the ballot would make matters worse, as open voting at least enabled non-electors to distinguish friend from enemy, upon which basis they could exercise exclusive dealing and other forms of pressure. Having promoted the ballot as an exercise in improved class relations, Mill and the Philosophic Radicals hastily withdrew, refusing to regard the working class as adequately prepared for universal suffrage. The ballot was abandoned for Corn Law repeal or non-political literary pursuits.[26]

The Philosophic Radicals were no match for the Whig grandees and their political mongering. No candidate of suitable stature and parliamentary expertise emerged to unite and energize a distinct Radical party, despite the presence of a number of experienced politicians trained in the unreformed parliament, such as Joseph Hume, persistent, pedantic and interminable in condemnation of government extravagance. For all its limitations, the Reform Act enhanced the powers of the Commons, encouraging Hume and his colleagues to persist in radical 'independence'. Guardians of parliamentary sovereignty, they sought to control the executive, to dismantle the Hanoverian 'fiscal-military' state, through the vigilance of independent MPs, a style of politics in which parties were still disparaged as factious, sectional concerns. Apart from the ballot, there was little programmatic or ideological agreement on the Radical benches. Alongside the Benthamite prescriptions of the Philosophic Radicals, opinion extended from the untrammelled free trade of the Manchester school through the inflationary currency reform of Attwood and the Birmingham Radicals to the alternative popular political economy of regulation and protection upheld by John Fielden, Cobbett's political heir and Radical MP for Oldham. The inadequacy of parliamentary Radicalism dismayed middle-class 'moral radicals' and the wider Nonconformist constituency. Previously, political Dissent had tended to be the preserve of the Unitarian and Quaker mercantile and professional elite. After the Reform Act, however, this urban patriciate enjoyed a good working relationship with the Whigs in pursuit of a common agenda of civil liberty, the moral improvement of the people, and structural reform of urban government. While the old Dissenters were incorporated, members of the socially more modest evangelical sects, politicized by the slavery and reform agitations, stood forward to demand immediate action to rectify Nonconformist grievances. A United Committee of Dissenting bodies was formed in 1833 to campaign against church rates, religious tests at Oxbridge and Anglican supervision of the rites of passage. Disappointed in their expectation of Whig reform in Church and state, the more militant Dissenters advocated 'voluntaryism'. While working to undermine the church rate system at local level, they rejected any government reform short of disestablishment. In similar fashion, abolitionists defiantly adopted the label 'Radical' to distinguish themselves – and their insistence on an immediate and total end to slavery – from those who accepted the compromise legislation of 1833. In the temperance movement, moderation and compromise were repudiated in favour of total abstinence. As Alex Tyrell has noted, anti-slavery immediatism, religious voluntaryism and teetotalism exhibited similar characteristics of 'expressive' politics: an uncompromising emphasis on principle; an upsurge of Dissenting self-confidence; a suspicion of parliamentarians and other bearers of traditional authority; a belief that moral and political virtue would have to be forced on London by plain men from the provinces; and the adoption of the label 'Radical' to highlight the contrast with others who claimed to be working for similar ends.[27] However, this increased dissidence of dissent, was at odds with wider developments in the reformed electorate. As practised by Russell and the 'Foxites', the Whig–Liberal project of active rule was in advance of the 'public opinion' which counted at elections. In the all-important county and small-town seats, electors were increasingly disposed to conservatism, having come to distrust the Whigs (yet alone the Radicals) for their over-responsiveness to popular pressure in general and Irish Catholicism in particular.[28]

Disillusionment with the Reform Act thus took different forms, leading to the formation of distinctive working-class and middle-class radical movements by the late 1830s. The switch from the ballot to the corn laws emphasized the ideological thrust (and cultural style) of middle-class radicalism. The Anti-Corn Law League (ACLL) grew out of the Manchester Anti-Corn Law Association into a national body in March 1839, bringing a new vigour and unity to middle-class radical endeavour as it campaigned against the symbol of aristocratic misrule and the major impediment to free trade. Its leading figures, Richard Cobden and John Bright, were committed radicals in search of a rallying cause. Cobden, a Lancashire industrialist originally from Sussex farming stock, had previously concentrated on municipal reform under the slogan 'Incorporate your Borough', while Bright, the son of a successful self-made Rochdale cotton manufacturer and Quaker, was a prominent anti-church rate campaigner. By focusing on the corn laws, middle-class radicals looked to maximize their appeal from their Manchester base. It was a single issue which would attract the funds and support of millowners and industrialists otherwise averse to political involvement, while enlisting the provincial pride, moral superiority and agitational expertise of the 'moral radicals'. 'Never, never talk of giving up the ship', Cobden wrote to his disillusioned brother in October 1838, lamenting the 'apathy of the three years when prosperity (or seemingly so) made Tories of all'. Insisting that he did not 'feel at all inclined to give up politics in disgust, as you seem to do, because of the blunders of the Radicals', he expressed his hopes for the new campaign:

> I think the scattered elements may yet be rallied round the question of the corn laws. It appears to me that a moral and even a religious spirit may be infused into that topic, and if agitated in the same manner that the question of slavery has been, it will be irresistible.[29]

At the same time, popular radicalism acquired a defiant and independent working-class tone. Viewed through the popular mythology of the times, the implementation of the Reform Act marked dramatic change, reflected in the various applications of the language of class. In popular perception, the carefully-calculated £10 franchise left the 'working class' alone as the unrepresented people, separated from the middle class, the 'shopocrats' who acquired the vote and joined the ranks of the politically privileged. Political exclusion, then, brought a sense of inverted class pride. Henceforth, the virtue of the people resided in the working class alone. At the same time, however, 'class' implied pejorative connotations when applied to those who monopolized political power. Excluded from parliament, the working class regarded themselves as the particular victims of 'class legislation', new laws and 'reforms' to protect and promote the economic self-interests of the politically privileged. Viewed from the perspective of exclusion, the 'modernizing' reforms of the 1830s were a comprehensive assault on traditional rights and expectations. To the voteless, indeed, it seemed that the state, having shed its old inefficiency and corruption, was taking on the form of an interventionist and exploitative dictatorship. Reform of national and municipal government along propertied lines removed old areas of popular political influence; the amendment of the Poor Law, the new 'Starvation Law', took away time-honoured social and welfare rights; the new factory legislation undermined the efforts and programme of the short-time movement; trade unions were under constant attack in parliament and the courts; and professional police forces, those 'plagues of blue locusts', were extended throughout the land, enforcing the new discipline upon the traditional leisure activities of the working class.[30]

By exploiting the different meanings of class, Chartism constructed a working-class constituency of support. Addressing the politically excluded, Chartism promised to protect working-class property in labour and skill against the depredations of 'class' legislation. In so doing, Chartism distinguished itself from Tory protectionist paternalism and middle-class liberal radicalism. On the factory and anti-poor law platform in the north, Feargus O'Connor, proud and worthy heir to Henry Hunt, brought a radical edge to Tory-sponsored campaigns against the reforms introduced by the Whigs and their 'sham' radical allies. The dreaded new Poor Law exemplified the 'new system of the political economists':

> The auxiliaries to this infernal law are the Factory scheme, the rural police, and the complete destruction of the Trades' Associations, which was the last remnant of power in the hands of the working classes by which supply and demand could be wholesomely regulated.[31]

By insisting on direct political representation for the working class to ensure regulation and protection, O'Connor left the Tory paternalists behind. The Charter, however, made no reference to economic matters: a traditionally-phrased programme of parliamentary reform, it was endorsed by some middle-class Radical MPs. Once adopted by O'Connor and other popular radicals, however, the Charter acquired a different image and meaning. As projected and interpreted on the revitalized mass platform, it was closely identified with a political economy of regulation and control widely at odds with the laissez-faire prescriptions of middle-class radicals.

5

RADICALISM AND CLASS, 1835–50

Early Chartism

At first, O'Connor and the northern radicals regarded the Charter with suspicion, as a diversionary ploy by those opposed to the thrust and tone of the anti-Poor Law agitation. Such fears were not ungrounded given the provenance of the document in the 'elite politics' of the London Working Men's Association (LWMA) and the attempt to revivify the reform alliance. When the war of the unstamped came to an end, metropolitan radicals withdrew into educational activity. An artisan forum of mutual self-improvement, the LWMA was restricted to 'the *intelligent* and *useful* portion of the working classes'. Jointly signed by the LWMA and a group of parliamentary Radicals headed by Daniel O'Connell, the Charter was drafted with the assistance of Francis Place on the agreed understanding that it would neither attack the Poor Law nor advocate socialism. It was not until it was linked to the national petition and the national convention – schemes which emerged from the revived BPU – that the Charter was adopted in the provinces as the symbol and focus of radical endeavour.[1]

Having waited patiently for the reformed parliament to implement the requisite 'inflationist' financial policy, the BPU returned to political agitation with the onset of economic depression in 1837. Taking account of procedural changes in the reformed Commons where – to the detriment of 'petition and debate' – the presentation of petitions no longer conferred the right to speak, the BPU called for a 'national petition' for universal suffrage. Weariness and inertia were swept aside by enthusiasm for the proposal. One great mass supplication, the national petition was to be 'the last petition', a final test of the contractual relationship between government and the sovereign people. Wary of the consequences, the BPU suggested that the presentation of the petition be entrusted to a national convention, a proposal which immediately (if unintentionally) aroused the old ultra-radical enthusiasm for an 'anti-parliament'. Once the Charter was linked to the Birmingham proposals, preparations for the convention – the election of delegates and the collection of the national rent – fused the various local agitations into a campaign of national dimensions, extending the coordination already established within O'Connor's Great Northern Union.[2]

Trade societies provided the necessary framework for political mobilization in large cities. The Manchester Combination Committee, established in the wake of O'Connell's denunciation of the Glasgow spinners, marshalled an impressive display of support at the first Chartist demonstration on Kersal Moor, drawn from a wide variety of 'insecure' trades: shoemakers, tailors and other proletarianized artisans; craft workers in the building trades in conflict with the new 'general' contractors; spinners, dyers and other male factory workers, along with smiths, metal workers and engineers whose aristocratic status was yet to be established.[3] The real Chartist strongholds, however, were not the cities but surrounding towns and out-townships, the typical industrial communities of the manufacturing districts – the textile towns of Lancashire, Cheshire and the West Riding; the hosiery, lace and glove-making areas of the east midlands; the depressed linen-weaving centres of Barnsley and Dundee; and the industrial villages of

the mining and iron-working districts, the north-east coalfield, the South Wales valleys and the Black Country. Here
the structural foundations for collective action were closely
interwoven. Occupational ties were reinforced by other
loyalties, by networks of mutual knowledge and trust which
facilitated powerful and effective political organization.

Diverse in composition and character, the localities were
united in national protest by the press and the platform
as Chartism extended the techniques of mass agitation
deployed by Hunt and the post-war radicals. Local and
regional initiatives were accorded national significance
through reports in the *Northern Star*, which quickly established itself as the comprehensive and definitive voice of
the movement, a role which earlier radical papers had
been unable to fulfil. The platform acted as an integra-
tive and cumulative force as the movement rallied around
the indefatigable O'Connor, the itinerant champion of
the people. True to the memory of 'ever-to-be-loved Hunt',
O'Connor toured the country, deliberately exploiting his
platform appeal as a gentlemanly and charismatic demagogue to connect and unify the movement, to lay the
foundations for more regular (and elected) forms of
working-class organization.[4]

Chartism consolidated its hold on the manufacturing
districts in the autumn of 1838 through torchlight meetings and mass 'defensive' arming, tactics which challenged
the accepted limits of open constitutional agitation. As
the Convention assembled, excitement and expectation
reached fever pitch in an apocalyptic mood which the
movement was never to recapture. Delay, deliberation and
dissension, however, characterized the Convention's early
proceedings.[5] The Cobbettites withdrew once the Convention refused to restrict its competence to the supervision
and presentation of the petition, to be followed by another group of financial reformers, the Birmingham middle-
class radicals, isolated in condemnation of any discussion
of 'ulterior measures'. Steeped in images of the French
Revolution, the insurrectionary rhetoric and conspiratorial

plans of George Julian Harney and the London Democratic Association – an ultra-radical Jacobin body which
aspired to purge the convention of traitors and initiate
the necessary rising – failed to attract support as fears
grew of the government spy-system.[6] Finally, after having
moved to Birmingham, the Convention adopted a series
of extra-parliamentary expedients which, with the exception of the proposed 'sacred month' or general strike,
were drawn (inappropriately) from the middle-class repertoire of the fabled 'Days of May'. Throughout these delib-
erations, O'Connor continually called upon the Convention
to assume the bellicose posture essential for 'forcible intimidation'. The leading exponent of the rhetoric of
menace, he spoke ominously of a defensive rising, of spontaneous and invincible armed resistance to government
repression. Events, however, belied the rhetoric, exposing the fallacy of forcible intimidation.[7]

Constrained by undue delay in the presentation of the
petition and by the non-occurrence of some Peterloo-like
act of outrageous provocation, the 'constitutional' Chartists lacked a universally agreed point at which resistance
was deemed to be justified. There were a number of local clashes – Birmingham magistrates, prominent members of the BPU, enlisted the Metropolitan Police to
disperse crowds gathered in the Bull Ring in support of
the Convention, a violent end to the spurious local unity
of the 'productive classes' – but there was no major outrage.[8] The Whigs, indeed, acted with unexpected forbearance, keeping the state and the military out of provocative
confrontation. Once the much-delayed petition was finally
rejected, Chartists were compelled to advocate positive
action, to move beyond the rhetoric of righteous retalia-
tion to the threshold of violence, at which dangerous point
they were pulled up short by O'Connor's unexpected disavowal of the 'sacred month'.

Adapted from William Benbow's scheme for a *Grand
National Holiday and Congress of the Productive Classes*, the
'sacred month' was predicated on the active involvement

(and disciplined behaviour) of the overwhelming majority of the population. In the absence of the required nation-wide support, a fact sadly confirmed by the Convention's missionaries in agricultural and other districts, O'Connor refused to lead the Chartists into an unequal struggle against the disciplined armed forces at the government's disposal. Together with Bronterre O'Brien, the 'school-master of Chartism', he persuaded the Convention to cancel the 'sacred month' and to substitute instead an innocuous three-day withdrawal of labour. This retreat was a bitter and disorienting blow in the forward areas, particularly in the Lancashire cotton district where Chartists had eagerly armed themselves for the decisive confrontation. A sorry end to the 'constitutional' phase of the first Chartist campaign, the abortive 'national holiday' dispelled the myths that had sustained forcible intimidation.[9]

The cotton districts took little part in the various conspiratorial schemes of the winter of 1839–40. As in 1819–20, the initiative passed to the West Riding. Plans for a national rising in early November were hastily abandoned, however, when Peter Bussey, chairman of the West Riding secret delegates, sent the word round to desist before suddenly quitting Bradford. While the north was quiet, thousands of colliers and ironworkers armed with clubs, muskets and pikes marched on Newport in the early hours of 4 November, the most significant Chartist excursion into physical force. Chartism enjoyed remarkable popularity in South Wales, where radicalism had previously attracted little interest outside of artisan and lower middle-class circles in the established towns. With the arrival of Chartism, however, working-class radicalism took control of the industrial valleys – in 1839 there were over 25,000 enrolled or committed Chartists in Glamorgan and Monmouthshire, one in five of the total population. Here there was no loss of momentum following the failure of the Convention and the clampdown by the authorities. Chartists proceeded with plans to rise throughout the region, to occupy all the towns amid the traditional saturnalia of 5 November.

Rather late, the scheme was modified by John Frost who advised an earlier concentration on Newport, where he had once been mayor and magistrate. On the fateful night the Chartists succeeded (albeit sometimes by impressment) in mobilizing the workforce, native and immigrant, skilled and unskilled, in a brave attempt to capture Newport, the symbol and inspiration for decisive action by workers across the border. As it turned out, the Newport rising confirmed O'Connor's worst fears. Partial outbreaks were doomed to bloody and ignominious failure. Delayed by atrocious weather and indecisive leadership, the marchers were finally confronted by the well-prepared military in Newport: 22 Chartists were killed and many more injured, the greatest casualties inflicted by the military on the British civilian population in the nineteenth and twentieth centuries.[10]

The campaign to save Frost, Williams and Jones from the gallows reopened the field of constitutional protest: indeed, petitions for their reprieve collected more signatures than the National Petition itself. In calling for a 'second convention' to coordinate the legal efforts, O'Connor found himself at cross-purposes with physical-force militants who looked to such an assembly to instigate the insurrection without which Frost could not be saved. O'Connor duly absented himself from the convention, a gathering of working-class militants closely linked to the underground movement, but he was asked to endorse the plan, first proposed by the northern delegates committee at Dewsbury, for a concerted rising on 12 January. Having bided his time, O'Connor exposed the scheme in the *Star*, after which there was no prospect of success, but abortive risings took place at Dewsbury and Sheffield. A fortnight later, physical-force Chartism came to an end with the failure of Robert Peddie's Bradford rising.[11] After the government wisely commuted the Newport death sentences, tension subsided but the Chartists still remembered the Welsh leaders and campaigned persistently for their pardon and return from transportation.

The National Charter Association, the Anti-Corn Law League and the 'New Move'

Chastened by defeat, the Chartists regrouped in the summer of 1840 around a permanent organizational structure with a national executive, weekly membership payments and elected officers. Here the Chartists tried to maintain the essential democratic and inclusive character of platform agitation, a principle which distinguished the National Charter Association (NCA), the first working-class political party, from other forms of working-class associational culture in the general trend towards more sophisticated structures based on regular subscriptions and the election and payment of permanent officials. Committed to members unlimited, the Chartists sought to enroll the poorly paid and the casually employed, the otherwise excluded workers who had little or irregular time to spare when in work, and unlimited time but nothing to subscribe when unemployed. At the top end of the structure, accountability became a critical issue. The Executive was kept under scrutiny by a short Annual Delegate Convention, an additional cost beyond the means of several localities, a typical example of the poverty which impeded internal democracy and often left the Executive without proper payment and adequate resources. Economic problems were compounded by legal difficulties. Self-governing societies were still not allowed to federate: a national movement could exist only without separate branches or divisions, a centralized and undemocratic structure adopted without demur by the ACLL.[12]

The struggle for political power remained the essential consideration, but within the 'movement culture' of the NCA the emphasis changed from confrontational 'ulterior measures' to collective self-provision, offering a stimulating pre-figurative experience of the shape of things to come. The boycott of excisable articles was transformed into Chartist teetotalism with tea-parties, soirees and balls; the practice of exclusive dealing developed into the Chartist cooperative store, the profits of which were often given to imprisoned comrades; and the 'occupation' of parish churches, the religious confrontation of 1839, was replaced by a non-sectarian form of radical preaching and worship. The NCA was the cornerstone of a democratic counter-culture of Chartist schools, stores, chapels, burial clubs, temperance societies and other facilities for education, recreation and the celebration of radical anniversaries.[13]

A grassroots complement to political struggle, branch culture held the movement together during the lean periods, preserving the structure intact and in readiness for the return of excitement and the next great national agita-tion. In the interim, considerable care was taken to prevent deviation or exclusivism, organizational characteristics which, George White warned, 'might lead to the estab-lishment of a sort of aristocracy in our ranks or take the attention of our most active men from the great question of the Charter'.[14] O'Connor has incurred much criticism for his (in)famous condemnation of 'Church Chartism, Teetotal Chartism, Knowledge Chartism, and Household Suffrage Chartism'. A tireless promoter of the new organ-ization, O'Connor strongly approved of collective self-help within the democratic and inclusive framework of the NCA. What he opposed was divisive elitism, the establishment of exclusive standards of Chartist membership, the with-drawal from mass action, developments which led back to the middle-class embrace.[15]

The 'new movers' denounced by O'Connor sought to reformulate the reform alliance, to reinvigorate the elite politics and ideological alignments of the LWMA in ac-cordance with important changes in political culture and communication. In a broad cultural shift towards greater 'respectability', the open-access procedures of the past – the ritual and street theatre of open elections, the open-air carnival of the mass platform – were being challenged by more organized and disciplined forms, by more efficient policing which restricted access to public space, and by the rapidly-expanding press which encouraged personal and political development in the privacy of the home. The ACLL was one of the pace-setters in this process of cultural and political adaptation. Having encountered fierce Chartist opposition in its initial efforts to maximize extra-parliamentary support, the League quickly took steps to avoid unwelcome intervention. The unruly crowd was excluded by ticketing, direct mailing (up to three and a half tons of tracts distributed weekly via the penny post), door-to-door canvassing, registration of voters (numerous solicitors were engaged in 'experimenting on the Reform Act') and other mechanisms of what D. A. Hamer describes as the 'politics of electoral pressure' – the mobilization of electoral pressure to persuade candidates and political parties to commit themselves to promote particular legislation. In Cobden's unashamed words, the League became 'rather a middle-class set of agitators', concentrating its efforts on existing and 'respectable' voters, to whose numbers provident free-trade supporters were to be appended by building-society purchase of forty-shilling freeholds. However, this was not the point of closure for middle-class radicalism.[16]

Through changes in style and agitation, middle-class radicalism was transforming itself into Victorian liberalism, a vehicle of political moralism in which the extension of the franchise was not a matter of constitutional balance or citizenship rights but a question of 'character', of moral entitlement. An inclusive character test, respectability served as a cross-class (and cross-gender) cultural counterweight to the self-interested prescriptions of laissez-faire political economy, to the egoistic possessive individualism scarcely concealed in some ACLL propaganda. As it flourished into liberalism, middle-class radicalism offered no licence for unrestrained satisfaction of wants and desires: laissez-faire extended no further than political economy. Respectability, the prerequisite qualification for full membership of the political nation, consisted in the ability to rise above sensual instincts and passions through sobriety, self-help, frugality, duty, effort, industry and 'temperance in all things'.

As the great conference of ministers of religion organized by the ACLL attested, middle-class radicalism was infused with the Nonconformist conscience which stressed individual responsibility for redemption through the overcoming of sin.[17]

As the respectable individual replaced the riotous freeborn Englishman as the emblematic figure of popular politics, middle-class radicals and disaffected Chartists found common ground in behaviorial reform. The cultivation of respectability offered a way forward after the ignominious collapse of platform agitation. 'New movers' distanced themselves from vainglorious demagogues, from volatile crowds of 'fustian jackets, blistered hands and unshorn chins', and from the 'illegal' NCA.[18] By eradicating ignorance, drunkenness and thraldom, William Lovett's National Association for Promoting the Political and Social Improvement of the People offered the working class the self-respect necessary for the attainment and exercise of the franchise.[19] The means, facilities and method of instruction in the virtues of working-class self-reliance, however, were assisted by middle-class patronage, exercised in a manner which tended to subvert the democratic ethos of collective self-help. Acting in the spirit of Christian stewardship and philanthropy, middle-class patrons displayed an unthinking arrogance, assuming the right of leadership and control.

Such tensions came critically to the fore in the Complete Suffrage Union (CSU), the most notable attempt to reconstruct the old cross-class reform alliance of 1832. Promoted by Edward Miall, owner–editor of the *Nonconformist*, the CSU was formed in response to the Whigs' defeat in the 1841 general election, an unexpected reverse which united voluntarists, free traders and parliamentary radicals. The CSU straddled old and new styles of political agitation. Although unconnected officially with the initiative, the ACLL and its leaders secretly welcomed the CSU as a reprise of the old 'brickbat argument', as 'something in our *rear* to frighten the Aristocracy – And it will take the masses out of the hands of their present rascally leaders.'[20] Not surprisingly, O'Connor denounced the scheme as 'complete humbug', a plot to gain working-class support for Corn Law repeal just as the Leeds Parliamentary Reform Association – the 'Fox and Goose Club' – had attempted in 1840 with a programme rigidly restricted to household suffrage. The preliminary conference at Birmingham, however, proved surprisingly radical: delegates rejected the name 'Chartist' but accepted all six points of the Charter. Sturge then took to the country, mobilizing pressure from without through the abolitionist techniques of lectures, petitions, lobbying, intervention in elections and the nominations of parliamentary candidates. As economic distress intensified in the summer of 1842, he contemplated a nationwide campaign of passive disobedience, but the next conference of the CSU was postponed until December by which time O'Connor and the NCA had seized the initiative.

This time Chartists were in the majority at the conference, but the Charter was ruled out of discussion. Sturge's friends on the organizing committee presented the six points in the form of a Bill of Rights, a document prepared in typically high-handed manner without even consulting Lovett and the working-class promoters of the new move. While sincere in his commitment to democratic government, Sturge refused to acknowledge democratic organization within the movement for parliamentary reform itself, to accept working-class independence and self-sufficiency. The Chartists, indeed, were required to repudiate their past, to renounce their independence, their very identity. In a remarkable outcome, Lovett and O'Connor, otherwise diametrically opposed, united to defend the hallowed name of the Charter, 'the legislative text book of the millions'. Defeated by this unlikely alliance, Sturge and his colleagues withdrew from such 'uncongenial fellowship', unable to fulfil their social function 'to do the people a little good'.[21] 'There was no attempt to bring about a union – no effort for conciliation – no generous offer of the right hand of friendship', Thomas Cooper, one of the Chartist delegates, recorded: 'We soon found that it was determined to keep poor Chartists at "arm's length". We were not to come between the wind and *their* nobility.'[22]

Cross-class endeavour in the 1840s was disabled less by ideological dispute over political economy than by differences in style, organization and political culture, the very stuff of class identity. Chartists detested the ACLL far more than the programme of free trade itself, to which they displayed considerable ambivalence. Having rejected the CSU, Chartist leaders took consolation in the imminent discomfiture of the 'steam lords', the 'mushroom' millionaires of the League who left the home economy distressed in reckless pursuit of profit and markets overseas. Come the long-predicted disintegration of the Whigs, the middle classes would surely fracture: the workers would be joined by the 'industrious portion of the middling classes', the impoverished 'shopocrats' whose economic interests coincided with their own in a stable and prosperous domestic economy.[23] While the leadership patiently awaited this fundamental realignment, the rank and file favoured direct action in the form of the postponed national holiday or general strike.

It was grassroots pressure, not Chartist 'dictation', which transformed the wage disputes of 1842 into a general turnout for the Charter, an escalation ratified and legitimized by a rapidly and democratically-convened trades' conference in Manchester. In the severe depression of 1842 workers from across the spectrum of 'combined and uneven development' turned to the Charter as their best hope of economic protection, of ensuring 'a fair day's wage for a fair day's work'. Most delegates at the trades' conference were cotton-factory workers (spinners, powerloom weavers, calico printers, dressers and dyers) or members of the engineering and metal-working trades, the supposed beneficiaries of industrial change but who had yet to acquire 'aristocratic' status and security. Artisan trades were also well represented, particularly in the less secure clothing and building sectors, and there was also a small number of distressed textile outworkers, mainly silk-weavers and fustian cutters. On their fortuitous arrival in Manchester, the NCA Executive displayed less unity and resolve. Dr Peter Murray McDouall advocated the extension of the turnout into all-out confrontation with the authorities as the best means to secure cheap food, high wages, low taxes and 'protective political power to labour', but the Executive refused to assume command. Having rebuilt the movement after the disastrous confrontationalism of 1839, O'Connor and the national leadership were again fearful of partial and incomplete insurgency. Although at its height the strike involved up to 500,000 workers from Dundee and the Scottish coalfields to South Wales and Cornwall, support was patchy and uneven outside the cotton districts. In the words of Hill, editor of the *Northern Star*, 'there was no element of nationality, and consequently, no element of success in it'. To facilitate the necessary withdrawal, the Executive expressed support for the strikers, but then castigated the factory owners of the ACLL, claiming that they had deliberately forced the working class out on strike in a conspiracy to coerce the government into Corn Law repeal. A contributory factor in the collapse of the CSU–Chartist negotiations, this myth was not entirely without substance. More than 1100 people were tried in connection with the turnouts, after troops and special constables were called into quash the strike. In 1842, indeed, more people were arrested and sentenced for public-order offences than in any other year. O'Connor, the prize catch, was charged in a 'monster indictment' along with other members of the Executive (including McDouall, who had fled to France) and the Lancashire strike-leaders. He escaped imprisonment, however, through delay, legal technicalities and a tactical retreat by the Tory government, seen by some historians as the first indication of 'liberalization' by the ruling orders.[24]

Initiated or not at O'Connor's trial, this much-vaunted

policy break has been accorded undue emphasis in the linguistic 'rethinking' of Chartism. The movement, it is now argued, was undermined less by socio-economic change in the 1840s than by the rigidity and obsolescence of its public political language. The old predictions of ever-worsening political immiseration, oppression and exploitation lost resonance and appeal once the 'moralized' Peelite state introduced beneficent reform.[25] The extent of this 'liberalization', however, is open to doubt. By no means a coherent policy (Peelite or Whig), it was halting, begrudging, delayed in impact and punctuated with repression. A more important factor undermining Chartism's purchase and appeal was the broader shift to 'respectability', exemplified in increasing competition from 'new model' forms of associational culture. Resolutely committed to members unlimited, bad risks included, the NCA was unable to stem seepage to exclusive and secure forms of collective mutuality. Affiliated friendly societies, amalgamated trade unions, retail cooperative societies steadily gained what the NCA was denied: public approval and legal recognition.

The Land Plan

O'Connor's Land Plan, often misunderstood and undervalued by historians, was an attempt to reverse this process. This was a time of general enthusiasm for spade husbandry and small farms: a gamut of politicians, philanthropists and political economists promoted a variety of schemes for settling 'surplus' or dispossessed workers on the land. Radical options ranged from utopian communitarianism to peasant proprietorship, but the distinction between communal and private ownership, a split which went back to Spence and Paine, was of little significance. All agreed that misery and oppression were attributable to the usurpation and monopolization of the land, 'the people's farm'. Working their own plots of land on Chartist estates, workers would reap the full fruits of their labour, thereby establishing the real or 'natural' value of labour, upon which basis other workers could freely choose between entering the factories or working the land. A means of escape from 'artificial' society, the Land Plan was also designed to reverse the downward pressure on urban wage rates.

O'Connor's plan was distinguished by its democratic and participatory nature. Under his proposals, access to the land was neither dependent on upper-class patronage nor restricted to the high-wage 'aristocracy of labour' through the conventional priority system of 'first pay first served'. Advertised through the *Star*, shares were payable in small weekly instalments: when an estate became available, a 'ballot' or lottery was used to allocate farms and home-steads on a random but fair and exciting basis (a pro-cedure with several echoes in modern popular culture and promotional journalism). A Land and Labour Bank was established to attract working-class deposits and mortgage the estates so as to give the Land Company more cash in hand with which to purchase more land more quickly. At this stage, legal registration was essential, but attempts to register under either friendly society or joint stock legisla-tion were unsuccessful – limited liability was denied to a company based on mass share-holding among poor people. These legal problems added to the practical difficulties experienced on the estates, where most of the lucky early allottees were industrial workers with no knowledge of agriculture.[26]

In the doldrums of the mid-1840s, the administration and organization of the Land Plan not only gave a new sense of purpose to NCA localities but also facilitated an expansion of support among otherwise excluded or marginalized groups. Agricultural labourers, still the largest occupational category, were unable to participate in open political agitation for fear of dismissal and eviction. Rural protest was perforce covert and violent. The Swing riots

of 1830 were exceptional, the unique conjuncture of reform excitement, political crisis and economic depression
for once enabling farm labourers to protest openly and
defiantly, supported by other groups in rural society.[27]
Subscription to the Land Plan, however, offered a form
of participation without the usual risks and soon proved
very popular in rural areas. Traditional forms were not
displaced, however: incendiarism reached its peak in East
Anglia in 1843–5 when villages in Bedfordshire and Cam-
bridgeshire were left desolate by spectacular blazes.[28]

In similar fashion, women could support the Land Plan
without infringing the 'respectable' re-gendering of politics which otherwise served to marginalize their participation. Women were prominent in early Chartism, the
climacteric of open-access protest on the streets. As the
movement developed a more organized and structured
form, however, women were marginalized, leaving the
routine (and drink-assisted) organizational management
of the NCA localities to the men. In accordance with the
new cultural style promoted by (indoor) middle-class organizations in which 'respectability' was displayed by wel-
coming the passive attendance of women and family groups
at orderly meetings and festivities, women were still encouraged to join the NCA. However, it was increasingly
unusual for them to act as officers or committee members other than in specific female localities, which dimin-
ished in number in the early 1840s along with other purely
female radical and democratic societies.[29]

In programme and methods, organized Chartism conformed to the hegemonic ideology of separate spheres.
The movement made no formal demands for female suffrage, although many Chartists favoured votes for unmarried
women and widows on the assumption that such women
would not be represented by a male household head. From
this position, Chartists were able to manipulate the dominant discourse of domesticity to arouse middle-class guilt
about female factory work. Such rhetorical appropriation
was of dubious and temporary advantage, failing to advance

the cause of political reform. In subsequent formulations
of the 'Condition of England Question', Chartism was
designated as a symptom of the degradation of woman, a
problem to be solved by special legislation for women and
children.[30] Unable (or unwilling) to reject the dominant
ideology, Chartists offered no alternative to domesticity,
the best in a narrow range of unhappy options for working-class married women. Subscription to the Land Plan,
however, offered some connection to a wider sphere,[31]
causing an upsurge in female membership as Chartist
women dreamt of joining the lucky allottees on the first
estates – 'With their freehold for their empire / And their
fireside for their throne'.[32]

1848

The success of the Land Plan apart, there seemed little
prospect of a revival of Chartist agitation in the late 1840s.
The worst trough had been experienced amidst the crisis
of 1839–42. Thereafter a number of growth factors carried the economy through the commercial crisis of 1847
with remarkable resilience and strength. There was some
temporary distress but industrial Britain was now out of
sequence with continental Europe (and famine-stricken
Ireland) where catastrophic economic distress – the combination of famine prices and high unemployment – immediately preceded the revolutions of 1848.

While Chartists sought to exploit the excitement generated by European revolution in 1848, they were determined to display constitutional good order and discipline.
Here was the irony which disabled their long-sought alliance with the Irish repealers. Previously blocked by
O'Connellite proscription, alliance with the Chartists was
approved when new leaders in Dublin, inspired by revolution in Europe, removed all former restraints, not least
the rejection of physical force. Deeply disturbed by the

security implications, the British government feared its
military resources would be overstretched by simultaneous
and diversionary insurrectionary activity. Confronted by
the three-pronged threat of revolutionary Paris, insurgent
Ireland and revitalized Chartism, the authorities mounted
a massive display of coercive power to defend English
freedom and constitutional liberty.

As public opinion sided firmly with the government,
the Chartists were at hopeless disadvantage in the politics
of public space. Against the odds, however, Chartists strove
to secure an acceptable image. The British platform was
to be distinguished from European revolution by strict
observance of the constitutional proprieties of extra-parliamentary agitation, conduct in accordance with the new
culture of respectability. Unhappily, the first mass meetings
called in the wake of revolution in Paris were the occasion
for unseemly disorder provoked by trouble-making youths,
pickpockets, criminals and other members of the 'dangerous classes'. In secret, platform militants like Harney shared
Bronterre O'Brien's misgivings about the monster demonstration and procession to parliament planned for 10 April,
fearing it would 'let loose hundreds of rogues and thieves
upon society, thus bringing down upon themselves the
indignation of the reflecting people of this country'. A
sustained press campaign accompanied the excessive
security precautions for the ill-located demonstration on
Kennington Common, portraying Chartism as criminal,
unconstitutional, unEnglish and, most damning of all, Irish.
'The present movement', The Times warned on the morning
of 10 April, 'is a ramification of the Irish conspiracy. The
Repealers wish to make as great a hell of this island as
they have made of their own.' Quite as much as the fear
of continental 'red republicanism', of Parisian 'démoc-soc'
ideals of socialism and the organization of labour, it was
the spectre of crime, disorder and Irish violence that im-
pelled the middle classes to protect the established order.[33]

Contrary to mythology, O'Connor served the movement
well on 10 April: it was 'Feargoose' indeed who ensured

the day's events were not a fiasco. Considerable crowds were attracted to Kennington Common – acting on police instructions, the anti-Chartist press reported the total as 15,000, a figure ten times lower than the latest historical estimate. Thanks to O'Connor's oratorical skills, unpropitious confrontation was avoided: the right of assembly was asserted, but the mass procession to present the national petition was wisely abandoned. Having salvaged some self-respect for the movement on Kennington Common, O'Connor was nevertheless forced to withdraw the motion for the Charter when the Commons Committee reported (with undue haste) that the national Petition had not been signed by 5,706,000 as the Chartists claimed, but by 1,975,496, a figure which included many bogus, fraudulent and obscene signatures. In these embarrassing circumstances, O'Connor refused to sanction an escalation in extra-parliamentary pressure. No longer prepared to appear more insurrectionary than he actually was, he abandoned forcible intimidation to promote discussion of the Land Plan, his practical (non-socialist) solution to the 'labour question'. Some of the more ardent Chartist spirits proceeded to convene a National Assembly, only to be drawn into languishing discussion of tactical and constitutional niceties. A sparsely-attended, dispirited affair, it marked a sorry end to the 'anti-parliament' in radical politics, replaced in mid-Victorian agitation by the stage-managed conference.

The Irish Confederates, by contrast, displayed no such debilitating self-doubt. Where their presence was strong, as at Bradford, the town with the highest concentration of Irish-born in the West Riding, they were to boost Chartist morale and activity. A Chartist 'National Guard', primarily composed of woolcombers threatened by machinery, drilled openly on the streets until military reinforcements arrived. Investigation revealed that half the Bradford Chartists were Irish, nationalist radicals preparing to make a diversion should Mitchel be convicted, in order to prevent the government from sending more troops to Ireland'. News of John Mitchel's conviction and transportation, the first victim of the new Crown and Government Security Act, enraged Irish immigrants, prompting them to abandon the restraints of open Chartist alliance for a secret conspiratorial framework linked to Dublin. The Chartist rump, however, hoped to channel the anger over Mitchel's fate into renewed platform agitation. Ernest Jones planned for an exact count of heads to be taken at simultaneous Whitsun meetings, a combined display of Chartist and Confederate numerical strength to stand in lieu of the discredited petition. At this point, however, the authorities introduced repression. Refusing to distinguish between Irish conspiracy and Chartist agitation, they declared the Whitsun demonstration illegal and issued warrants against Jones and other leaders.

As in the past, repression and arrests pushed some militants towards physical force, but there was little coordination in the underground politics of conspiracy and insurrection. When news came that Ireland was 'up', Confederates insisted on 'an immediate outbreak of a serious nature'. They were criticized for precipitate haste by Chartists who had yet to complete plans, coordinated by Cuffay and the 'Orange Tree' conspirators, for simultaneous risings in London and Manchester. In the interim, as relations deteriorated, the authorities prepared for decisive action. Come the day, they arrested the conspirators, and then issued 'monster' indictments, as at Manchester, listing 'all the leading agitators who have for some time past infested this City and the neighbouring Towns'. Cuffay, the veteran black radical, was an easy target for the cartoonists, but *Punch* and the press preferred to highlight the Irish element in the August conspiracy, a dastardly affair involving the likes of 'MOONEY, ROONEY, HOOLAN, DOOLAN'.[34] The trials followed a standard format well summarized by Harney:

> Place *Fustian* in the dock, let *Silk Gown* charge the culprit with being a 'physical force Chartist', and insinuate that

he is not exactly free from the taint of 'Communism', and forthwith *Broad Cloth* in the jury box will bellow out 'GUILTY'.[35]

Middle-Class Radicalism and Internationalism

As the middle classes rushed to defend the established order in 1848, middle-class radicals were left with little political space for their on-going mission. Two years previously they seemed to have secured an epochal victory, but contrary to Cobden's confident expectation, repeal of the Corn Laws in 1846 did not presage 'rule through the middle classes'. In agitating for repeal, the ACLL was impressively efficient, harnessing the complementary talents of Cobden, Bright and George Wilson who had acquired considerable agitational expertise as secretary of the committee which obtained a charter of incorporation for Manchester in 1839. The building of the Free Trade Hall on the site of Peterloo, the establishment of *The Economist*, and the pioneer implementation of what were to become familiar propaganda devices prompted *The Times* to acknowledge that 'a new power had arisen in the land'. The ACLL, however, had no say in the timing or terms of the 'high political' settlement of 1846. Directed towards the election expected in 1848, its 'politics of electoral pressure' merely restricted Peel's room for manoeuvre, removing his preferred option of temporary delay until repeal became a non-contentious issue. As with the Reform Act, the repeal of the Corn Laws, once passed, served to consolidate 'modern conservatism'. Lacking another rallying cry of such emotive and unifying force, middle-class radicals became increasingly isolated and disillusioned with the deference, parochialism and quiescence of the middle classes in general.[36] Then the events of 1848 underscored their cultural and ideological distance from the Chartists.

These differences were already apparent in the rival forms of internationalist associations established in the prelude to the revolutions of 1848. Since the mid-1840s, Harney had been trying to reinvigorate the Chartist platform by incorporating 'red republicanism', the creed of revolutionary European artisans exiled in Britain. Known to Marx and Engels as 'Citizen Hip-Hip Hurrah!', he managed to unite diverse nationalities and social philosophies in the Fraternal Democrats, a pressure group formed to hasten the necessary changes in the NCA programme and agitation: 'henceforth mere Chartism will not do, ultra-democracy, social as well as political, will be the object of our propaganda'.[37] Ironically, progress was curtailed by the outbreak of revolution: the repatriation of the political refugees and the introduction of a tough new Alien Act in 1848 deprived Charter-Socialists of their continental red-republican allies. Rival internationalist bodies suffered a similar loss as aristocratic nationalists and other non-socialist exiles rushed home to enjoy the 'springtime of the peoples'. The People's International League, the Mazzinist successor to Lovett's Democratic Friends of All Nations, was reduced to a domestic rump of advanced middle-class liberals, social reformers and dissident Chartists, 'rational reformers' who regrouped as the People's Charter Union, an avowedly 'moral force' association which condemned the violence of the Chartist platform but applauded physical-force revolution abroad.[38]

Henceforth, as Margot Finn has shown, there was a pronounced ideological and class gulf within radical discourse. Chartists displayed their working-class credentials, prioritizing events in France where Louis Blanc's 'Organization of Labour' pointed to social as well as political rights, towards a positive social-democratic view of liberty and the state. Middle-class radicals, by contrast, remained committed to classical political economy and a negative definition of liberty. Insisting on the distinction between the social and the political sphere, they condemned socialist revolution in France while applauding liberal and nationalist revolution in Germany, Italy and later Hungary.[39] Class polarization, however, should not be overdrawn. Mazzinist ideals, emphasizing respectability and the 'inward conscience of the Universal Duty of the Suffrage', exerted a powerful cross-class appeal, embracing a new generation of working-class radicals disillusioned with unruly (and unsuccessful) platform agitation.[40] Furthermore, there were competing (if not contradictory) versions of middle-class radicalism.

While eschewing conflictual social relations, state interventionism and socialism, Mazzinists condemned the excesses of economic liberalism. Here they endorsed the kind of voluntary cooperative schemes promoted by the Christian Socialists, who were staunch critics of political radicalism in general and the Chartist mass platform in particular. Other middle-class radicals, no less enthusiastic than the Mazzinists for liberal nationalism, sought to extend the principle of non-intervention beyond economics to international diplomacy, in line with Cobden's morally empowered vision of free trade. After the repeal of the Corn Laws, 'peace' became the symbolic key issue for moral radicals, inspired by the presence of Elihu Burritt, the 'learned blacksmith' from Connecticut. In promoting the League of Universal Brotherhood (alongside the Peace Society), Burritt spoke of a movement which would be to 'Slavery, War, Intemperance, Ignorance, Political and Social Inequalities what the Anti-Corn League [*sic*] was to Monopoly'. While an active force in this radicalization of the peace movement in the late 1840s, Joseph Sturge was prepared to compromise his pacifism to secure an agreement with Cobden for arbitration and international disarmament. On this agenda, described by Sturge's biographer as 'very much an Anglo-Saxon Protestant businessman's version of internationalism', the peace movement became a major radical crusade.[41] Criticized for his pragmatism, the carnivorous Sturge was also condemned on the 'expressive' wing of middle-class ultraradicalism, newly organized in the Vegetarian Society, for the inadequacy and inconsistency of his pacifism. The latest addition to the regime of 'physical puritanism', this 'Vegetarianism of the *mind* as well as of the *body*' represented the acme of individual reform: 'If a man abstain from a certain kind of food for *conscience sake*, it reminds him every day of the connexion between his outward conduct and his inward feeling: his sense of justice, of mercy, or of truth.'[42]

Middle-class radicals of a more pragmatic and 'instrumental' disposition were no less divided in the absence of a convincing programme of parliamentary reform. Although adopted by the veteran Joseph Hume as the basis for the 'Little Charter' movement in 1848, the traditional household suffrage proposals stood in need of revision. Some expended their energies on devising a formula which would exclude the undesirable while incorporating the lower middle-class heroes of the day, the young clerical workers living in lodgings who had so conspicuously proved their respectability and worth by enrolling as special constables and defending London against the 'unconstitutional' Chartist challenge on 10 April. Others sought to 'garrison' the constitution, to use John Bright's expression, by extending the franchise to the skilled working class. Much disillusioned by the course of events since 1846, Cobden argued against political agitation, although he clearly recognized the need to recruit the aristocracy of labour: 'as we descend in the ranks of the middle classes, and approach the more intelligent of the working people, the feudal prejudice diminishes; and this brings us to our only hope for progress . . . an increase in the popular element in the House of Commons'. Looking to the formation of a broad-based 'liberal' alliance in support of non-intervention and retrenchment, Cobden put his trust in 'systematic organization and step-by-step progress', virtues enshrined, the *Nonconformist* noted, in the burgeoning freehold franchise associations: 'For the breaking down of a dangerous monopoly of landed property – for the cultivation of forethought, frugality and self reliance by working

men – and for the redistribution of political influence
and power, they are equally and admirably adapted.' The
freehold movement, the *Manchester Examiner* commented
approvingly, 'appeals exclusively to the industrious, intelligent, and provident members of the working class'.[43]

Although averse to political agitation, Cobden campaigned for financial reform, hoping to build upon the
initial success enjoyed by the Liverpool Financial Reform
Association. While offering blistering attacks on govern-
mental extravagance and the injustice and inefficiency of
taxes on commerce and industry, financial reform failed
to develop into an effective rallying-point. It lacked a
positive programme of its own, other than the extension
of probate and legacy duties on land. The subsequent
merger of financial and parliamentary reform, a move
repudiated by the Liverpool body, failed to excite much
interest outside of London. To the consternation of Manchester liberals, metropolitan radicals like George
Thompson sought to recruit former Chartists – Feargus
O'Connor included – by projecting household suffrage
not as a criterion but as an attainable instalment towards
manhood suffrage.[44]

By the end of the 1840s, then, middle-class radicalism
appeared in disarray and decline. Economic progress
enabled governments to gain increased revenue from stable
rates of taxation, confounding the predictions of Cobden's
'People's Budget'. The peace movement was overwhelmed
by the welter of jingoistic nationalism surrounding
Palmerston's Don Pacifico speech in 1850. Although Lord
John Russell and other leading Westminster politicians
were beginning to abandon their 'finality' stance, it seemed
that middle-class radicalism, no less than Chartism, was
out of touch with public opinion.[45]

The Charter and Something More

After 1848, Chartism entered a final period of revision and adaption, a brief coda characterized by both ideological advance and reformist pragmatism. The pressures for change were overwhelming. After the final collapse of the mass platform in 1848, traditional ways and means were totally discredited. The initiative had passed from confrontational politics to 'new model' forms of collective mutuality, associations which negotiated successfully with the state to secure legal protection for their members' interests. These new model forms were better adjusted to economic change. Still committed to the underconsumptionist language of irreversible slump and crisis, Chartism was unable to explain, yet alone compete with, the ultimate resilience of industrial capitalism. Then there was the impact of revolution and reaction in continental Europe. Heroic in defeat, republican exiles enjoyed considerable prestige. Their presence, however, may have constrained the process of change, hindering the transition from green flag to red. Mazzini and Kossuth, respected voices in the stock-taking which followed in the wake of 1848, deflected attention away from 'démoc-soc' experiments – red republicanism, socialism and the organization of labour – back towards more traditional radical concerns.[46] Their impassioned condemnation of centralized state power encouraged some radicals to reject 'mongrel Socialism' imported from 'the Parisian school of philosophers'. Implacable opponents of 'Communistic Chartism', the Manchester-based National Charter League (NCL) continued to campaign against 'Old Corruption', henceforth identified with government centralization. Unable to support the Charter-Socialists or the NCL, O'Connor, the 'worn-out warrior', was left stranded in political isolation, vainly seeking the illusive 'union of the veritable middle classes and the working classes ... an alliance between mental labour on the one hand and manual labour on the other'.[47]

Having captured control of the NCA Executive in pursuit of 'the Charter and Something More', Harney and the Charter-Socialists sought a social-democratic alliance with social reform, trade union, cooperative and other organizations. The response was mixed. Organizations sponsored by the Christian Socialists were negative and critical, insisting that the Chartists first recant their past folly. Others favoured a progressive understanding which would combine ameliorative social reform with gradualist political advance, a rational reformism personified by George Jacob Holyoake. Editor of the *Reasoner*, Holyoake, a post-communitarian Owenite and a practical 'secularist' (the respectable term which replaced earlier infidel and atheist labels), disapproved of demagogic Chartists and other 'foundation reformers' who dismissed any progress short of their never-to-be-realized 'grand ideal'. For Holyoake, indeed, Cobden was the 'Model Agitator'. Holyoake, Thornton Hunt and other luminaries of the *Leader*, a new progressive journal, were largely responsible for the draft programme presented to the famous 1851 Chartist Convention, a document much criticized by Bronterre O'Brien who regretted that 'the cloven foot of the old Anti-Corn Law League peeped out in every proposition'. Led by Ernest Jones, the Convention amended the programme, transforming it into the blueprint for a 'socialist' democratic state in which the land, cooperative endeavour, credit and welfare provision were all to be nationalized prior to 'the complete adjustment of the labour question'. 'Henceforth', Harney joyously proclaimed, 'Chartism is *démocratique et sociale*', but the new programme failed to revivify the movement. The initiative, he was forced to admit, had passed to the 'respectable' agencies of collective self-help. In an effort to engage their support, Harney joined W. J. Linton and the 'middle-class literati' of the *Leader* in a single-issue campaign for the suffrage, dropping the name and details of the Charter. By an irony of the times, the campaign for 'the Charter and Something More' ended with the sacrifice of the six points, the original 'whole hog', abandoned in favour of 'respectable' and rational gradualism, moderation and expediency.[48]

Problems of a different complexion hindered the efforts to effect a social-democratic alliance with the trades. Through their encouragement of the new National Association of Organized Trades for the Industrial, Social and Political Emancipation of Labour (NAOT), the Charter-Socialists were to be stigmatized as Tory protectionists. Formed by a committee of 'lower' depressed trades, the NAOT rejected the craft exclusivism of the National Association of United Trades and its programme of 'self-reliance – self-respect – self-helpfulness'. Committed to legislative intervention, the NAOT adopted an eight-point programme of political, economic and financial reform, much in line with O'Brien's proposals for 'national regeneration'. In its campaigning, however, the NAOT prioritized the demand for 'legislative protection for native industry, against the present unfair and ruinous system of competition', and unwisely welcomed the patronage of prominent Tory protectionists. Damned by association, Charter-Socialists tried to extricate themselves, vainly insisting that it was 'absolutely dishonest and unfair to confound "Protection to Labour", with "Protection to Landlords"'.[49]

Trapped in on-going partisan debate over free trade, Chartism was disabled by its protectionist leanings and its liberal sentiments. Protectionist but not Tory, radical but not Liberal, Chartism failed to retain its distinct identity, its ability to transcend partisan divisions. Further research is required to understand the process by which Chartism was marginalized in the localities, reduced to insignificance by the emergence of new cultural alignments upon which formal party and constituency organizations were soon to be constructed. While Liberals incorporated the new model collective self-help agencies into a union of progressive and respectable sentiment, Tory paternalists, sponsors of working-men's clubs and outings, appropriated the populist traditions, spectacle and fun of the defunct radical mass platform.

6

RADICALISM, LIBERALISM AND REFORMISM, 1850–75

In the short term, response to the revolutions of 1848 accentuated cultural, ideological and class tensions within British radicalism, but continued interest in international affairs – the Italian Risorgimento, Polish freedom and the American Civil War – provided the space for subsequent compromise, conciliation and cooperation. Other factors contributed to the proverbial 'reformist' tenor of mid-Victorian Britain. Economic expansion, still an uneven process, reached its highest levels in the 'Great Victorian Boom' between the 1840s and the 1870s. Although substantial and lasting advances in real wages were not apparent for many workers until the late 1860s, the greater stability in employment – and the obvious resilience of industrial capitalism – belied the old Chartist rhetoric of underconsumption, irreversible slump and worsening crisis. Radical fundamentalism was duly replaced by a new pragmatism. Encouraged by the repeal of the Corn Laws and the final attainment of the Ten Hours Bill, energies were concentrated on specific achievable measures of ameliorative reform. At the same time, the extension of voluntarism was encouraged through the continuing growth and public approval of 'new model' forms of collective mutuality. For the increasing numbers who could afford regular subscriptions and no credit, dividend-paying cooperative societies (based on the Rochdale Pioneers), affiliated friendly societies and amalgamated trade unions offered respectability, security and other advantages, seemingly denying the need for structural change or 'organic' political reform.

Where voluntarism merged into labourism, however, collective self-help was problematic, a cause of much tension in the age of equipoise. Paternalist employers, Tory and Liberal, were reluctant to concede recognition, amend labour law and submit to collective bargaining. Robert Platt, a cotton manufacturer and leading light of the Stalybridge Liberals, offered trips and treats in order to 'beat all trade unions out of court'. In keynote speeches at Platt's various functions, Dan Lynne, a long-serving employee and 'trusted servant', underlined the message of deference and non-unionism, drawing upon populist suspicion of paid officials: 'They wanted no third party to interfere between them and their employer; they acknowledged no paid secretary or committee in a back room, drinking brandy and water, and smoking cigars at the expense of the public.'[1] Despite paternalist resistance, organized labour was to advance towards incorporation, carried forward in alliance with progressive industrialists and academics. These progressive middle-class radicals played a crucial role in a complex process of transition, a period of inter-active change unduly obscured in accounts of Liberal continuity. By contributing to what Trygve Tholfsen describes as the 'mellowing of liberalism', the abandonment of the harsh ideological laissez-faire stance of the 1830s and 1840s, they pointed the way forward to interventionist 'new Liberalism'.[2]

Progressive industrialists, pioneers of modern collective bargaining, promoted arbitration and conciliation schemes to give institutional expression to the new mood of mid-Victorian compromise in industrial and class relations. Radical intellectuals, most notably the Positivists, went further, seeking to enlist the unions as a progressive political force.

Proponents of Comte's religion of humanity, they hoped to moralize existing property relations, to reconcile capital and labour through the incorporation of the organized and respectable working class. Thus there was a strong current of convergence in the 1850s and 1860s. While pragmatic working-class radicals were carried away from Chartist fundamentalism, progressive middle-class radicals began to move in an interventionist direction, abandoning rigid adherence to laissez-faire political economy. Liberalism was no longer the narrow middle-class creed characterized by Matthew Arnold in *Culture and Anarchy* (1869) with 'the cardinal points of its belief the Reform Bill of 1832, and local self-government, in politics; in the social sphere, free trade, unrestricted competition and the making of industrial fortunes; and in the religious sphere, the Dissidence of Dissent and the Protestantism of the Protestant religion'.[3]

Despite such adaptation and convergence, radicalism remained a minority force in mid-Victorian Britain, over-awed by the dominance of Palmerstonian liberalism. After 1846, as Jonathan Parry has shown, the Liberals established something approaching political hegemony, attracting a vast range of support from aristocrats to artisans, industrial magnates to labour activists, zealous Anglican high-churchmen to militant secularists. Placing themselves above social classes, vested interests and divisive politics, the Liberals affirmed the virtue of parliamentary government, upholding the constitutional rules of the game in neutral and disinterested manner to ensure harmony and integration within the political nation. The Liberals stood too as the guardians of free trade, a policy which invoked similar values of fair play and impartiality in international affairs, in social relations and in the market, where workers looked forward to the 'free breakfast table', the abolition of all forms of taxation on the necessaries of life. In the 'workshop of the world', free trade was politically unassailable, interwoven in the master narrative of British freedom, prosperity and supremacy, the progress of the nation. Workers in some hard-pressed industries occasionally questioned the desirability of unilateral free trade but there was no political space for 'economic nationalism', for working-class radicals to campaign for reciprocity or protectionism. Under Palmerston, indeed, the Liberals squared the circle, retaining the moral virtue of free trade internationalism while pursuing diplomatic and other policies which unashamedly championed Britain's national interests. While maintaining a traditional balance of power policy, Palmerston mobilized radical libertarianism, calling upon constitutional Britain to fulfil its historic Protestant mission. Rephrased in chauvinistic and sectarian Palmerstonian form, constitionalism offered the most successful formula in British politics: patriotism, retrenchment and reform. Hence, the Manchester School radicals, advocates of a non-interventionist foreign policy, were despatched to the margins along with the radical protectionists. Admittedly, aristocratic incompetence during the Crimean War prompted the formation of the Administrative Reform Association to campaign for middle-class ideals of efficient government and careers open to talent, along with the traditional demand of the parliamentary Radicals for the purification of the legislature and greater powers for independent MPs. Palmerstonian patriotism, however, soon regained the initiative: the inadequacies of Crimea were attributed to the retrenchment demanded by the Radicals. Bright, Cobden and the handful of anti-war parliamentary Radicals all lost their seats at the 1857 general election.[4]

Although dominant, Palmerstonian 'Caesarism' was vulnerable to populist attack, particularly at times of internal tension and Radical disaffection within parliamentary Liberalism. On such occasions, David Urquhart, an unrestrained Russophobe, attracted large audiences to his condemnation of European and Asian entanglements which benefitted Russia at the expense of British commerce and constitutional liberties. Broadened from personalities into an attack on Whig apostasy, factionalism and diplomatic intrigue, Urquhart's campaigns gave vent to instinctive popular suspicion of politicians and the establishment. However, his particular remedy, restoration of the royal prerogative, confirmed his reputation as an eccentric. Audiences dwindled as soon as Whigs, Radicals and Liberals re-established a working relationship at Westminster.[5]

The Liberal ascendancy, Parry insists, depended essentially on party and parliamentary management, Palmerston's metier. Other historians, however, emphasize the role of the provincial press and the associational infrastructure of collective self-help and Nonconformist respectability which created and sustained the Liberal Party as 'a community of progressive sentiment' in the constituencies.[6] Palmerston, however, was reluctant to test his popularity at the polls, fearing that elections gave undue prominence to radical activists whether inside or outside party ranks. While marginalized in terms of policy and power, 'faddist' radicals could still cause problems through the politics of electoral pressure. Here a number of Nonconformist pressure groups, stirred into action by the educational controversies of the 1830s and 1840s, presented the most serious problem. Renamed in 1853 as the Liberation Society, the Anti-State Church Society was the first of the great single-aim militant Nonconformist pressure groups. Backed by substantial provincial support and funds, it quickly developed into an efficient electioneering organization. A model of rational agitation, it extended earlier *ad hoc* attempts to extract pledges from individual candidates into nationwide 'electoral pressure'. The United Kingdom Alliance, also established in 1853 with a membership predominantly drawn from militant Dissent, became particularly systematic – usually to the Liberals' peril -- in its exercise of such electoral 'coercion' in pursuit of temperance reform through the principle of local option.[7] After Palmerston's departure, Gladstone adopted a pro-active approach to the problem, seeking to enlist the 'faddists' in electoral crusades, his 'wars of religious liberalism'. Furthermore, Gladstone abandoned Palmerston's increasingly anachronistic prohibition of parliamentary reform. The very success of liberalism, Gladstone appreciated, necessitated further suffrage extension. Premised on notions of social equity and political justice, the 'social contract' of free trade and retrenchment raised expectations of full citizenship among the 'respectable' working class. In 1864, during the debate on the motion of a private member, Edward Baines, to reduce the franchise qualification in the boroughs from £10 to £6, Gladstone finally and decisively acceded to the logic, opining that every man 'who is not presumably incapacitated by some consideration of personal unfitness or political danger, is morally entitled to come within the pale of the constitution'.[8]

By the time of Gladstone's public conversion, the case for parliamentary reform had already made substantial progress. Within parliament itself, however, there had been little advance. Various proposals were introduced, promoted from across the spectrum of partisan positions, but no legislation was passed other than the unduly neglected Irish Reform Act of 1850 and the abolition of the property qualification for MPs in 1858. Having abandoned his 'finality' stance in 1848, Lord John Russell brought forward a number of limited measures the progress of which was halted first by ministerial instability, then by the increasing preoccupation with foreign affairs, and finally by the insurmountable obstacle of Palmerston's acquisition of the Liberal leadership. On the Tory side, Disraeli, in his ambition for office, took an early interest in parliamentary reform, realizing that the abandonment of protection was inadequate to restore the party to power. His emphasis, however, was on redistribution rather than suffrage extension, on ways of making existing Conservative votes count for more in terms of parliamentary seats, primarily by sharpening the distinction between counties and boroughs. The introduction of one such 'country gentleman's bill' during Derby's minority ministry in 1859 precluded discussion of far more radical proposals newly-drafted by John Bright.

Following his defeat at Manchester and subsequent adoption for a vacant Birmingham seat, Bright stood forward with new vigour as the leading Radical spokesman for parliamentary reform. The old animus against the aristocracy, much intensified by the bitter experience of the Crimean War, was now complemented by the proverbial (if specious) Birmingham ethic of class harmony to produce a radicalism of pronounced moral fervour. His new crusade for parliamentary reform promptly gained the support of former opponents – most notably J. A. Roebuck and other pro-Crimean War Urquhartite Radicals – and inspired the formation of a number of Reform Unions in the midlands and north. Bright's specific proposals, however, were too narrow to elicit support beyond the middle class. On redistribution and the ballot he advocated radical change: on the suffrage, however, he went no further than household suffrage in the boroughs and a £10 householder franchise in the counties.[9]

Irrespective of specific proposals, it was the moral force of Bright's rhetoric – the sense of suffering in the cause of justice, of unwillingly taking up a burden that must none the less be borne, of leadership as a trust or stewardship in a higher cause – which steadily drew in the crowds. Within a few years, Bright stood at the head of a substantial movement for reform, aloof from specific faction or programme, holding the various radical strands together through the kind of moral authority which Gladstone was soon to emulate. If Gladstone was the Christ of popular liberal democracy, Bright, it has been observed, was his John the Baptist.[10] Bright's pre-eminence apart, the development of the reform movement from the late 1850s was driven and distinguished by two factors: the congruence of middle-class and working-class radicals through joint involvement in campaigns to advance continental nationalism; and the steady politicization of skilled workers.

Rapprochement gathered pace during the Orsini affair of 1858, following the attempted assassination of Louis Napoleon by the eponymous Italian exile. Radicals were drawn together in defence of Britain's vaunted constitutional freedoms, rights which they claimed extended to those who sought political asylum, including Simon Bernard, the French démoc-soc exile accused of assembling Orsini's bombs. Angered by the French emperor's determination to rid Britain once and for all of political refugees, radicals appropriated the Palmerstonian language of 'Britishness' to secure a series of notable victories: Bernard was acquitted; prosecutions were abandoned against publications which raised the question *Tyrannicide: Is it Justifiable?*; and the Conspiracy to Murder Bill (a measure introduced by Palmerston under pressure from the French government) was defeated. Secured by middle and working-class radicals working in unison and through the 'national' idiom, these victories, Margot Finn perceptively notes,

> served to affirm received beliefs in the impartiality of the institutions of the state, in a legal system responsive to the just claims of the disadvantaged against the ruling elite, and in a parliamentary system capable of registering the decrees of the people even in an unreformed state. In this manner, the national idiom of Victorian radicalism undercut the language of class, encouraging collaboration between liberals and Chartists by underscoring their shared ancestry in a radical tradition that predated industrial capitalism.[11]

Significantly, it was in 1858 that the National Charter Association was wound up. Having advocated a 'Labour Parliament' during the Preston lock-out of 1853–4, Ernest Jones finally abandoned the hope of reviving the Chartist mass platform and accepted the need for class collaboration.

On the middle-class side, collaboration was embraced with particular fervour by 'proto-republicans' and 'progressive' intellectuals. Joseph Cowen, newspaper entrepreneur, leader of the Newcastle school of radicalism and the outstanding supporter of foreign republican revolutionaries, recruited the talents of such former Chartists as Harney, once notorious for his Jacobin enthusiasms, and the Lintonite–Mazzinist republican W. E. Adams.[12] Positivist intellectuals like Frederic Harrison, E. S. Beesly and J. H. Bridges, evangelists of Comte's religion of humanity, signally failed to win converts among the working class, but their belief in interventionism – whether in continental nationalist struggle or in ordered industrial progress at home – helped to wean middle-class radicals from the laissez-faire orthodoxies of the Manchester School. By reintegrating political and social spheres in radical discourse, they were able to forge alliances with labour leaders.[13]

The Positivists became actively involved with the trade union movement during the London building disputes of 1859–61, the watershed of mid-Victorian labour history. In demanding a nine-hour day, the first large-scale attempt to control working conditions by the modern device of an hour's reduction, the building craft unions made tactical use of the language of improvement, stressing the moral and social benefits of a shorter working day. Although unsuccessful, the disputes led to important new alignments in labour and politics: the adoption of exemplary new model unionism in the building trades; the establishment of the *Bee-Hive* newspaper; and the formation of the London Trades Council, through which Beesly and the Positivists hoped to effect a radical departure. The Trades Council, however, was dominated by union bureaucrats, professional guardians of the official non-political stance, who generally discouraged political initiatives. The Trade Unionists' Manhood Suffrage and Vote by Ballot Association was established in 1862 but it attracted little support.[14] Undeterred, the Positivists turned to campaigns in support of Italian nationalism and Polish freedom. Here the web of committees, organizations and contacts provided a structure open to individual labour leaders without compromising union rules against collective involvement in political agitation. Furthermore, these campaigns accelerated the 'leftward' shift in middle-class radicalism.

The shift was perhaps most noticeable in the National League for the Independence of Poland (NLIP), which, in embracing continental nationalism and French conceptions of social relations, attracted middle-class radicals, labour leaders and radical artisans. Under the presidency of the barrister and former liberal Edmond Beales, the NLIP committed itself to democratic procedures, interventionism and the cultivation of working-class support. Support for Garibaldi strengthened such cross-class alliance, carrying it further in a leftward direction as the united radicals repudiated the attempts of aristocratic liberals to restrict the General's visit to England to the exclusive confines of elite culture. The Garibaldi Trades Committee was instrumental in the emergence of the First International, assisted by the NLIP, which sponsored a visit to London by a deputation of French workmen. It was this deputation which laid the groundwork for a congress of European working men at St Martin's Hall in September 1864, chaired by the indefatigable Beesly, where the International Working Men's Association was established, committed to both nationalist aspiration and the international solidarity of labour.

Despite the involvement (but limited initial participation) of Marx and Engels in the International, there was no new ideological thrust or polarization. Through its culture of tea parties, soirées and public meetings, the First International, Finn notes, reinforced the confluence of class and nationalist conviction with internationalist symbolism and interventionist argument. Whether in foreign or labour relations, English members of the International deployed Polish nationalist sympathies to justify political intervention against the laissez-faire prescriptions of Manchester radicalism. In ideology and personnel, there was remarkable continuity back to 1848 and the démoc-soc enthusiasm of late Chartism. These red republican aspirations had been kept alive in democratic clubs, composed mainly of radical artisans in unmechanized trades, in Soho and other parts of London. Most English members of the General Council of the International were habitués of the clubs and hence disciples of Bronterre O'Brien, while others like Benjamin Lucraft and George Howell were former followers of Ernest Jones.[15]

A new and distinctive feature of the International was the scale of *formal* trade union involvement, notably among the building trades. While abandoning the strict non-political stance, labour leaders were divided in their priorities, divisions which were to accentuate tensions within radicalism in the late 1860s and early 1870s. While some looked to démoc-soc interventionism to secure the rights of labour, others were concerned simply to enhance their collective bargaining position: for many, indeed, affiliation to the International was a tactical and industrial matter enabling unions to take advantage of arrangements to prevent foreign blacklegging during disputes. Then there were those whose priority was to secure the legal framework for trade union autonomy.[16] Here the perceived 'respectability' of the members was the crucial issue. During the American Civil War workers seemed to have established the requisite image for Liberal incorporation.

The dire distress of the cotton famine following the Federal blockade of Confederate ports drained the savings and resources of cooperative, friendly society and other collective self-help institutions, the means by which 'Rochdale Man' maintained working-class pride and respectability. In the circumstances, the forbearance of the cotton workers, their refusal to despair, riot or condemn the American North, was remarkable, reviving middle-class confidence in the innate liberalism of the working class. It was this behaviour, indeed, that prompted Gladstone's conversion to reform as he considered it 'a shame and a scandal that bodies of men such as these should be excluded from the parliamentary franchise'. Once again, the Positivists offered their services to effect the necessary class and political alignment. Denigrating those who sympathized with the South as old-fashioned, anti-capitalist Tory radicals, Beesly hoped that support for the North would initiate a progressive alliance between modern trade unionism and advanced middle-class radicalism under the morally-inspired and indispensable leadership of John Bright.[17] The champion of the hour, Bright uninhibitedly linked domestic politics with the moral cause of the American North, establishing himself as undisputed leader of the growing movement for parliamentary reform.

In April 1864 the National Reform Union was established in Manchester to campaign for household suffrage, the ballot, equal electoral districts and triennial parliaments. A reprise of earlier initiatives by Bright, Cobden and Hume, the League, with George Wilson as president, stood in direct lineage from the Anti-Corn Law League, propounding the virtues of capitalist growth and liberal individualism. There was no uniform or rigid orthodoxy of middle-class radicalism within the Union, however. The ranks extended to interventionists in foreign affairs (most notably, militant and anti-pacifist Nonconformists like Joseph Cowen, George Dawson, James Stansfield and P. A. Taylor) and to liberal academics, such as Henry Fawcett and Thorold Rogers, who now accepted trade union intervention in market relations. At this end of the spectrum there was considerable overlap with the Reform League, established in London in February 1865, under the leadership of Edmond Beales, to promote manhood suffrage and the ballot. Here the presence of Harney, Ernest Jones, Holyoake and Reynolds suggested a parallel lineage back to Chartism, but the veterans' role was essentially symbolic, leaving the management of the League to a new generation of working-class radicals – Howell, Odger, Leno, Cremer, Applegarth and Lucraft – associated with the 'new model' unions, the London Trades Council and the First International. The affiliation and financial contributions of progressive employers, liberal academics and other middle-class reformers added substantially to the League's image, status and resources.

The overlap extended beyond membership to programme, tactics and ideology, seemingly confirming the reformist tenor of mid-Victorian radicalism. From the outset members of the League pledged themselves to work alongside adherents of the Union 'without animosity'. As understood by leading figures within the League, there was now little to distinguish between manhood suffrage and household suffrage, an indication of the impact of the dominant ideology of respectability and improvement. A symbol of virtue and independence, manhood suffrage was not to include the 'residuum', Bright's term for those lacking the capacity for organized self-help, for those 'sunk in almost hopeless poverty and dependence'. This lack of sympathy for the rough and 'undeserving' poor was endorsed by the upper ranks of the working class, the League's target audience, disabling any Chartist-style appeal to a 'ragged' radicalism of enslavement and pauperization.[18]

In return for funds from advanced liberals, the League agreed to mount an earnest agitation – a respectable mid-Victorian application of the old brickbat argument – in support first of the Union's household suffrage proposals and then of the more limited bill introduced by Russell's government after Palmerston's death. When the Liberals were defeated in June 1866, however, the internal dynamics changed, giving the League the tactical advantage in the reform alliance. Following the defeat of Gladstone's bill and the formation of Derby's Conservative ministry, middle-class radicals were compelled to rely on old-fashioned mass pressure from without to wrest the reform initiative from Disraeli and the Tories, at which point the League insisted on 'a thorough and unequivocal commitment to the Chartist principle of manhood suffrage'.[19]

A further factor accentuated the transformation of radical class relations: the politicization of the main body of trade unions. The conjuncture of economic depression, a rising tide of strike activity and the defeat of the Liberal Reform Bill finally provoked the mainline unions out of political lethargy. Where previously labour leaders had moderated their claims to secure liberal support, middle-class radicals were henceforth compelled to amend their ideological prescription in order both to sustain and to contain large-scale popular enthusiasm. In these circumstances, Finn observes, middle-class radicals endorsed lines of political argument earlier denounced as 'socialist' delusions of the working class – the legitimacy of abstract political rights, the efficacy of trade unions as political agents, and the power of parliamentary institutions as instruments of social reform.[20]

Reformism, then, was a two-way dynamic much influenced by tactical needs and considerations, a complex relationship in which the ascendancy of liberal values was a contingent and a contested process. Liberal politicians and academics set the tone of the reform debate, encouraged by the new mid-Victorian precision in constructing and classifying the working class as a tripartite grouping. At the apex, urban artisans were judged worthy of enfranchisement by the very criteria previously expected of 'independent' representatives: wealth, lack of venality and propensity for civic virtue. Through residential, educational, savings and other 'fancy franchises', liberals sought the appropriate formula to incorporate the respectable working class in the political nation, drawing them away from dangerous and contaminating contact with those below them, a project endorsed in the latest cheap improving periodicals such as *The Working Man's Friend* and *The Working Man*. Such carefully-demarcated parliamentary reform was part of a three-tier approach to social harmony and order: philanthropy and paternalism would encourage the upward movement of the strategic intermediate group within the working class, while social policy would isolate and discipline the residuum. To the Positivists and other university liberals who contributed to the *Essays in Reform* (1867), there was an urgent need to respond to the current moderation and goodwill of the respectable working class, to garrison the constitution by incorporating their virtues. Denial of the franchise would lead to hatred, suspicion and class hostility. 'The real danger', Bryce observed, 'is not from the working classes, but from the isolation of classes.' John Stuart Mill, the most celebrated liberal intellectual, took an individual line, wishing to extend political citizenship to women while protecting minority and educated interests by adoption of Thomas Hare's proposals for proportional representation. In parliamentary debate, Robert Lowe argued the Benthamite case for retaining government by the educated in a series of brilliant speeches which thrilled the Commons but angered the unenfranchised. Ironically, Lowe's 'insults' provoked a wider interest in the reform issue than Gladstone's rhetoric of moral entitlement.[21]

As extra-parliamentary agitation developed, the liberal programme and premises of reform were challenged by more militant voices, echoes from the Chartist past. Unduly neglected by those historians who regard the Liberal ascendancy as unproblematic, this radical alternative was to be carried beyond the Reform Bill agitation into an attempt to establish an independent labour politics in the 1870s. Beginning with internal differences within the trade union movement, the radical challenge developed into a démoc-soc republican movement at odds with the Lib-Lab alliance seemingly sealed by the events of 1866–67.

Having been forced out of the London Trades Council for his defence of the pro-Southern editor of the *Bee-Hive* during the American Civil War, George Potter, a staunch critic of the 'Junta' – the coterie of full-time 'new model' leaders and bureaucrats who dominated union politics – established the London Working Men's Association (LWMA). As the champion of the small, non-amalgamated and militant trade unions, Potter and the LWMA campaigned for manhood suffrage and labour legislation.[22] By the time he arranged the first Trades Reform Demonstration, however, the militant political radicals, led by the Chartist veteran Benjamin Lucraft, had already seized the initiative with a series of outdoor meetings on Clerkenwell Green where they condemned the inadequacies of Gladstone's Reform Bill. When the bill was defeated, these radical demonstrations were transferred to Trafalgar Square, a provocative move which the Reform League, encouraged by the Reform Union, felt compelled to match, not least to capitalize on the popular indignation aroused by the disparaging anti-democratic remarks of Lowe and the 'Adullamites'. A programme of official demonstrations was arranged culminating in a national gathering in Hyde Park on 23 July, a revival of the mass platform which involved the League in the controversial question of the right of assembly in London's public spaces – there had been violent clashes when the police tried to clear the park during the Sunday trading demonstrations of 1855 and the Garibaldi festivities of 1862. Under pressure from the militants, the League decided to proceed, despite the ban imposed by the authorities. Denied entry to the park, Beales led the first column of the procession peaceably away to Trafalgar Square, but many remained at the scene, gaining ingress to the forbidden territory when the dilapidated railings collapsed under the pressure of numbers. There followed three days and nights of intermittent skirmishing with the police. Order was not restored until Beales returned to the scene, an intervention which Spencer Walpole, the Home Secretary, welcomed with tearful relief.

Parliament was prorogued for several months but public interest in reform remained at a high and irresistible level as Bright toured the country addressing huge working-class audiences. When parliament reassembled in 1867, the militant radicals convened a series of meetings in Trafalgar Square at which Potter and others advocated a 'universal cessation of labour', reviving the old Chartist rhetoric of a 'Grand National Holiday' and a 'People's Parliament'. Unwilling to be upstaged, the League announced another official demonstration in Hyde Park, overruling the cautious advice of Beales and Howell. The government immediately banned the proceedings and mobilized the forces of order, but this time it was they who capitulated. Led by the Clerkenwell branch of the

Reform League, carrying a red flag surmounted with a cap of liberty, some 150,000 demonstrators marched through the open park gates on 6 May to attend a peaceable and triumphant meeting. The hapless Walpole, scapegoat for the humiliation, resigned his ministerial post.[23]

In these circumstances, the minority Tory administration could not withdraw from parliamentary reform. However, it was 'high politics' not extra-parliamentary pressure that prompted Disraeli to accept Radical amendments which transformed the government bill into an extensive household suffrage measure by enfranchising lodgers and removing the distinction between compounders and personal ratepayers. By conceding these points, Disraeli was able to outmanoeuvre Gladstone and 'dish the Whigs'. With Radical support he maintained command of parliament, keeping control of the redistribution of seats, enabling the Tories to exploit their strength in the counties – in these party-political terms, indeed the nature of the urban franchise was of little significance since large urban constituencies were mostly Liberal already.

As it emerged from parliament, the Reform Act of 1867 awarded the vote to 'registered and residential' male householders, the respectable urban working class on whose behalf the League had campaigned. Although seemingly vindicated, the 'Lib-Lab' alliance, as it has come to be known, entered a difficult period, hampered by structural and internal inequalities and by the contentious issue of trade union rights. Soon after the Act was passed, Howell, the secretary of the Reform League, negotiated a secret financial agreement with Glyn, the Liberal chief whip. An ex-bricklayer turned professional labour leader, Howell lacked a permanent union post and was thus dependent on precariously financed political appointments. In return for personal security, Howell undertook to use League machinery to investigate the intentions of the much enlarged urban electorate, to promote designated Liberal candidates and thereby prevent independent working-class candidates from splitting the vote. Too susceptible to Liberal blandishments, Howell, it seems, sacrificed the independence of the League without securing any real concessions over policy and working-class representation. A handful of League members, Howell included, were encouraged in their candidacies in hopeless constituencies, but other labour leaders were compelled to withdraw in favour of Whigs and other official party nominees. As negotiated by Howell, Lib-Labism was a poor deal for organized labour, but an asset for the Liberals, who secured a remarkable electoral success in 1868. The Reform League was disbanded in post-election recrimination, but Lib-Labism was by no means discredited. Through the new, Labour Representation League, Howell and the moderate trades leaders hoped to renegotiate the terms of the pact, to prevail upon elitist Liberals to accept a small band of working-class MPs in return for electoral support throughout the land. This limited objective was briefly but dramatically revised when Gladstone's government introduced the Criminal Law Amendment Act, an unexpected reverse which underlined the radical argument for an independent labour party to guarantee trade union rights.[24]

In the midst of the Reform Bill agitation the legal status of trade unions was called into question by adverse court decisions and a hardening of middle-class attitudes following the violence and 'rattening' of the Sheffield 'outrages'. When a Royal Commission was appointed, the Junta – studiously avoiding contact with either Potter's militant unions or the congress convened by the Manchester and Salford Trades Council, the precursor of the TUC – worked closely with two of its members, Frederic Harrison, the leading Positivist, and Thomas Hughes, novelist, sportsman and Christian Socialist, to ensure a favourable outcome for respectable new model unions. The minority report, signed by Harrison, Hughes and the Earl of Lichfield, served as the basis for government legislation in 1871 according legal recognition and financial protection to unions. However, the new trade union law was accompanied by the Criminal Law Amendment Act, a forceful restatement of anti-strike legislation which made those on the picket line liable to prosecution for intimidation, molestation and obstruction. The Junta were thus betrayed by their own moderation. Having projected themselves as friendly societies, unions gained legal status precisely on those terms without any advance on legal rights during disputes. Furious with the Liberal government, labour leaders – Howell included – called for an independent labour party, but neither the Labour Representation League nor the newly-formed Parliamentary Committee of the TUC possessed the necessary resources. Despite their initial enthusiasm for independent working-class politics and the creation of a 'third party', the Positivists confused the issue by also supporting Joseph Chamberlain's 'firmly drawn quadrilateral' – Free Church, Free Land, Free Schools, Free Labour. As the 1874 election approached, the Positivists, Royden Harrison critically notes, 'wavered between a conception of a third party organized *de novo* in the country and a reconstruction of the Liberal Party on the basis of Chamberlain's programme'.[25] Lacking clear leadership, delegates at the 1874 TUC decided against any specific commitment on labour representation, leaving themselves free to adopt whatever policy seemed most appropriate in their own constituencies. The Liberals were badly defeated at the election as middle-class activists, disillusioned by other legislation, withheld their support, but they were saved from disaster by the absence of a coordinated labour challenge. Working-class estrangement, it has been calculated, cost them no more than ten to fifteen seats. The two labour candidates elected, Thomas Burt at Morpeth and Alexander McDonald at Stafford were returned without Liberal opposition on orthodox programmes unexceptionable to middle-class radicals.

Throughout these difficult times a small number of advanced liberals and progressive industrialists kept open a line of communication between unions and party leadership. The matter was resolved in bipartisan manner in 1875 when the Liberal opposition, spurred on by its ad-

vanced wing, amended and extended the Tory government's legislation into a comprehensive and final settlement.[26] For their part, the Conservatives gained little by
way of gratitude. Once the labour legislation was safely
on the statute book, the unions rallied behind the Liberals,
supporting Gladstone's latest war of religious liberalism,
his moral crusade against the wicked Turk and the 'prestige politics' of Beaconsfieldism. The Lib-Lab tradition was
firmly enshrined in the TUC when Henry Broadhurst replaced the exhausted Howell as secretary of the Parliamentary Committee.

While the issue of trade union rights preoccupied labour
leaders, militant radicals turned their attention to those
outside the ranks of organized labour and beyond the
newly-extended franchise, the unemployed poor of the East
End of London. Although generally associated with Charles
Bradlaugh and middle-class meritocratic radicalism, the
republican movement derived its initial impetus from socio-
economic protest in the East End where the distress of
the poor stood in marked contrast to the profligacy of
the royal family – the insatiable financial demands of the
Prince of Wales and the continued absence from public
life of Victoria, still mourning the death of her husband
ten years after the event. The Unemployed Poor League,
established in the autumn of 1868, demanded that parliament give precedence to the condition of the poor over
that of royalty and aristocracy. When the League's public
meetings were transferred to Hyde Park in June 1869,
another organization, the International Democratic Association, appeared on the scene with an avowedly republican programme. The ideological thrust for this démoc-soc
republicanism, however, was provided by the Land and
Labour League, founded after the disbandment of the
Reform League by denizens of London's radical and republican clubs where Bronterre O'Brien's formulations
for national regeneration still held sway. To ensure that
'labour should receive the full share of the products of
all industry', the League proffered a nine-point programme

for the republic of labour, a medley of old Chartist, Owenite and currency-reform schemes, within which particular prominence was accorded to land nationalization and home colonies. Considerable numbers were attracted to unemployed demonstrations in Trafalgar Square in 1870, but then the republican movement entered its 'second phase' and acquired a different socio-political character.[27]

Here the inspiration came from France with news of the collapse of the Second Empire and the Declaration of the Republic in September 1870. Secularist republicans like Bradlaugh, radical trade unionists led by Odger, Positivist intellectuals such as Frederic Harrison and Richard Congreve joined members of the International Democratic Association, the Land and Labour League and the First International in support of the French. Parliamentary Radicals and advanced Liberals soon joined the bandwagon, most notably Sir Charles Dilke, although he was to abandon his extensive schedule of republican speech-making outside parliament when the Prince of Wales fell ill in 1871. Republicanism briefly became the symbolic defining issue of middle-class radicalism, embodying the meritocratic aspirations of those who wished to advance further than the parliamentary Liberals on a range of issues from disestablishment and reform of the House of Lords to land reform and reform of the marriage laws. Even so, republican propaganda still tended to be phrased in the traditional British and populist manner. An expression of anti-monarchist sentiment against 'Mrs Brown', Victoria's sobriquet, it seldom argued the case for a republic as a more rational and democratic form of government, concentrating instead on the expense of monarchy and attacking personal extravagances and failings.[28] Enthusiasm for republicanism was soon undermined by further developments in France where the Commune raised the dread spectre of what Bradlaugh described as 'class dictation'. A model of orthodoxy in his commitment to classical political economy, his reputation for militant and unorthodox rhetoric notwithstanding, Bradlaugh distanced himself from the social republicans. Although specifically moderate and political in programme, his newly-formed National Republican League failed to stop the erosion of middle-class support. The démoc-soc republicans were left to argue amongst themselves about how best to emulate the social and democratic Communards. One faction, led by John Hales, tried to regroup radical forces through the International by establishing an English section, a Federal Council, which would unite trade unions and O'Brienite republicans in an independent political party. The attempt fell victim to other sectarian disputes as Marx decided to transfer the International to New York to prevent a takeover by Bakunin and the anarchists.[29]

By this time, some radical-republicans, encouraged by the economic upturn of the early 1870s, transferred their energies to the industrial front, seeking to establish independent labour politics through the extension of trade unionism throughout the ranks of the working class. Here, as in their other initiatives, they were unable to counter the institutional power of the Lib-Lab leaders. Furthermore, they lacked a new ideology to inspire and sustain such a major leap forward. New unionism among the unorganized was brought to an abrupt halt in the mid-1870s by the onset of the 'Great Depression'.

The north-east set the lead in the new industrial policy through the Nine Hours League. Having started as an unofficial movement among Tyneside skilled engineers, the League secured notable victories throughout the region and other industrial districts by uniting various grades of workers, unionized and non-unionized, skilled and unskilled. It was an example that members of the Land and Labour League tried to emulate in the London docks, with limited and brief success. In the north-east, the leadership of Joseph Cowen, as Nigel Todd has shown, was a decisive factor: 'his mixture of Chartism and Mazzinism, a blend of revolutionary and reformist principles and tactics finely tuned to the conditions of the early 1870s, supplied the motivation to encompass a form of plebeian democracy'. Cowen's inspirational leadership, and the coordination provided by his paper, the *Newcastle Chronicle*, covered a wide range of initiatives to extend the boundaries of working-class collective endeavour in the early 1870s: the Nine Hours strike, agricultural trade unionism, cooperative production, franchise reform (the 1867 Act had been applied in a particularly restrictive way in the north-east), and women's agitation in consumerism, trade unionism and the suffrage. Exhausted by these efforts and his new parliamentary responsibilities, Cowen was forced by ill-health to withdraw from active politics between February 1874 and spring 1876. Much had changed by the time of his return. Economic downturn had undermined the new unions, and politics had come under the control of the local Liberal caucus, an exclusive middle-class group 'indifferent to the condition of their less favoured and less fortunate fellow-countrymen'.[30]

While there were pointers towards independent labour politics, the most famous of the new unions of the early 1870s, Joseph Arch's National Agricultural Labourers' Union, carried Lib-Labism into the rural counties. By 1874 the union boasted a membership of 100,000, many of whom enjoyed substantial wage rises, thanks to favourable market conditions and selective strike action. The onset of agricultural depression and the return of a Conservative government led to a dramatic reversal of fortune as the power of the union was crushed in conflict with farmers' defence associations and the imposition of a lock-out in the eastern counties. Defeated and demoralized, the union abandoned industrial action to concentrate on emigration schemes, friendly society activities and campaigns for land reform and suffrage extension in the counties, issues which were steadily moving up the Liberal agenda.[31]

The variety and persistence of radical alternatives indicate some disquiet with Liberal values, an unease absent in the current historiographical orthodoxy which insists on the salience and appeal of Gladstonian Liberalism. In the formative years around the Second Reform Act, Lib-Labism established itself as the dominant expression of popular radicalism, aided by the rhetoric of Bright and Gladstone which imbued a new reciprocal respect and moral affinity between leader and audience. Incorporated in the discourse of moral entitlement, the subaltern classes, Biagini asserts, continued to support the Liberals through rational choice, impressed by a programme of reforms – for example, abolition of the taxes on knowledge (the stamp and paper duties), continued reduction of taxation on items of working-class consumption, and relaxation of Poor Law administration – which offered convincing solutions to pressing problems. Having proved himself at the Exchequer as the first 'People's Chancellor', Gladstone extended his 'social contract' with the people as the prospective 'Premier of the working classes'. By no means the formula for a minimalist state, his shibboleth of liberty, retrenchment and reform actually encouraged an expanding framework of social policy in which non-expensive forms of state intervention (such as factory legislation) were combined with ever-increasing local government provision. Here, the Public Health Act of 1848 had established the trend, beginning the transformation of the discredited municipal corporation into the proud Victorian civic authority. Once converted to interventionism through cooperation with working-class radicals and labour leaders in the international and reform campaigns of the 1860s, the seed-bed of new liberalism, middle-class radicals emerged as 'municipal socialists', providing social services supervised by central government inspectors and subsidized by loans and grants-in-aid made available by Gladstonian budgetary surpluses.[32]

It is questionable, however, whether such intervention was desired or appreciated by the working class. Suspicion of the state, the authorities and the law ran deep in popular culture, as evinced by the appeal of *Reynolds's Newspaper* and by the remarkable popularity of the Tichborne claimant. According to Thomas Wright, *Reynolds's* attracted a working-class circulation of over three hundred thousand in the mid-1870s, a successful commercial adaptation of old-style radicalism in which sensation and voyeurism were blended with what Patrick Joyce describes as 'classical populism': deep distrust of the state and the vaunting of voluntary activity.[33] In his struggle to regain his supposed standing and fortune as Sir Richard Tichborne, the claimant – the generously-proportioned Charles Orton – established himself as popular martyr and hero, attracting mass support throughout the 1870s in his manly pursuit of 'fair play'. This 'sporting' struggle (melo)dramatized popular antagonism towards the state and the law, drawing upon the motifs of radical patriotism: a lost golden age, messianic leadership and an excluded people against a corrupt and conspiratorial ruling class and legal system. While venerating masculine independence, the claimant's supporters, marshalled by Kenealey and the Magna Charta Association as freeborn Englishmen, expressed deep resentment of outside intrusion, whether by the state in the form of taxes and the poor law, or by law courts which operated one law for the rich and another for the poor.[34]

Successful as it may appear, the Liberal project was severely disabled by the persistence of popular distrust of the state. Popular mentalité remained little altered by the extension of trade union and political rights. For all their rhetoric of incorporation, the Liberals failed to transform the image of the state: indeed, they left important areas of transparent class discrimination in the civil law unreformed, including institutional and legal constraints on thrift and personal indebtedness. Minimalist or not, the Liberal state still seemed to operate on one law for the rich and another for the poor. Despite the growing acceptance of collectivist ideology and action and the public promotion of social opportunities via education, housing, health and welfare policies, Victorian class law, Paul Johnson has noted, continued to discriminate against many manual workers and to sustain the moral basis of class division well into the twentieth century.[35] At the popular level, the state had yet to be redefined and accepted as a neutral force responding sympathetically to a plurality of interests. Furthermore, popular cynicism extended beyond the state and the authorities to politicians and parties – part of the appeal of the Tichborne claimant was his very 'independence'. This distrust was in no way dispelled by the new constituency organizations, Liberal caucuses dominated by local notables. Thus, the rise of Lib-Labism concealed a number of tensions, pressure points where there was space for other political formations to gain a popular audience. Militant radicalism secured an intermittent presence but failed to effect the necessary breakthrough to mass support. Popular Toryism proved more successful.

Upholding the interests of nation rather than party, the Tories defended traditional ways of life – not least good old-fashioned fun – against the moralism of Liberal interventionism. The success of 'clog Toryism' in urban Lancashire demonstrated the powerful purchase of paternalism and employer influence when extended to the 'manly' idioms of popular culture. Masters of the common style, Tory employers championed the working man's right to his glass of beer and idle pastimes. There was no condescension or moral preaching in the manful paternalism of 'Sir Harry' Hornby, the latest 'gamecock' of the Hornby dynasty, a family of squire-employers whose Tory politics were proudly followed by their loyal and devoted Blackburn workers.[36] Ethnicity was a further factor as English anti-Celt prejudice concentrated into enmity of the Irish, reinforced by a popular redefinition of anti-Catholicism in which poor Irish immigrants replaced cunning continental emissaries of Rome as the cause of alarm. Popular Toryism flourished as the volume of anti-Irish, anti-Catholic propaganda increased, rallying freeborn Englishmen to protect the Protestant constitution from the enemy within. Defenders of the faith, the Tories were also the guardians of a robust popular culture which mid-Victorian liberalism failed to amend.

7

GLADSTONE, LIB-LABISM AND NEW LIBERALISM

In its heyday, Gladstonian liberalism left little space for independent radicalism. The old protest politics of exclusion were undermined by substantial (but not democratic) franchise extension, satisfactory trade union legalization and the Grand Old Man's persuasive rhetoric. Charismatic but still patrician, Gladstone represented a new form of gentlemanly leadership in which ethical substance and ethical character were fused in a powerful platform of moral populism. Embodying the moral claims of the people's cause, Gladstone's campaigns facilitated popular incorporation in liberty, retrenchment and reform, in joint and zealous struggle for self-government, economy and Christianization. Eschewing any crude appeal to class at elections, Gladstone invoked a wider frame of reference, a single overarching issue in the struggle between good and evil – Irish disestablishment, condemnation of 'prestige' politics or 'Beaconsfieldism', Irish Home Rule – within which individuals, sections, 'faddists' and classes could transcend the narrow limits of their own 'selfish' interests.[1] Here ideology coincided with electoral realism. The foe of sinfulness, selfishness and fiscal extravagance, Gladstone campaigned against the abuse of power and privilege, attracting the votes of those who had neither. About half the working class were enfranchised in 1867, but subservient small shopkeepers and tradesmen still dominated most electoral rolls, 'individualist' voters who relished the opportunity – enhanced by the introduction of the secret ballot in 1872 – to exact political revenge, to belittle the high and mighty at the polls. In his electoral crusades, Gladstone, the people's William, offered the 'psychic satisfaction of ruling to the ruled'.[2] Beyond electioneering, however, Gladstone's appeal extended throughout the subaltern classes (to use Biagini's terminology), often accompanied by a strong sense of working-class collective pride and dignity. In this manifestation, an image enshrined in working-class autobiographies (and in popular pilgrimages to Hawarden), Gladstonian liberalism approached its own self-righteous evaluation as the culmination of popular radical tradition.

As an expression of working-class aspirations and values – as perhaps 'the first Labour party' – Gladstonian liberalism tended to be strongest in areas of distinctive religious affiliation and/or occupational composition. Although a high Anglican, Gladstone exuded a 'vital Christianity' which transcended differences over Church establishment, Rome and denominationalism, attracting the support of the Nonconformist conscience in political crusade against the sinfulness of natural man. The strength of Lib-Labism in isolated mining, fishing and agricultural communities where Primitive Methodism prevailed has long been appreciated. Recent research has drawn attention to the continuing importance of Old Dissent among the urban working class, and not just in traditional Nonconformist strongholds in the east midlands. The Congregationalists, generally seen as one of the more middle-class of Nonconformist churches, contributed much to the flourishing of Lib-Labism. Increasingly liberal in theology, social attitudes and politics, they retained significant support among skilled workers and leaders of organized labour. In education and other social provision, Congregationalist separatism exemplified the key tenets of Lib-Labism. Where voluntarism was inadequate, public intervention was an unpleasant necessity, to be conducted in local and representative manner, free from aristocratic patronage, clerical control and Whitehall dictation. Through advocacy of arbitration and conciliation schemes, Congregationalists and other Old Dissenters provided a means of intellectual convergence between liberalism and trade unionism, reinforcing existing institutional ties. For Robert Knight, Congregationalist and leader of the Boilermakers' Union, active trade unionism, a practical (and voluntarist) manifestation of Christian belief, would regulate the market in accordance with considerations of humanity and social justice.[3]

Nonconformist attitudes informed the political economy of trade union leaders and the radical politics of the first Lib-Lab MPs. Between 1874 and 1906 some twenty four members of working-class parentage and background were returned to the Commons as Lib-Lab MPs, a label which seems to have originated as a term of political abuse by socialist opponents. For the most part self-educated workmen who had progressed from manual occupations to influential positions as professional trade union officials and labour organizers, over half were former miners.[4] This was a reflection of political geography, as the location of the industry enabled miners to exert overwhelming influence within coalfield constituencies. In his three-tier typography of Lib-Lab MPs and constituencies, Biagini has shown how electoral success was most likely where the Lib-Lab candidate was 'one of ours', closely identified with the dominant local industry, religion and culture. Miners' MPs in South Wales and in the north-east coalfield enjoyed lengthy Lib-Lab parliamentary careers: in the Rhondda constituency, where nearly 80 per cent of the electors were miners, 'Mabon' Abraham was opposed only twice between 1885 and 1910. Electoral chances were much less secure where a local trade union leader stood in an economically and culturally diverse constituency, or where national labour leaders put themselves forward – figures like Howell and Broadhurst (who contested six seats and represented four constituencies) with illustrious careers in central organizations of the labour movement but who lacked committed trade union support or community identification with their constituents.[5]

Much influenced by Nonconformity (and often also by temperance), Lib-Lab MPs exercised a cultural style which was both 'puritan' and working class, belying the image of self-satisfied careerist upward mobility often attributed to them by opponents. Proud to remain members of the respectable working class they represented, they quickly established an *ouvriériste* tradition that working-class interests could only be directly represented by those who had worked at a trade. Deeply suspicious of power, privilege and wealth, they displayed what Biagini calls the 'anthropological pessimism' of Victorian Nonconformity.[6] The greater the power and wealth of individuals and classes, the greater their power to do evil – unless checked by active democracy. In theology, as in traditional radicalism, the struggle was with 'the classes', those aristocratic sections of society most corrupted by unchecked power and unearned wealth.

In certain circumstances, then, the practice of Lib-Lab politics by working men and their leaders gave formal expression to genuine attachment to Gladstonian liberalism. Underlying this commitment was a fundamental faith in the goodness and rationality of humankind (the corrupt and privileged apart), a religio-political belief that individual moral improvement would lead to social progress. As a vehicle of moral populism, Gladstonian liberalism mobilized the 'respectability' of all who stood above the instincts and passions of unbridled licence, whether through force of will, religious conviction and/or collective self-help. Voluntarism remained the essential creed of working-class Liberals whose political affiliation, Robbie Gray notes, embodied a sense of plebeian self-assertion and independence, even class pride, underpinned by a dense cultural network of chapels, schools, trade unions, mutual associations and other manifestations of collective self-help, the organizational infrastructure, as it were, of the 'first labour party'.[7] Where interventionism was required, as in elementary education, it should uphold and extend civil and religious liberty through popular control exercised by local representative bodies. Thus working-class Liberals looked to the School Boards to counteract privilege and established interests, to exercise democratic control over the way public money was spent and their children educated. In opposing provisions within the 1870 Bill which allowed rate-aid for voluntary Anglican schools, the object of hostility was not religious teaching as such, but its manipulation as an instrument of political and social control. The struggle for popular control of education, along with the parallel campaign for Church disestablishment (Mabon's maiden speech in the Commons called for the disestablishment of the Church of England in Wales), spearheaded the wider radical battle against the 'cruel and selfish principles of feudalism, of aristocracy, of the plutocracy, of capital, and of masterdom'.[8]

In localities where community-based trade unionism in agriculture and mining had strong links to Dissent, the union lodge and the chapel were to all intents and purposes the local organizational presence of the Liberal Party, the base from which elections were conducted. Elsewhere, however, particularly in the large towns, the operation (and pretensions) of constituency organization revealed class and other tensions within Lib-Labism. No longer the preserve of time-serving oligarchies, local Liberal associations became more professional and middle-class after the Second Reform Act. Birmingham set the lead in Liberal constituency organization with a model democratic structure, manipulated and controlled by a powerful middle-class 'caucus' that demonstrated its canvassing prowess by capturing all three city seats despite the minority-vote clause, which gave local voters only two votes. The trend continued as local government reform, more regular elections at all levels, and the elimination of disreputable old ways and means by the Corrupt and Illegal Practices Act (1883), underlined the need for efficient organization. At constituency level, electioneering relied upon party management and voluntary endeavour, harnessing the resources of those with time and other means to spare, women included.

Although excluded from the two main party organizations until 1918 (the year of their partial enfranchisement and eligibility for Parliament), women were welcomed into subsidiary associations to assist with canvassing and other electioneering chores. However, there were pronounced cultural and organizational differences between the parties. The Liberals established women-only organizations, in which those already active in suffrage societies and branches of the Ladies' National Association for the Repeal of the Contagious Diseases Acts were joined by those new to the world of organized endeavour. Most recruits were predominantly middle-class in character: it was infinitely easier for those with servants to find time for political work in a busy day. At the cost of some dissension, the associations began to cultivate 'female political power', progressing beyond canvassing, as Linda Walker has observed, to a fourfold set of practical objectives: 'to improve women's political education, to make sure that women voters used their prerogative in local elections, to encourage women candidates for Poor Law Boards, School Boards, town and county councils and, ultimately, to enhance their claim to the Parliamentary suffrage'. Such feminism, however, lacked the pan-class appeal achieved by the Tories through the Primrose League, by far the most popular political organization in the country, almost half the total membership of which was female. The Tories saw no need for single-sex organization or the specific promotion of women's issues. In recognition of their electioneering and other talents, women were accorded considerable space within the League. Offices and status were determined by class and financial standing rather than by gender: about a quarter of the leading officers were women. Furthermore there was a warm welcome for working-class women seeking sociability and acceptance, a much-appreciated alternative to the middle-class homilies on self-denial, hard work and social purity which characterized Liberal women's politics.[9]

Dominated by middle-class elites, the rise of the caucus displeased popular radicals like Joseph Cowen who hankered after the old hustings with its direct relationship between politicians and the people, unmediated (and uncorrupted) by formal organizational structures. The selection of candidates became the major point of contention as middle-class electoral logistics came increasingly into conflict with working-class claims for labour representation, sadly confirming the fears of radical papers like *Reynolds's* and the *Bee-Hive*. In Birmingham itself, staunchly Liberal trade unionists such as W. J. Davis of the brassworkers sought independence from the middle-class caucus by forming a Birmingham Labour Association to run independent Labour candidates at local elections during the 1870s.[10] Mining constituencies apart, local Liberal associations often refused to adopt labour parliamentary candidates on the grounds of social class and finance. It was this provincial short-sightedness, not central Liberal Party policy, which accounted for the exiguous increase in the number of Lib-Lab MPs. The leadership at Westminster spoke encouragingly of the need for more working-class representatives, but local political practicalities precluded their selection. Constituency associations chose not to offend rich local notables by asking them to stand aside and then defray the expenses of working-class candidates. Labour leaders were to react increasingly angrily to such exclusion. Ramsay MacDonald joined the ILP in 1894 after the local Liberal association rejected Charles Hobson, president of the Sheffield Federated Trades Council, for the Liberal nomination at the Attercliffe by-election. 'We didn't leave the Liberals', MacDonald protested: 'They kicked us out and slammed the door in our faces.'[11]

While the caucus system led to working-class anger at

their renewed exclusion, it provided the point of entry for middle-class radical activists and 'faddists', still busily engaged in agitation – between 1868 and 1872 an all-time record 101,573 petitions were presented to the Commons.[12] Acting within constituency organizations, activists from the various pressure groups could intensify the politics of electoral pressure. While generally unsuccessful in attempts to dictate terms to prospective parliamentary candidates, they tried to impose a policy agenda on party leaders. Here their usefulness, if not indispensability, in turning out the Liberal vote in large urban constituencies appeared to give them considerable bargaining power. Tactics differed, however, as some 'faddists', most notably in the United Kingdom Alliance, continued to threaten independent or coercive electoral action, while the Liberation Society, once incorporated in the caucus system, preferred to emphasize loyalty and commitment. Whether in gratitude for their continuing loyalty or through fear of their withdrawal and abstention, activists expected the party leadership to give legislative priority to their particular nostrum: temperance, disestablishment, secular education, international peace, repeal of the Contagious Diseases Act, or whatever.[13] Such tactics, however, failed to take account of political realities. After the Second and Third Reform Acts, as after the First, the electorate was considerably less radical than activists assumed. Indeed, as Disraeli and the Tories appreciated, there was widespread concern at the prospect of 'incessant and harassing legislation'. Furthermore, Liberal governments had to legislate for the nation rather than for the party. Although a Peelite not a Whig by upbringing, Gladstone generally recognized the need (at least until 1886) for conciliation, compromise and consensus, for national settlements above class or sectional interests. Liberal reforms continually (and necessarily) failed to satisfy the purist criteria of middle-class radical activists.[14]

This was the context in which Joseph Chamberlain sought to extend caucus control into programme politics, to transfer power and policy-making from Westminster to radical activists in the constituencies. Although an industrialist and a Unitarian, Chamberlain was by no means an archetypal middle-class radical–Liberal. Little influenced by the religious ethos of militant Dissent, his radicalism was practical, utilitarian and ambitious, unencumbered by old pacifist and individualist shibboleths which hindered strong and efficient imperial government. From the ruins of the National Education League, a militant pressure group which had failed to secure free, national and secular elementary education, he constructed the National Liberal Federation (NLF). The aim was to coordinate and rank the various reforms demanded by constituency activists. In seeking control of policy-making, however, the NLF failed to establish adequate representative credentials, to extend either its membership or programme much beyond standard big-town radicalism. Having returned from retirement to protest against the Bulgarian atrocities, Gladstone graced the platform at its inaugural conference in 1877, captivating the delegates with his impassioned denunciation of Beaconsfieldism, prestige politics and the wicked Turk. By keeping his grip on radical affections, especially in foreign and imperial affairs, Gladstone seemed able to thwart caucus control and programme politics.[15]

Carried forward to the Midlothian campaign – an attempt to stir up the country to a new and high standard of political awareness, discussion and citizenship – Gladstone's rhetoric brought the Liberals back into power in 1880 on a wave of moral righteousness. Soon at odds over policies and priorities, internal party divisions deepened as an unfortunate conjuncture of colonial, Irish and domestic problems took Gladstone's attention further away from party management and reform. The government was finally defeated over the 1885 budget, but elections were delayed pending the completion of the new registers of the Third Reform Act, the one positive achievement of the ministry. The new electoral possibilities of the Act – and the prospect of Gladstone's final retirement –

prompted Chamberlain to bid for power. He resigned shortly before the ignominious ministerial collapse to canvass support for an alternative 'Radical Programme', a conspectus of progressive proposals advocated by allies and friends, 'the advanced party', in articles in the *Fortnightly Review*.

Old issues were to be resolved through devolution and local government reform, enabling the party to progress, as Chamberlain had first proposed in the *Fortnightly* in 1873, to his 'four Fs': the 'quadrilateral' of free schools (no fees, and certainly no rate-aid for voluntary schools); free church (disestablishment); free land (removal of ancient laws restricting the sale of land); and free labour (legalization of peaceful picketing). As brought up to date, and confidently commended to the newly-enlarged electorate, the 'Unauthorized Programme' of 1885 called for the extension of local government powers to acquire land at a fair price to let as allotments, smallholdings and artisans' dwellings; the establishment of elected authorities in counties; free and efficient elementary education; and graduated taxation to reduce the burden on the poor (and also, though seldom stated, to maintain adequate levels of defence spending). The accompanying 'hype' was perhaps more important than the specific details. Chamberlain hailed his 'constructive' proposals as 'the death-knell of the *laissez-faire* system', the necessary extension of the 'municipal socialism' he had pioneered in Birmingham where public enterprise was responsible for gas, water, sewerage, lighting and slum clearance. Social reform and limited collectivism, he insisted, were the 'ransom' which property had to pay to ensure security of tenure. In this respect the 'Unauthorized Programme', like tariff reform later, was an ambitious exercise in pre-emptive politics, a clarion call to the middle class to prevent class polarization and socialist dispossession. Funded by graduated taxation, death duties and other financial reforms, constructive social reform would ensure social harmony, keeping the working and middle classes united, the industrious and productive sectors of society whose worth was still denied by parasitic landowners and idle rentiers, 'those who toil not, neither do they spin'.[16]

In demonizing the landlord, Chamberlain struck a familiar radical chord, all the more resonant as household suffrage was introduced in the counties. Through compulsory purchase by local authorities, the programme held out the promise of 'three acres and a cow'. Urban workers were offered less tangible benefits, a programme of reform little in advance of traditional Liberalism, the 'Radicalism of the crochet-mongers'.[17] In the absence of an 'urban cow', the programme failed to arouse enthusiasm among the working class. At the same time, however, its 'advanced' nature frightened middle-class voters away from Liberalism, now perceived as the thin end of the socialist wedge.

The fate of Chamberlain's radical programme gave early but unheeded warning of the structural, rhetorical and other obstacles which were to hinder subsequent attempts to reformulate Lib-Labism. Financed without impeding capitalist enterprise by taxing the wealth of landowners and rentiers, Chamberlain's collectivism was predicated on the old radical division – the sociological foundation of both Chartist and Anti-Corn Law League rhetoric – between the industrious and the idle. On the economic surface, the distinction still appeared valid. Rentiers not industrialists, the late-Victorian elite derived their wealth from the City through control of political, legal and financial services, the monopoly against which radicals had always protested. The profits of 'Old Corruption' had fallen victim to reform and 'cheap government', but overseas trade and investment, the 'invisible empire' of finance proved a lucrative alternative. Much to the envy of provincial industrialists, London's financial dynasties enjoyed equality of wealth and prestige with the landed aristocrats – City investors themselves – who still occupied the highest positions in political and social life.[18] Within the late-Victorian transformation of Conservatism, however, property interests were merging in a manner which belied the old radical sociology. In a process that still awaits due historical analysis, the Tories succeeded in attracting the various strata of the propertied middle class, down to the rapidly-expanding marginal white-collar groups of the lower middle class, irrespective of level or source of income. Redistribution, the *quid pro quo* for the franchise proposals of the Third Reform Act which Salisbury and the Lords would otherwise have blocked, was an important factor. By creating a system of overwhelmingly single-member seats, roughly apportioned on the basis of population, the Redistribution Act (1885) allowed 'villa Toryism' to flourish in the new separate suburban constituencies.[19] 'The middle-class', the *Fortnightly* regretfully observed, 'has swung round to Conservatism. . . . The sleek citizens, who pour forth daily from thousands and thousands of smug villas round London, Manchester and Liverpool, read their *Standard* and believe that the country will do very well as it is.'[20] Thenceforth, Tory rhetoric refused to distinguish between different fractions of capital – industrial, commercial, financial, rentier, landed, etc. – as it invoked the security of defensive solidarity against incessant and harassing legislation, radical finance, socialism and working-class spoliation. The party of property, the Conservatives were increasingly to define themselves relationally and differentially against the mythical class enemy, the crude (hence effective) stereotype of a unionized, militant and greedy working class.

Refracted through the progressive lens of Chamberlain's social radicalism, this stereotype, or rather the dread prospect of working-class socialist politics, brought added urgency to the need for social reform. In looking to state social reform to transcend class divisions, promote social harmony and pre-empt socialist spoliation, Chamberlainite new liberalism not only misjudged middle-class electoral sociology, it also misread working-class attitudes and needs. Rising real wages and increased leisure time enabled the labour movement to shed its former exclusiveness, to extend beyond the ranks of Lib-Lab voluntarism, but suspicion of the state (and of politicians) persisted. Hence the 'statist' demands which accompanied the unionization of the semi-skilled and unskilled in the 1880s were restricted to basic economic fundamentals concerning the right to work, minimum wages and the eight-hour day. Ironically, Chamberlain and the progressive Liberals refused to intervene on these terms, rejecting these working-class demands as 'sectional', beneath the dignity and higher social purpose of the radical collectivist state.[21]

In proto-type Chamberlainite formulation, new Liberalism lacked electoral purchase. As a radical leader, Chamberlain's credentials were further compromised by his aggressive stance on foreign and imperial issues, a maverick approach which antagonized parliamentary colleagues, middle-class Radicals reared on the creeds of Cobden and Bright. Lacking an adequate power base, Chamberlain entered negotiations with Hartington, trusting to secure a position of influence (not least over domestic reform) once the latter assumed the leadership. Contrary to expectations, however, Gladstone chose not to retire or to allow himself to be ousted. By elevating Home Rule to a moral crusade, the Grand Old Man occupied the radical high ground in the political crisis of 1885–6, establishing a criterion which Chamberlain and the Whigs were unable to meet. A test of Liberal orthodoxy, Home Rule enabled Gladstone to effect what might appear a salutary purge.[22]

The split, Jonathan Parry contends, was damaging and unnecessary. Despite the tension between 'Whig' and 'Chamberlainite' factions, there was no fundamental fracture on ideological or socio-economic matters: questions of economic principle, domestic reform or class tension were not important enough to tear the party asunder. Most Liberal MPs, men of studied moderation and party loyalty, were neither whig grandees nor activist radicals. At the beginning of 1886, 110 of 339 Liberal MPs were from the landed classes, 164 were professional men, 142 were active businessmen, and 12 were from the working classes. Essentially a political force, the Liberals were never the party of doctrinaire political economy: the requirement of political reconciliation always came first. As the (natural) party of government, they aimed at national settlements which, however they might displease faddist activists and purist radicals, managed to conciliate non-party interests and viewpoints. By pragmatic and constructive use of central and local government, they followed a successful agenda – order, economy, free-market conditions, and 'self-improvement' – which stood above class interest or programme politics. Under the Liberals, 'self-government' proved compatible with the extension of moral guidance, the preservation of class harmony and the continuance of elite (but accountable) leadership. This considerable achievement, Parry contends, was all but ruined by Gladstone's catastrophic adoption of Irish Home Rule.

Home Rule, seemingly a natural development of the principle of responsible self-government, directly contravened powerful Liberal myths inherited from the Whigs: national and imperial integration under the rule of law (Home Rule struck a devastating blow at the notion of a truly national supra-factional parliament); and the responsibility of the propertied to uphold law and morality, to resist anti-social minorities of any sort. Much more than in his previous ventures, this latest war of religious liberalism – as judged by the Whig-Liberal tradition of government – displayed Gladstone's disastrous inability to distinguish between unconsidered sectional clamour and the matured wishes of reasoning opinion. His subsequent conduct compounded the error. In an impetuous action which institutionalized division in the party, Gladstone dissolved parliament on the defeat of his Home Rule Bill. Campaigning behind the slogan, 'the masses against the classes', his platform rhetoric was unduly divisive, subverting the essential cross-class collaboration of the Liberal project. For once, his relentless crusader politics failed to elicit a mass popular response, damning evidence, Parry maintains,

of Gladstone's spectacular misinterpretation of the popular will. Chamberlain and Bright, two of the most high-
profile Liberal tribunes, moved to the Unionist side, as
did Whigs, radicals and others who believed in an administrative, rational, consensual and parliamentary conception of liberalism. Out of line with many in his party,
Gladstone was increasingly out of tune with the mood of
the nation. Prior to the Home Rule crisis, there was considerable concern that his remorseless opposition to government expenditure – his refusal to pursue a
Palmerstonian strategy of national assertion – was jeop-
ardizing British interests abroad at a time when Britain's
economic and strategic superiority was coming under challenge. The crisis of 1885–6 destroyed the Liberals' status
as the natural governing body of the world's greatest
empire.[23]

Gladstone's last years of leadership witnessed what
Michael Bentley describes as 'the death-throes of an individualist politics based on the language of mission and
prophecy'.[24] Alternative approaches were held in abeyance
while Ireland 'blocked the way', until the all-important
Home Rule mission had been accomplished. After the
Parnell divorce scandal, however, critics of this Irish ob-
session gained the upper hand, committing the party to
programme politics. The omnibus resolution passed at the
NLF conference in Newcastle in 1891 was a catch-all of
demands, embodying four fundamental principles to which
all Liberals, old and new, subscribed to a greater or lesser
degree: the extension of political and religious liberties;
community self-government; the eradication of privilege
and vested interests which conflicted with wider community
interest; and social reform to improve the condition of
the working class.[25] Popular with constituency workers, the
Newcastle Programme helped the Liberals back into power
in 1892 when Gladstone duly reverted to the theme of
'Irish obstruction'. Ailing but still obsessed, he wished to
challenge the Lords at the polls after the upper house
rejected Home Rule. He was unable to persuade colleagues,

however, who now realized it was not Ireland or the Lords which blocked the way, but the Grand Old Man himself. His final retirement, however – over the cost of naval rearmament – was not the occasion for a new departure. Without his commanding presence the governing party soon collapsed in disarray, its attention diverted from social reform and labour policy – crucial considerations at a time of trade depression and industrial discontent – by personal rivalries and internal divisions. While Rosebery, Harcourt and Morley each hinted at different Liberal programmes at the 1895 election – reform of the House of Lords, local option and Home Rule – the Unionists were able to extend both their class and their populist appeal. Liberalism stood condemned not only for undermining middle-class business confidence but also for infringing the liberties and rights of the freeborn Briton. Local option would deny the poor man his beer while allowing the well-off to enjoy the privilege in hotels and restaurants; Welsh disestablishment threatened the endowments of the poor; and reform of the Lords would remove its 'democratic veto' – 'the heritage of the people for the people' – its ability to block 'faddist' measures that lacked an overwhelming popular mandate.[26]

Amid the recrimination which followed the Liberal débâcle of 1895, some social radicals looked to a better future, trusting to transform Liberal politics along the lines discussed in the Rainbow Circle and in the *Progressive Review*, founded in 1896 to advocate 'an enlarged and enlightened concept of the functions of the State'.[27] With its emphasis on a 'national minimum', this 'new Liberalism' reflected heightened awareness among the professional classes of the problem of poverty, a 'consciousness of guilt' raised by social science and social service, by the shocking revelations of urban surveys and post-Oxbridge experience of the 'nether world' of the slums through the settlement movement. Broader in scope than Chamberlain's 'constructive' proposals, new Liberalism drew upon a substantial intellectual lineage, extending back through

Green and the Liberal Idealists, academics who resisted the anti-Home Rule drift of the intellectual establishment into Conservatism, to John Stuart Mill, the 'transitional thinker between old and new, *laissez-faire* and collectivist forms of liberalism'. True liberty, Mill concluded, was concerned with the full development of the self and society, with the cultivation of man 'as a progressive being', a process which might necessitate state intervention to ensure the requisite social conditions for self-realization.[28] Before his premature death in 1882, T. H. Green took the argument further in a doctrine of citizenship which posited a positive role for the state, no longer regarded as incompatible with liberty. As in earlier formulations of Victorian Liberalism, however, 'character' remained the essential consideration. The role of the state was to secure sufficient personal freedom for citizens to act as rational moral agents, to structure society so that only certain types of conduct brought success. Green's principal aim, Richard Bellamy notes, 'was to reinforce the desirable character traits which were essential to Victorian self-help and voluntary schemes, he did not seek to substitute them by the direct provision of welfare services or redistribution by the state'. Second-generation Idealists underlined the point.[29] In his *Principles of State Intervention* (1891), D. G. Ritchie, whose fusion of Idealism, Darwinism and utilitarianism was the proximate intellectual inspiration for new Liberalism, outlined a collectivist radicalism in which the state created the conditions which allowed individuals to realize their potential.[30]

New liberalism acquired a specific agenda of economic and social reform through the recommendations of the Rainbow Circle (whose members insisted on differentiating themselves from the old Manchester school of radicalism by according the state a central role in their philosophy), the *Progressive Review*, and the writings of J. A. Hobson and L. T. Hobhouse. Based on the Idealist principle of distributive justice, the proposals embodied an ethical and efficient political economy which would reward the industrious while securing minimum standards for all. Nationalization was eschewed in favour of steeply graduated taxation of rent and unearned income, to be accompanied by pensions and other measures of economic redistribution. Social reform was no longer to be considered a cost or burden on the productive economy: through redistributive taxation, the unearned 'surplus' could finance positive measures of welfare relief without infringing the traditional Liberal emphasis on individual desert and merit. Furthermore, by redistributing purchasing power, collectivist social reform would eliminate the under-consumption of the masses, reducing waste and inefficiency throughout the economy.[31] Here new Liberalism aligned with other discourses. Concern about 'national efficiency' spread across the political spectrum as the economy reached its climacteric, soon to be outpaced by the productivity and welfare levels of industrial latecomers. The quest for 'national efficiency' led some social radicals away from the Gladstonian (and radical Nonconformist) vision of the state as a moral force, the agent which maintained ethical values between itself, its citizens and other states, to an activist economic notion of the state, a power entitled to pursue the prosperity of its citizens, if necessary in conflict with other states. By supporting imperialism during the Boer War, however, they had to abandon links with the progressive intelligentsia and the traditional radicals for whom anti-jingoism remained the crucial political dividing-line.

As a broad ideological and cultural phenomenon, new Liberalism was undoubtedly influential: it was to shift the nature of political discourse and thought, forging a social welfare ethos endorsed and embellished by future (pre-Thatcherite) generations. For all its intellectual vitality and influence, however, its immediate electoral and political purchase was minimal. New Liberalism, Michael Freeden notes, was unable to penetrate beyond its natural urban professional base and arouse the type of mass enthusiasm required for political success.[32] Furthermore, any possibility of a progressive realignment in British politics – as explored by the Rainbow Circle – was blocked by the electoral system and the inflexibility of existing party structure.

In reaching the reform and redistribution settlement of 1884–5, Gladstone and Salisbury had both strongly endorsed the single-member plurality system of election by bare majority, or first-past-the-post: indeed, only a handful of MPs supported an amendment for proportional representation proposed by a couple of academic Liberals. Backed by powerfully-entrenched party organizations in the constituencies, single-member plurality was the best guarantee of party unity and discipline, denying dissidents and new formations any prospect of independent electoral breakthrough. Labour was the one exception, a new party which gained a foothold through the social–geographical concentration of the working-class vote, but even here electoral survival was to depend upon alliance with the Liberals.

8

LABOUR'S TURNING-POINT?

Through an electoral understanding with the Liberals in the Edwardian years, the newly-formed Labour Party was incorporated in 'Progressive Alliance'. A tactical and ideological accommodation, Labour's role in the alliance, historians insist, attests to the continuity of radicalism, preserving the spirit of Lib-Labism in reconstituted form.[1] As this chapter demonstrates, the formation of independent Labour was not a dramatic or decisive break. In its public political language, independent Labour kept within the mainstream current of radicalism, drawing upon conventional (and accessible) idioms and motifs. The following chapter will review the relationship of Liberal and Labour in 'Progressive Alliance', stressing points of increasing tension – cultural, organizational, class and gender – which call into question the extent of ideological harmony and continuity.

Throughout the late Victorian and Edwardian period, Liberalism displayed considerable ideological vitality. Having purged 'old corruption' by administrative and financial reform, Liberals advanced from laissez-faire to a programme of 'progressive' interventionism through the 'neutral' state. Given the adaptability and continuing popularity of Liberalism, there seemed neither space nor need for an independent Labour Party. In certain localities and industries, however, Lib-Labism was perceived as dysfunctional, failing to meet radical and/or 'labourist' requirements. Here activists began to contemplate an independent (and more responsive) alternative. Once established – and that was the difficult task – the continued institutional independence of Labour was to become the focus of class pride. Having secured a foothold, Labour was increasingly perceived as the workers' party, better attuned to labourism, voluntarism and participatory democracy, more sensitive to continuing suspicion of the state and the political 'classes'. For non-Tory elements of the working class, Labour gradually replaced the Liberals as the guardian of radical and working-class values.

Labour's origins are best explained in tactical and contingent terms: its fragile emergence and uneven early progress reflect the first fractures within the complex geography and ideological variants of popular Liberalism. Where Lib-Lab activists were able to exercise influence in policy-making and candidate-selection, independence from the Liberals was unnecessary. Elsewhere the inflexibility of caucus Liberalism prompted labour radicals towards independence, the next stage, as it were, in the politics of electoral pressure. Local factors were an important determinant, but there was often a national dimension in these tactical equations. Following the high political crises and realignments of the 1880s, Lib-Lab activists constantly reviewed the national electoral prospects of the Liberals, an assessment in which opinion differed widely. Furthermore, Lib-Lab activists had to position themselves within the changing contours of organized labour and industrial relations. From the late 1880s trade unionism extended (or rather exploded) into the ranks of semi-skilled and unskilled workers. In certain instances this leap forward into non-craft sectors brought forth a different kind of 'labourism', a set of workers' demands for protection and reward which stretched the 'progressive' Liberal agenda of legislative intervention. Furthermore, Lib-Lab allegiance came under strain in industries where market pressures were particularly intense as employers adopted new managerial strategies hostile to organized labour.

Lib-Lab activists were divided not only in assessment of Liberalism but also in response to socialism and the call for a 'labour alliance'. Independence was not simply a tactical consideration, but a question of ideology. In the 1880s, independent (and extra-parliamentary) radicalism, previously upheld by démoc-soc republicans and ultra-radicals, became associated with socialism. This was a complex and problematic process. At the intellectual level, Marxist ideas were mediated and recast through utilitarianism, the romantic critique of capitalism and other indigenous traditions.[2] None of these adaptations of scientific socialism pointed directly towards independent electoral politics. Having crossed a watershed, socialist ideologues resolved to sever all links, to establish a distinctive (or purist) political identity by shunning contact with reformist trade unions and other Lib-Lab organizations. Extending beyond the ideologues, however, there was a wider process of cultural adjustment, a creative interaction with the language and values of Nonconformist radicalism.[3] At popular level, this 'ethical socialism' held out the promise of a higher social ethic, a new way of life predicated not on dialectical materialism and the revolutionary proletariat – on the internal contradictions and inevitable collapse of capitalism – but on the triumphant crusade of the virtuous people against materialism. Speaking a familiar language, converts to this 'religion of socialism' chose to proselytize from within, hoping to radicalize and maximize the institutions of Lib-Labism. At the same time, socialist activists took to the streets, agitating among the poor and unemployed, seeking to halt the advance of urban popular Toryism. In such practical efforts, socialists sought not to subvert but to extend and complete the radical project. They hoped to construct a broad 'labour' alliance which would harness the moral fervour of Lib-Labism and the funds and resources of its collective associations, the necessary foundation for independent labour representation. In this practical and ethical formulation, socialism offered a revitalized language for united radical advance.

Renewed interest in land reform, prompted by the visit of the celebrated American land-reformer Henry George, opened the way to the socialist revival of the 1880s. The history of land reform, one of 'the *idées fixes* of middle-class Radicalism from Cobden to Lloyd George', neatly reflected wider change in the radical movement.[4] After the repeal of the Corn Laws, Cobden and Bright failed to carry the middle class forward to 'free trade in land'. Interest languished despite their insistence that the only way to eradicate 'feudalism', to break up inefficient and unwieldy estates and erode the privilege and influence of large landowners, was through the free market, by composite abolition of primogeniture, entail, settlement and private conveyance. When interest revived in the 1860s, in part in reaction to attempts to appropriate some of London's most famous commons, land reform helped to forge the Lib-Lab alliance. There was a new interventionist tone, reflecting the input of Liberal academics, members of the professional middle class, and labour leaders. Lib-Lab supporters of 'home colonization' advocated direct state intervention to bring aristocratic waste land into profitable cultivation and extend peasant proprietorship, anticipating the 'Free Land' proposals of Chamberlain's radical programme. Once again, J. S. Mill provided the ideological bridge between old and new radicalism and between middle-class and working-class radicals. Founded in 1870 by academics, middle-class professionals and members of the First International, Mill's Land Tenure Reform Association went beyond free trade in land to advocate taxation of the unearned increment of rent.[5] In the early 1880s, at a time of intensifying agricultural distress and in the context of imminent franchise reform in the counties, Henry George's more radical single-tax proposals attracted vast attention – annual sales of his controversial *Poverty and Progress* (1879) reached 400,000 in 1882. No socialist himself, Henry George opened the way for the socialist revival as he toured the country, challenging the 'invisible hand' of orthodox political economy in campaigning for 'single tax' on the incremental value of land. Furthermore, his platform provided a rallying-point for radicals disillusioned with Gladstone's second ministry and its 'illiberal' Irish and imperial policies. Discussion soon progressed beyond George's proposals and land nationalization, the *ne plus ultra* of the old démoc-soc radicals, to the full socialist programme, Marx's exposition of which was soon widely available in English translation.

Carried along by this ideological advance, the Democratic Federation altered its name to the Social Democratic Federation (SDF). Established in 1881 to promote 'a new independent and working-class party' or 'labour party', the Federation had attracted a range of radicals and disillusioned Gladstonians, including Joseph Cowen, who was regarded by the denizens of the Soho radical clubs (and also by Engels) as 'the obvious leader'. Having stood forward in anger at Liberal coercion in Ireland (and in support of the Land League), Cowen remained deeply attached to the concept of private property ownership, and thus promptly withdrew from the SDF. Cowen's brand of democratic radicalism, a militant inflection of Lib-Labism, lost direction and purchase in the 1880s. He supported social reform, but not socialism; he advocated Irish Home Rule while adulating the empire as his sense of Englishness expanded; and he endorsed the Land League but rejected land nationalization.[6] W. E. Adams, former Mazzinist-republican and editor of Cowen's *Newcastle Weekly Chronicle*, followed a similar path. He abandoned radical politics to publish his memoirs, which extolled the virtues of self-reliance and individual freedom against new-fangled socialist collectivism.[7]

The departure of Cowen and his like notwithstanding, the ideological divisions of the 1880s should not be overdrawn. The leading critic of the caucus system, Cowen was alienated as much by Hyndman's organizational dictatorship – his determination to use the SDF as the 'centre of organisation' to direct working-class politics – as by his socialist prescription. On Cowen's departure, Hyndman, a top-hatted ex-army officer and county cricketer, sought to impose a narrowly mechanistic reading of scientific socialism. His *England for All* (1881) contained chapters lifted straight from Marx alongside demands for a strong navy to protect the colonies, a vestige of his Tory–radical jingoist past. Denouncing the 'trade union fetish', he proscribed all contact with existing working-class organizations, labourist bodies. Led by 'stodgy-brained, dull-witted, and slow-going time-servers', unions were 'the chief drawback to our progress'. According to *Justice*, the SDF paper, the TUC was a 'reactionary caucus "bossed" by a few fat, well-paid wire-pullers'.[8]

Prompted by the rise in unemployment (a word which first appeared in the *Oxford Dictionary* in the 1880s), Hyndman pointed the SDF towards street marches and demonstrations to rally those excluded by Lib-Labism. Also intended to halt the advance of urban popular Toryism, outdoor agitation among the poor, unemployed and less politically-motivated sectors of the working class involved SDF activists in violent confrontational rivalry with Tory Protectionists. Without endorsing the SDF agenda, various radical groups offered support to uphold the right of free-speech and public assembly. When the Tory Fair Traders called a demonstration in Trafalgar Square on 8 February 1886, the SDF decided to sabotage the proceedings, to capture the crowd for the socialist cause, symbolized by the red flag brandished by John Burns. They soon lost control of events as the crowd, an unpoliticized force of unemployed casual labourers, rioted its way through Pall Mall and adjacent streets, before returning to the East End singing 'Rule Britannia'.[9]

'Black Monday' aroused anxiety among socialists and others critical of Hyndman and the SDF, but they joined together in a broad-based campaign to defend the right of open-air public assembly, threatened by the return of a Tory government and the appointment of a new metropolitan police commissioner. The year 1887 was a crucial one in the politics of public space, confirming the power of the authorities through both festival and repression. Victoria's Golden Jubilee offered the crowds a stage-managed package of 'jingoism, circuses and guff'.[10] Once the celebrations were over, however, Trafalgar Square and other public places were occupied by the homeless unemployed. These outdoor camps, refuge of 'outcast London', were soon the scene of rival initiatives, philanthropic and socialist. As hot summer gave way to chilly autumn, charitable agencies distributed food and lodgings tickets, while the SDF rallied the unemployed in meetings and demonstrations under the slogan 'Not charity but work'. When Sir Charles Warren, the new commissioner, banned all meetings in the Square, socialists, radicals, secularists, Irish nationalists and members of the Salvation Army united to defend the right of assembly. The Metropolitan Radical Association announced a monster demonstration on 13 November to defy the ban and protest against William O'Brien's imprisonment in Ireland. On the fateful day – 'Bloody Sunday' – mounted police and troops dispersed the assembly with brutal ease and ferocity, inflicting fatal injuries on three of the crowd.[11]

While socialists, radicals, secularists and others were united in anger at police brutality and the suppression of free speech, 'Bloody Sunday' accentuated internal divisions within socialist groupings and exposed the wider isolation of the SDF within late-Victorian radicalism. Although attention has focused on Hyndman's dictatorial and crude Marxist determinism, the SDF, it has recently been suggested, properly belonged to metropolitan ultra-radicalism, a long tradition extending back through the Land and Labour League and Harney's London Democratic Association to the post-Napoleonic 'revolutionary party' and the Jacobins of the 1790s. As such, the SDF established a good working relationship with the more radical elements of the London press: *Reynolds's*, in particular, often extolled the organization and its socialist objectives. In this two-way process *Reynolds's* embraced socialism not as a critique of the existing economic order but as a vision of the ideal society that would be created after the state had been wrested from the hands of the 'parasitic' classes. In return, the SDF placed political reform at the top of the agenda: in its official programme, old Chartist demands for adult suffrage, annual parliaments, and payment of members headed the list, followed by such political measures as abolition of the standing army, legislative independence for Ireland, and free and equal access to education and justice, leaving the call for collective ownership of the means of production, distribution and exchange until the end. Presented in this unobtrusive manner, socialism was not the barrier to popular support. In its failure to effect a nationwide response, the SDF was disabled by image, not by ideology. By taking the rhetoric of violent revolution onto the streets, a revivalist exercise in forcible intimidation, the SDF exposed the cultural fault-lines, widened by Lib-Labism, which separated ultra-radicalism, militant, secular and metropolitan, from organized labour, respectable, Nonconformist and provincial.[12]

For other socialists 'Bloody Sunday' was an object lesson in the overwhelming physical power of the state. Visionary or utopian socialists withdrew from this unequal struggle to concentrate on the 'education of desire', offering a morally-compelling vision of the socialist future. Disgusted by Hyndman's sham insurrectionary tactics, his predilection for 'adventure, show and advertisement', William Morris had already quit the SDF to found the Socialist League (SL). Inspired by Carlyle, Ruskin and the romantic critique of bourgeois industrialism, Morris, a wealthy designer, artist, poet and writer, found in socialism the promise of a qualitatively different way of life. Morris envisaged a society without money, markets, legislation, unnecessary economic growth or pollution, an inversion of Victorianism hailed by modern radical environmentalists as a blueprint for a non-authoritarian ecological society. Gender relations, however, remained unamended: Morris's utopia offered women romantic love, motherhood and happy housekeeping. Imbued with his vision of 'Nowhere', Morris sought first and foremost to make socialists of the working class, a project not to be compromised by entanglement in electoral politics, industrial militancy or futile violence on the streets. But the SL, a high-minded exercise in expressive politics, was soon appropriated by anarchists who looked to the bomb, not the revolutionary working class, as the agency of human liberation.[13]

Edward Carpenter, another important inspirational figure, was bewilderingly eclectic in support of rival strategies for labour's advance, from the ballot box to anarchist violence. Much influenced by Walt Whitman and by oriental spiritualism, Carpenter's religion of socialism promised a democratic utopia in which communalism and comradeship would replace class division and sexual inequality. Revered by converts to the new 'religion' for his alternative life-style of rustic simplicity, Carpenter was the prototype of the sandal-wearing, vegetarian, fruit juice-drinking socialist whom George Orwell was to traduce in the 1930s. Carpenter's socialism was premised on his homosexuality: as an 'uranian', he claimed to prefigure the new spirit which would reconcile differences of sex and class. Having insisted on a conceptual separation of sex and reproduction to legitimize his homosexuality, he chose not to extend the distinction to women, whose reproductive role was left unquestioned. In Carpenter's socialism, motherhood remained the pinnacle of womanly achievement and fulfilment.[14]

Divorced from Hyndman's agitational preoccupations, utopian socialists prefigured a 'new age' agenda of green issues and gay rights to which socialist-feminism was later to be added. 'Back to nature' became a middle-class fad in these early green politics as the wealthy were attracted to Carpenter's Fellowship of the New Life in the hope of therapy, of a solution to individual crisis, an elevation of individual life. Other critics of Hyndman's tactics pursued more conventional political goals. After Bloody Sunday, the Fabians abandoned all thoughts of working-class revolution. 'I object to a defiant policy altogether at present', George Bernard Shaw wrote to Morris after 'Bloody Sunday': 'If we persist in it, we shall be eaten bit by bit like an artichoke.'[15] Having adjusted continental theory to British circumstances, the 'Hampstead Marx Circle', the Fabian think-tank, elaborated a strategy of gradualist socialism, concentrating their efforts on 'permeation', on the rational conversion of politicians and administrators working within existing institutions.[16] Permeation, however, depended on circumstances. Fabian intellectuals in the metropolis encouraged the new London County Council towards progressive politics. In the provinces, Fabian activists involved themselves in the associational network of radical, Liberal and working-men's clubs, steadily encouraging a shift of allegiance to independent Labour politics.

Working within existing organizational and rhetorical frameworks, provincial Fabians facilitated an extension of the radical project by condemning the social, economic and political power of the 'idle rich', shifting the focus from state parasitism, the monarchical and aristocratic privilege which still preoccupied *Reynolds's*, to social parasitism, the power exercised by an idle, unproductive class living off unearned incomes. Rejecting Marx's theory of surplus value, Fabians said little about the exploitation of labour for profit. Fabian economics, Jon Lawrence notes, was essentially little more than a refinement of the traditional radical critique of capitalism. The condemnation of rent, an unjust tribute over land, was extended to include interest, an unjust monopoly over capital. Constitutional reform remained the essential preliminary since it was the political system that maintained the dominance of the idle monopolist classes. Once out of the control of hostile class interests, however, the 'neutral' state would be run by representatives of the working class, who would legislate on its behalf. As socialists, the Fabians reintegrated the political and the economic, applying a systematic analysis of the economic power of the 'class monopolists' and its political legitimation by the state. Committed to the socialization of land and machinery, the Fabian project 'remained squarely within Radical discourse: it claimed "to do away with the idle owners and to keep the whole product for those whose labour produces it"'. The Fabians' tireless advocacy of this new politics between 1890 and 1893, Lawrence contends, 'allowed them to wean many disillusioned and disoriented Radicals away from their traditional allegiances, while convincing large numbers of trade unionists who had previously remained aloof from organized politics that the working class could be "emancipated" under their leadership'.[17]

Prior to this Fabian initiative, attempts to construct independent labour politics had fallen foul (at least in England) of vested Lib-Lab interests, socialist ideological dispute, and all manner of financial and other wrangles. Through the *Labour Elector* and the Labour Electoral Committee (established by the TUC in the wake of the 1884–5 Reform Act), H. H. Champion tried to build an electoral machine to secure the return of a group of labour MPs who would represent working-class interests at Westminster in the same single-minded spirit as the Irish nationalists. Forced to quit the SDF, Champion supported a number of independent candidates, most notably Keir Hardie at the Mid-Lanark by-election of 1888, the beginning of the 'labour revolt' against Liberal domination of constituency politics. By no means a mere personal protest at Liberal control of the selection process, Hardie's candidature was a test of the Liberal Party's willingness to recognize 'Labour', and what it stood for, as a separate political force. Supported by Champion and by J. L. Mahon's Scottish Land and Labour League, Hardie managed to secure a mere 8.4 per cent of the poll, but sufficient interest was generated to establish a Scottish Labour Party.[18] South of the border progress was blocked by vested interests and internecine dispute. The TUC, still under Broadhurst's leadership, remained a bastion of Lib-Labism, opposed to any independent parliamentary initiatives. As an emblematic figure, Hardie failed at this stage to unite supporters of a labour alliance. Vague in detail, Nonconformist in spirit, his 'ethical socialism' offended against the secular and theoretical propensities of metropolitan and middle-class socialists. Caught in the middle of ideological, religious, financial and personal disputes, the hapless Champion, having closed the bankrupt *Labour Elector*, emigrated to Australia.

Soon afterwards prospects improved. As Jon Lawrence acknowledges, Fabian permeation of 'popular Radical subculture' was fortunate in its timing, coinciding with 'the unparalleled awakening of popular interest in the possibility of a distinct labour politics engendered by the trade union revival associated with the so-called New Unionism'.[19] In a sudden and dramatic burst, trade union membership doubled between 1889 and 1891. As in the early 1870s, the leap occurred at a time of cyclical upturn and a tight labour market. This time round, however, there was no shortage of suitable leadership or advice, as socialists, Georgeites and others came forward to organize the unskilled. Striking match-girls at Bryant and May secured the catalytic victory in 1888, encouraged and inspired by Annie Besant and W. T. Stead, co-publishers of *The Link*, a socialist–radical journal established in the wake of 'Bloody Sunday'. The next advance, the gasworkers' attainment of a three-shift system and eight-hour day, was organized by Will Thorne, a worker at Beckton Gas Works and member of the SDF. Not fully literate, Thorne was assisted by Eleanor Marx and an array of socialist intellectuals and activists. Working-class activists educated in socialist societies, most notably the engineers John Burns and Tom Mann, came to the fore in the famous London dock strike of 1889 which secured union recognition, a virtual closed shop and 'the full round orb of the dockers' tanner'. This sensational triumph encouraged other workers, unskilled, semi-skilled and previously unorganized, to mobilize for increases in wages and reductions in hours. In 1890, in response to the call from the founding Congress of the Second International, May Day demonstrations were held in London and other cities to demand the legal eight-hour day. A few months later, the TUC, briefly in tune with the new mood, decided to promote an eight-hour Bill, and elected Burns as the first socialist onto its parliamentary committee. The socialist societies, however, still remained aloof: the SDF officially dismissed the union work of Thorne, Burns and Mann as 'a lowering of the flag, a departure from active propaganda, a waste of energy'.[20]

Realists not revolutionaries, socialist activists offered practical assistance rather than ideological instruction to the new unions. Above all, they encouraged semi-skilled and unskilled workers to exploit their bargaining strengths, to adopt big structures and militant strategies alien to the craft-based traditions of conventional trade-unionism. This convergence of tactical and ideological considerations extended to legislation and independent labour politics. Unable to enforce craft regulation at the workplace or restrict the labour supply, new unions were compelled to advocate legislation to consolidate gains won by militant action in favourable market conditions. Through involvement in new unionism, socialist activists sought to reinforce the 'labourism' of metropolitan radicalism, to prioritize demands like the eight-hour day. The purpose was to secure popular support, to expose the limitations of Lib-Labism: any advance beyond the palliatives of labourism to full-blown socialism was a project for the future.

The success of new unionism depended on full employment, police tolerance of vigorous picketing and the absence of concerted employer opposition, factors which were not to persist. Abruptly halted in the early 1890s, new unions failed to capture control of the labour movement: indeed, the old Lib-Lab unions benefitted most from the membership explosion, sustaining their growth after the boom collapsed in 1891.[21] But the very weakness of new unionism prompted an important political response in the West Riding. Hit hard by depression and foreign tariffs, woollen workers were defeated in a series of disputes in which, as Edward Thompson noted, they 'confronted the face – sometimes complacent, sometimes oppressive, sometimes just plain stupid – of established Liberalism'.[22] The Manningham Mills strike, a bitter five-month lock-out during which the local Liberal authorities gave staunch political support to the Tory employers, underlined the political lesson. Radicals, trade unionists, members of the SL and other local socialists joined together in the Bradford Labour Union to promote labour representation on the town council and at Westminster 'irrespective of the convenience of any political party'. Similar labour unions and clubs, offering education, entertainment and political propaganda, spread throughout the West Riding, joining the new trades councils in demanding independent political action and an end to Lib-Labism.

Impressed by these and similar initiatives elsewhere, John Burgess and Robert Blatchford, talented journalists with a populist appeal, advocated a national federation to link these local independent labour parties of non-sectarian socialists, disaffected radicals and politicized trade unionists. As a further boost, independent candidates polled well at the 1892 general election, not least at Bradford where Ben Tillett, hero of the London dock strike, came near to victory in a three-cornered contest. John Burns and Havelock Wilson, the seamen's leader, were elected at Battersea and Middlesbrough respectively, but both were to seek an accommodation with the new Liberal government. Cloth-capped and proud of it, Keir Hardie remained defiantly independent, having won at West Ham on an anti-unemployment platform of land nationalization, municipal workshops and the statutory eight-hour day. At the TUC later in the year, Hardie chaired a small unofficial meeting which decided to call a national conference to unite the 'Independent Labour Parties in Great Britain'. In January 1893 the foundation conference of the Independent Labour Party (ILP) assembled in Bradford, an appropriate venue.

The delegates, more than one-third of whom came from Yorkshire, were overwhelmingly working-class, provincial and pragmatic. The object of the new party, they readily agreed, was 'to secure the collective ownership of the means of production, distribution and exchange', but the term socialist was not to appear in the party's title, or in its manifesto, a programme of reforms little in advance of progressive Liberalism. Here the important practical consideration was not to offend the trade unions, whose support was indispensable if independent labour representation, the desideratum of the ILP, was to be achieved at the earliest opportunity. A short-cut to political effectiveness, this 'labour alliance' was pursued with single-minded instrumentalism as Hardie, now a revered figure, exerted his influence over the new party. Alternative strategies were squeezed out of consideration, much to the chagrin of Blatchford and the Lancashire socialists, advocates of a United Socialist Party, a fusion of groups including the ILP and the SDF which belatedly purged itself of sectarianism.[23]

While the ILP asserted its instrumental political agenda, socialists in the labour movement gave expression to their creed through a variety of cultural forms. John Trevor's Labour Church extended the hand of ethical fellowship to all classes and creeds in a gospel of social amelioration, celebrated in music and texts, religious, democratic and socialist. An initial success – there were 54 Labour Churches by 1895 – the movement soon peaked, unable to compete with yet more convivial forms of socialist fellowship such as the new Clarion Cycling Clubs.[24] Sponsored by Robert Blatchford, author of *Merrie England*, a million-seller penny text which offered a popular view of a socialist (and autarkic) future, the clubs took the urban working class out into the country. Healthy exercise

161

was combined with political propaganda and 'making socialists': members dismounted to distribute socialist literature and hold impromptu meetings, disturbing the 'sabbath quiet' of remote country villages. Despite the socialist politics, the clubs conformed to English associational cultural norms: friendship and good cheer took precedence over party discipline, ideological rigour or organization. Socialism, it seems, took deepest roots in isolated districts, as in the new labour clubs of Colne Valley where trade unionism and other forms of working-class association were relatively weak.[25] Elsewhere socialists had to compete for popular support against other cultural forms. In the increased leisure time and rising real wages of late-Victorian England, socialism's advance was hindered not only by commercial mass culture but also by well-established forms of working-class associational culture, characterized by conviviality, mutuality and proud autonomy.

These obstacles to the construction of a socialist 'counter-culture' also precluded the rapid advance of independent labour politics. The 'labour alliance' sought associational and financial support to challenge the entrenched power of Lib-Lab politics. Support for independent Labour remained patchy, restricted to localities and industries where Lib-Labism was proving dysfunctional. For all its pragmatism, the new ILP failed to secure a significant breakthrough – all 28 candidates, Hardie included, finished bottom of the poll at the general election of 1895. To make matters worse, the TUC introduced new standing orders which strengthened the bloc-voting big battalions, the old brigade, at the expense of socialist trade councils, radical new unions and independent labour politicians, the proponents of the labour alliance. The political focus of the TUC reverted to more traditional issues: opposition to the Conservative government, renewed vigilance over changes in trade union law and the pursuit of increased labour representation within Lib-Labism. After the crucial battles of the early 1890s, industrial relations were relatively peaceful in the later years of the decade, a period of *détente* marked by the extension of institutionalized collective bargaining procedures. Such arrangements tended to reinforce union and worker commitment to Lib-Labism. However, in industries where the 'crisis of competitive capitalism' was particularly acute, with intense international competition and reduced profit margins, employers continued to apply the 'squeeze' on labour, asserting their undiluted right to manage in the face of 'obstructive' workers.[26] Here allegiance began to shift away from Lib-Labism towards independent labour politics, often encouraged by socialist activists. Defiant defenders of workplace autonomy, socialists acquired influence and respect among craft workers by leading resistance to employer prerogatives and the reorganization of production.[27]

In the complex (sometimes contradictory) industrial relations of the 1890s the question of political allegiance, the choice between Lib-Labism and independent Labour, was problematic. The political geography of industrial location was an important determinant. Lib-Labism remained strongly entrenched on the coalfields, separate parliamentary constituencies dominated by miners whose interests and needs could not be ignored. Here working-class candidates were encouraged to stand on the Lib-Lab platform, an arrangement which the Miners' Federation of Great Britain (MFGB), adequately represented in Parliament, had no wish to alter. Hence, they kept apart from the Labour Representation Committee (LRC), fearing that miners' funds would be purloined to support extraneous candidates. Scattered throughout the length and breadth of the land, railwaymen had no such clout at constituency level, a considerable disadvantage for workers in an industry without adequate safety legislation or union recognition. Along with the surviving new unions, the Amalgamated Society of Railway Servants (ASRS) led the call for independent labour representation, not to promote a socialist millennium but simply to protect the interests of workers ignored by Lib-Labism. In 1899 the TUC agreed that trade unions, cooperative societies, Fabian societies, the SDF and the ILP should confer together 'with a view of securing united political action'. At the conference the following year, Hardie and the ILP steered a skilful course between Lib-Lab attempts to restrict the new organization to limited trade union matters and the SDF's insistence on a clear socialist objective. The labour alliance was duly given institutional form as the Labour Representation Committee (LRC), subsequently the Labour Party.

There was no sudden surge of support until a further deterioration in industrial relations. Having crushed new unionism, employers returned to the courts to affirm their rights and authority. Unions, it seemed, could now be sued for tortious acts committed on their behalf, a point expressly denied by previous legislation. The principle was put to the test in a famous case in 1901 when the Taff Vale Railway Company was awarded damages against the ASRS for actions by its members during the strike of the previous summer.[28] Although the judgement virtually destroyed the right to strike, some trade union leaders were reluctant to press for its reversal, since the ruling addressed the crucial question of internal trade-union authority over militants and troublemakers necessary for the effective operation of the new collective bargaining arrangements. Union leaders, however, finally rallied behind the LRC and the campaign to reverse Taff Vale, a change of heart prompted by the strength of rank-and-file protest, the scale of the award, and the intransigence of the Tory government.[29] This was the moment of final breakthrough: union-affiliated membership of the LRC rose from 375,000 in February 1901 to 861,000 in 1903, when it was decided to raise a fund for the payment of Labour MPs – a practical necessity ignored by the Liberals – by means of a compulsory levy on the unions.

After hesitant beginnings, Labour began to acquire the financial and organizational resources to challenge the Liberals. In public political language, there remained little to choose between the two parties. As an independent electoral body, Labour sought to maximize its constituency, and duly rejected class-exclusive language. In partisan electoral politics, the 'populist' address to the people was a rhetorical necessity acknowledged by all political formations. Electors, however, were able to decode the rhetoric, to distinguish between different 'populist' appeals – Tory, Liberal and Labour – in accordance with their interests. Gradually and unevenly within the Edwardian Progressive Alliance, Labour acquired a distinctly 'working-class' radical image.

9

LIBERALS, LABOUR AND THE PROGRESSIVE ALLIANCE

In 1903 Herbert Gladstone, the Liberal chief whip, negotiated a secret electoral pact with Ramsay MacDonald, secretary of the LRC, to deny the Unionists the advantage of a split progressive vote. Building upon these electoral arrangements some social radicals wished to construct a permanent ideological accommodation. An 'organicist' intellectual synthesis, the project was to extend beyond traditional boundaries, Liberal and socialist, to embrace progressive concepts of distributive justice, industrial conciliation and social democracy, while upholding the principles of individual liberty, equality of opportunity and reward for initiative. No longer guaranteed by laissez-faire individualism, social harmony was to be underwritten by limited collectivism, by intervention sufficient to ensure distributive justice for the working class while preserving free trade and the continuance of capitalism.

No mere intellectual fashion, this progressive new liberalism established a prominent position in Edwardian political debate. An array of talented newspaper editors spread the message, including C. P. Scott of the *Manchester Guardian*, H. W. Massingham of the *Nation*, and A. G. Gardiner of the *Daily News*, the cheap radical paper read by provincial activists. The changing social composition

166

of the ranks of Liberal MPs strengthened the progressive element: each intake included increasing numbers of the professional middle class, often educated and trained in the Balliol–Whitechapel ethic of social responsibility. Although the Liberal business connection was weakening, there was no shortage of funds from a new generation of 'progressive' industrialists – Lever, Brunner and the Cadbury and Rowntree families – who appreciated the value of conciliation, collectivism and distributive justice.[1] Other industrialists, however, displayed no such interest. Representatives of the great staple industries, they responded to increased competitive pressure by retreating further into old-fashioned orthodoxy, rejecting protectionism and progressivism alike. As Michael Bentley has shown, the 'traditional Liberal industrialist in the West Riding of Yorkshire or the Lancashire mills, stiff with pound notes, chapel principles and free trade still existed on the Liberal benches in 1914'.[2]

Progressivism, then, did not carry all before it. Social reform was an unnecessary extra in 1906 when the Liberals maximized their vote simply by being the 'Not-Conservative' party. Outrage over 'Chinese slavery' – the exploitation of indentured Chinese coolies imported into South Africa – fuelled the reaction against costly and incompetent imperial adventures. Anger at the Education Act (1902) politicized the Nonconformist conscience, but it was the Unionist advocacy of tariff reform (Chamberlain's latest exercise in pre-emptive politics) which aroused the greatest passion, uniting Liberals of every description in defence of free trade (and the big loaf). For once, the Liberals were able to mobilize their full voting-strength, boosted by the whole-hearted cooperation of constituency activists, Nonconformist militants, Irish nationalists and Labour allies. Out in the constituencies, Liberal activists looked to the new government to complete the traditional agenda on temperance, education and Ireland, the unfinished business of the Newcastle Programme. Progressivism, indeed, was restricted in influence largely to

Lancashire, where C. P. Scott prescribed a programme of social reform to retain the former Tory working-class vote dislodged by tariff reform.[3] Elsewhere the new formula was seldom in evidence. Traditional loyalties still applied in north-east England where 'old Liberalism' enjoyed a continuing vitality among Nonconformists, industrialists, businessmen and working-class voters.[4] A bastion of Nonconformity, Welsh Liberalism continued to dominate the principality without any adjustment in programme or personnel, an unreconstructed force which Lloyd George could not ignore – a new Liberal in England, he was an old Liberal in Wales.[5] At Westminster, orthodoxy and retrenchment dominated the proceedings in Campbell-Bannerman's cabinet. After Asquith's succession, Churchill and Lloyd George enjoyed greater influence and power, but the new premier, a pragmatic imperialist, recoiled from any philosophical commitment, progressive or otherwise. Judged by the archives of those at the top, progressivism was not the administration's motivating force, merely an occasional rhetorical gesture.

When drawing up his famous budget of 1909, Lloyd George did not envisage its rejection by the upper house: rather he hoped to use the privilege of a money bill to gain legislative entry for measures recently rebuffed by the Lords' veto of unrepresentative 'fads'. But when the Lords acted in defiance of history and constitutional precedent, he exploited the controversy to the full. Promoted in progressivist rhetoric, his 'People's Budget' served to legitimize the leadership of the Liberal middle class, industrious and responsible citizens of wealth who recognized their obligations, fiscal and otherwise, to improve the nation's welfare and maintain its defences. A triumph of rhetoric, Lloyd George's tactics kept the Labour Party loyal and subordinate in progressive alliance. As in 1906, however, what brought out the vote was another revivalist campaign, an old-fashioned radical crusade against the abuse of power and privilege, the peers versus the people.

In a subsequent effort to rally progressive spirits – and

divert attention from his involvement in the Marconi scandal – Lloyd George launched his 'Land Campaign' in the autumn of 1913. The principle of minimum standards was to be extended to the countryside where the disastrous weakening of British agriculture had continued unchecked since the late-Victorian depression, causing serious social, economic and strategic problems. An intervention to improve the workings of the market, the campaign was distinctly new-Liberal and in no sense socialist, but a real economic transfer was perforce required to raise the level of agricultural wages. Once again, landowners were the target: the cost was to fall not on farmers' profits but on rent, already singled out for special taxation in the land-valuation clauses of the People's Budget. Although a 'wild-fire' success in the counties, where the prospect of a decent wage was irresistible, the Land Campaign failed to excite interest in the towns. Through site-value rating and other prescriptions of the vociferous land-tax lobby, Lloyd George hoped to stem the ratepayer revolt into Unionism, to relieve the burden on small property-owning ratepayers and small businessmen, as urban finance became trapped in the scissors of rising needs and stagnant revenue. In the urban context, however, it proved far more difficult to isolate and penalize rent. The bulk of urban property was composite in nature. In the absence of a clear-cut division between parasitic owners of the ground and enterprising capitalists, Lloyd George's rhetoric – as Chamberlain's before – served to antagonize urban capitalist proprietors. Confronted by progressive new Liberalism, property allied more firmly with the Unionist cause.[6]

In its political and ideological ambitions, as in its secret electoral base, the progressive project was disabled by irony and contradiction. By conceding the formal independence of Labour, the pact hardened the organizational divide between the parties and gave the LRC a valuable bridgehead in the Commons: in 1906, 24 of the 29 LRC MPs won by virtue of Liberal withdrawals. In so doing, the pact undermined the aspirations of Lloyd George

and others for a new Liberal coalition above and beyond
the sectional independence and 'class politics' of Labour:

> it is better that you should have a party which com-
> bines every section and every shade of opinion, taken
> from all classes of the community, rather than a party
> which represents one shade of opinion alone or one
> class of the community alone. . . . Liberals are against
> anything in the nature of class representation . . . it was
> a mistake for the Labour Party to go in for anything
> like independent class representation.[7]

In many respects, the pact was better suited to MacDonald's
version of progressivism, an organic evolution through liberalism to socialism: 'Socialism, the stage which follows
Liberalism, retains everything that was of permanent value
in Liberalism, by virtue of being the hereditary heir of
Liberalism.'[8] Defined in this way, socialism served to distinguish Labour as the vanguard of progressivism, leaders
of a cause which embraced the new Liberals. MacDonald
always aimed at replacing the Liberals at some stage, a
long-term goal which underpinned his enthusiasm for the
pact, the essential means in a plurality system of consoli-
dating Labour's initial precarious advance. An electoral
necessity, MacDonald's evolutionary approach also took
account of contemporary criticism of socialism. In accordance with the increasing complexity and interdependence
of modern society, the individual and the collective good
were to be maximized through greater public ownership
and central direction exercised on democratic participatory lines, retaining important roles for private property
and initiative, and for religion, the family and voluntary
associations.[9]

Other socialists were less patient. For a brief while after 1906, Labour MPs forced the pace on school meals,
workmen's compensation and other social reforms. They
were even allowed to dictate the terms of the Trades Disputes Act, restoring full legal immunity to trade unions,

the status quo before Taff Vale. But this was the last significant concession to labour 'sectionalism' as the Liberals seized the initiative with a series of progressive measures that Labour MPs could neither oppose nor amend. Left-wing discontent was voiced in Ben Tillett's polemic, *Is the Parliamentary Party a Failure?* (1908), an indictment of the careerist toadying of Labour MPs, repaying 'with gross betrayal the class that willingly supports them'. For activists on the left, unemployment became the test issue. Dismayed by the inadequate response at municipal level, the ILP, SDF and other advocates of 'Socialist Unity' mounted a 'Right to Work' campaign, extra-parliamentary pressure to encourage Labour to adopt an independent, if not socialist, solution. Jolted into action by the 1907 by-elections, when Pete Curran beat the Liberals at Jarrow, and Victor Grayson, an independent socialist, contested and won Colne Valley in defiance of party instructions, Labour (with the support of the TUC) placed itself at the head of the campaign and drew up a right-to-work bill. Having failed to pass beyond a second reading in 1907, the bill was to be overshadowed when it was reintroduced in 1909, on the day after Lloyd George presented his budget.

Intended to generate the resources for industrial development and social reform, the budget was an integral component of the progressive social strategy devised by Lloyd George and Churchill. Beginning with labour exchanges, the programme was to extend beyond the budget to invalidity and unemployment insurance. The unexpected constitutional crisis delayed the later stages and brought the parliamentary Labour Party firmly behind the Liberal ranks, tending to conceal differences over progressive reform. While restricted to the 'unfit', the pitiful and inefficient poor in the slums, progressive social engineering was welcomed and applauded by Labour. When extended beyond the 'residuum', however, Liberal interventionism – which often seemed to converge with employer requirements for greater discipline and control

– was far more contentious. Tawney noted a basic conflict of approach, a contrast of class interests:

> The middle and upper class view in social reform is
> that it should regulate the worker's *life* in order that
> he may *work* better. The working class view of economic
> reform is that is should regulate his *work*, in order that
> he may have a chance of living. Hence to working people
> licensing reform, insurance acts, etc. seems beginning
> at the wrong end.[10]

Although Labour MPs felt compelled to endorse Liberal interventionism, the party was divided – much like
its counterparts elsewhere in Europe – along 'revisionist'
and 'revolutionist' lines.[11] A handful of parliamentary
dissidents opposed the 'policing' aspects of National Insurance, echoing the wider criticisms of the Green Manifesto group, authors of *Let Us Reform the Labour Party* (1910).
These 'moral revolutionaries', optimistic believers in the
capacity of the working class to effect change, bemoaned
Labour's compliance in the construction of the Liberal
'servile state'. As implemented by the Liberals, and endorsed by MacDonald, collectivism was unaccountable and
bureaucratic, catering for the people without involving
them in any way. Far from leading to socialism, such public
control was strengthening capitalism. In the 'revolutionist'
perspective, the urgent need was to convert public opinion
to socialism, a task which required assertive independence
by Labour in its electoral tactics and reform agenda. Labour
should attack the Liberals at every opportunity – in parliament and at elections – to assert socialism's distinct
attraction, its readiness to use democratically-accountable
state interventionism to attack poverty, to transform the
material realities of working-class life.

Phrased in the idioms of radical Nonconformity,
MacDonald's revisionism carried the day, ensuring the continuance of the Progressive Alliance. While accepting a
stronger role for the state, MacDonald feared the conse-

quences of intervention: mechanisms for the organization of the state and the economy could not be dissociated from their role in 'advancing human character'. Through the democratization of the state, intervention should be limited, controlled and rendered compatible with individual liberty. A judicious blend of 'old' and 'new' ideological elements, MacDonald's 'revisionist' socialism ensured that Labour was an acceptable option for newly-disaffected Lib-Lab supporters. Although implacably hostile to state socialism, Lib-Lab radicals were not opposed to 'labourist' intervention: indeed, they were far more willing than their middle-class 'progressive' partners to extend collective self-government into market regulation. As radicals, they were sceptical about the social reform promoted by the new Liberals, interventionist proposals which took insufficient account of popular liberty and democracy, and the corruption and inefficiency inherent in the state.[12]

Whatever the divisions over the role of the state, the Parliamentary Labour Party was united in staunch defence of 'voluntarism', the framework in which organized workers negotiated with employers and undertook their own collective mutuality. Protected by Labour, unions were able to resist repeated attempts to curb the strike weapon and separate their benefit and bargaining functions. A cushion against adversity, the 'friendly' funds were an indispensable part of union strategy for attaining high wages. The defence of trade union rights and procedures distinguished Labour from the Liberals in a manner appreciated by those in the working class who regarded welfare as second best to secure, fairly paid employment.[13]

Impressed by Labour's sedulous defence of voluntarism, leaders of the refractory unions, miners included, abandoned their Liberal allegiance. News of the MFGB's conversion caused dismay in some quarters, prompting Shaw to ask: 'What then becomes of socialism?' As it was, this transfer of allegiance, the effective end of Lib-Labism, guaranteed Labour's long-term independence. There were immediate financial problems, however, provoked by the Osborne judgement of 1909, which rendered illegal the political levy by which affiliated unions financed the party. Despite considerable pressure, Liberals offered no assistance to their progressive allies – Lloyd George even entered secret negotiations with the Unionists to block a reversal of the Osborne judgement – although they did introduce payment of members in 1911 as a *quid pro quo* for Labour support of National Insurance. The ruling was not reversed by the Trade Union Act of 1913, but unions were permitted to hold a secret ballot on the issue. By 1914 ballots had been held in unions with an overall membership of 1,207,841: of more than 420,000 members who voted, 298,702 were in favour of financing Labour candidates and 125,310 against. While union leaders clearly favoured the Labour alliance, a minority of the membership – nearly 40 per cent of those who voted in the nine largest unions – were opposed to funds being used to support independent Labour. As Chris Wrigley has suggested, this opposition, by no means an indication of popular support for progressive new Liberalism, reflected the residual loyalty to old Gladstonian Liberalism, most notably among miners.[14]

While Labour was pressing for the reversal of the Osborne judgement, the trade union movement underwent an explosion of militancy and organization, a much greater leap forward than the new unionism of 1889–90. Throughout the country industrial unrest strained the Progressive Alliance to breaking point, often prompting the decisive switch at local level from Liberalism to an independent working-class position. Unions tended to resent government intrusion, fearing that the state would inevitably favour the employers, but the dramatic and not unsatisfactory nature of Lloyd George's last-minute interventions in strikes and lock-outs seems to have encouraged some of the stronger unions to eschew compromise within their conventional bargaining arrangements. But there was another side to government intervention: the use of troops and the deployment of gunboats against strikers. This repressive violence and display of force was favoured by some previously noted for their progressive views. By the middle of 1912, Churchill 'was practically in a "shoot 'em down" attitude'.[15] C. P. Scott, the *éminence grise* of progressivism, failed to understand the realities of industrial action. Oblivious of the consequences to the working-class Liberal vote in the Lancashire heartland, editorials in the *Manchester Guardian* castigated the 165,000 powerloom weavers locked out over their demand for a closed shop.[16]

Socialists and syndicalists stood forward to advocate direct industrial action in preference to the parliamentary methods and lacklustre performance of the Labour Party. In the first flush of industrial enthusiasm, the British Socialist Party (BSP) came into being, an alliance of the SDF (known since 1907 as the Social-Democratic Party), Clarion groups, forty or so defecting branches of the ILP, and other unattached local socialist groups. Its initial success owed much to the popular appeal of Victor Grayson, to a personal flamboyance which displeased the 'ethical socialists' of Colne Valley, where he was unseated by the Liberals in 1910.[17] Grayson, however, was soon to withdraw, in part out of ill-health, but mainly in anger at Hyndman's ruinous behaviour. Having gained control of the new party, Hyndman and the old guard of the SDF enforced old-style sectarianism, refusing to interfere with the industrial responsibility of trade unions, a prime example, James Hinton notes, of the triumph of dogma over realism in socialist politics.[18] In seeking workers' control through industrial action, syndicalists appeared to reject parliamentary methods out of hand. 'There never was, and there never will be "independence" in parliamentary politics', *The Syndicalist* insisted in September 1912: 'Even with a separate Labour Party, compromise reigns supreme; there are conferences, committees, bargainings, and what not, with the political parties of our employers. . . . *Down* with parliamentary politics that divide the workers, and *Up* with Direct Action that unites them.'[19] In practice, however,

syndicalism shaded over into a militant parliamentarian-
ism which stressed the necessity of coordinating industrial and political tactics, a point conceded by the authors
of *The Miners' Next Step* (1912). In the 'Triple Alliance' of
miners, railway workers and transport workers, syndicalism was subsumed as a tactical ploy within the voluntarist
framework of collective bargaining. The threat of combined stoppage was designed to lessen industrial conflict,
not to promote a revolutionary general strike.[20] Syndicalism failed to re-orientate the unions or replace Labour.
When put to the vote in 1912, the TUC reaffiirmed its
commitment to parliamentary action and the Labour Party
by 1,123,000 votes to 573,000.

Committed to parliamentary ways and means, the constitutional 'rules of the game', Labour strengthened its
hold on organized labour as trade-unionism expanded.
No longer the preserve of the labour aristocracy, national
trade unions steadily eradicated regional and traditional
loyalties, promoting a wider working-class identity. Some
Lib-Lab sympathies remained, as the ballots on the political levy evinced, but the decision to support Labour,
once confirmed in this way, was not to be reversed. In
Wales and other bastions, Lib-Labism was in rapid retreat,
overwhelmed by the explosion in union membership, the
scale of industrial disputes and the emergence of a younger,
more militant leadership. In the newly-unionized industries where there was no Lib-Lab inheritance, support for
Labour was a corollary of union membership, a point of
(class) pride and loyalty which quickly acquired the force
of tradition.

In electoral terms, however, Labour failed to register
any significant advance. Boosted by the secret Gladstone–
MacDonald pact, Labour reached its peak in 1906–7, after which support fell away, although losses were obscured
by the addition of all but three of the remaining Lib-Lab
MPs when the MFGB affiliated to the party in 1909. The
elections of 1910 revealed the weakness of the independent Labour vote: in the 35 three-cornered contests in the

two general elections, Labour candidates came third in
29 cases, second in six and first in none. Worse was to
follow in subsequent by-elections. The deaths of three
miners' MPs, former Lib-Labs, led to unseemly squabbles
over the right of succession, three-cornered contests which
left Labour at the bottom of the poll. All told, Labour
contested 14 by-elections between 1910 and 1914, losing
four seats and never finishing higher than third. On the
eve of the First World War, Labour did not appear an
irresistible electoral force.[21] Similarly in municipal politics there was no decisive breakthrough, but accumulat-
ing evidence of the class and gender tensions which were
to deny long-term viability to the Progressive Alliance.

At local level there was less discrimination in the electoral system against women, the working class and minority
interests. Married women were given the vote on the same
terms as men by the Municipal Franchise Act of 1869,
which enfranchised all compound householders. Taking
advantage of these arrangements a number of women stood
for election. Women advanced beyond philanthropy into
local government service, elected on the basis of their
gendered aptitude for 'caring' social policy. By 1900 there
were few substantial School Boards without at least one
or two women among their nine to fifteen members. Even
anti-suffrage women, Patricia Hollis notes, 'agreed that
local government was "social housekeeping", the school
and the workhouse an extended family, the municipality
and the locality women's parish'. Applied in this way, the
language of separate spheres allowed women 'both to
reorientate perceptions about local government, infusing
it with more humanistic values, and also to extend the
boundaries of what local government did'.[22]

Local School and Poor Law Boards were elected by cumulative voting, a system that enabled well-organized minority groups, socialists included, to gain some official
representation. In 1894 Mrs Pankhurst was nominated by
the Manchester ILP on a programme of free education,
free pre-school breakfasts and 'equal pay for equal work,

irrespective of sex'. On the Bradford School Board, Margaret McMillan emerged as the champion of needy schoolchildren and pioneer of school meals and medical inspections, while her contributions to Blatchford's *Clarion* pointed to a wider agenda: 'Women work in mills, workshops, homes, and therefore the question of Social Reform concerns them.... The wage-struggle has taught woman that she even more than man is influenced by all that takes place in the economic and industrial world.'[23]

Council contests were considerably cheaper than parliamentary elections, hence the readiness with which Labour activists, otherwise hard-pressed for funds, encouraged working-class candidates to stand. By 1900 the ILP boasted 106 local councillors, 66 members of School Boards and 51 Poor Law guardians. This local advance was strongest at West Ham, where Hardie and his Labour colleagues gained control in 1898 to promote a compulsory eight-hour day, improved housing, and public ownership of the tramways.

By standing forward on a collectivist platform Labour attracted increased support in localities where 'old Liberalism' prevailed, as at Bradford, whose Liberal councillors, still staunchly individualist, preferred self-help and charity to municipal provision. In other towns Labour advanced as the realities of municipal politics belied the rhetoric of progressivism, exposing the limitations of Liberal social policy. In competition with the Conservatives for the allegiance of rate-burdened lower middle-class electors, Liberals shunned proposals which would raise the rates or interfere with the local labour market. Labour alone defied the tenets of orthodox municipal finance. Local campaigns reflected the needs and demands of ILP socialists and other activists, members of the affiliated bodies responsible for constituency organization in the party's federal structure, the socialist counterparts, as it were, of Liberal 'faddists'. While campaigning to extend 'municipal socialism' beyond natural monopolies to the provision of milk, coal, health care and other services, Labour activists insisted on the right to work or relief, a basic demand which their Liberal allies generally failed to acknowledge.[24] As Labour abandoned the alliance, the progressive vote split, enabling the Tories to consolidate their control of most of the larger cities. At this stage, hard-pressed Liberals often sought an 'anti-socialist' accommodation with the Conservatives, a municipal alliance in negation of their progressive pretensions.

Progressive unity continued to operate during general elections, special occasions when the lowest common denominator – free trade in 1906, the defence of the constitution in 1910 – temporarily prevailed over the contentious issues of local social policy. After 1910, however, these parliamentary arrangements were increasingly defied by constituency activists. Self-restraint, the necessary precondition for the operation of the pact, disappeared on both sides. Liberal Party stalwarts were no longer prepared to make the constituency a sacrificial offering to Labour, while Labour activists, for whom the very purpose of the party was independent working-class representation, refused to stand aside for a Liberal middle-class candidate:

> Labour's desire for continued expansion came up against the Liberal party organization's instincts for self-preservation. . . . It made little practical difference to Labour whether the Liberal candidate was a Radical or not: it made little practical difference to the Liberals whether the Labour man was a professed Socialist or not.[25]

As antagonism intensified, ideological differences mattered less than pride and identity, fundamental 'class' opposition that no alliance could bridge. 'The division', Brougham Villiers noted in 1912, was 'upon the independence of Labour, not upon any economic or political doctrine in any ordinary sense at all.'[26]

For those with the vote, Labour offered the working class the chance to elect one of their own kind. Ill at ease in the Commons and unimpressive in debate, Labour MPs, David Martin observes, were 'closer than their political rivals to the working class; they did not have to change their basic character in order to embody proletarian attitudes'.[27] Its limited electoral advance notwithstanding, Labour was acquiring a working-class image, but there were organizational, cultural and other limits to the party's appeal. Labour organizers had yet to make contact with the urban poor. In Scotland, for example, Labour activists 'moved in a rarefied atmosphere of the politically militant'.[28] Impervious to working-class organization, slum-dwellers survived through a life apart, protecting their interests, enjoying their fun in a self-enclosed world of casual labour and neighbourhood support, primary networks into which politics, Labour or otherwise, were generally an unwelcome intrusion.

Indifference and/or hostility to politics spread far beyond the casual poor as increased leisure time and rising real wages brought forth rival attractions. The rapid growth of the working-men's club movement, organized nationally through the non-political Club and Institute Union, the foe both of Liberal temperance reformers and monopolist Tory brewers, signalled a growing resistance to the politicization of popular leisure. Previously, the Tories had seized the initiative with a beer-barrel populism, which not only defended the poor man's traditional 'cakes and ale', the target of dour Nonconformist moral reformers, but also celebrated the new commercial mass culture, the professional sport and other delights available in 'Ally Sloper's Half-Holiday'. Labour was unable to match this populist style, restrained by the earnest seriousness of leaders trained in chapels and mutual improvement classes. This cultural gap extended to journalism, where Labour struggled to find the formula – as well as the funds – for a national daily. 'The British working classes', Ross McKibbin notes, 'maddeningly refused to read a Labour newspaper, at least one that did not in more than equal parts report sports and sensations'.[29] In coming to terms with successive electoral defeat, the Tories displayed considerable flexibility, abandoning tariff reform and adjusting their popular cultural style to defend the sanctity of the home, the Englishman's castle, against the unwarranted intrusions of an increasingly interventionist (and 'socialist') state. Effective or not as a rebuttal of Edwardian progressivism, this change of emphasis – from the right to a quiet pint to the right to a quiet home life – stood the Tories in good stead for the transformed conditions of the post-war 'feminized' franchise.[30]

Labour was constrained by a number of factors which precluded any advance towards socialism or the unorganized poor: the jealously-guarded autonomy of working-class collective associations; the rival attractions of commercial popular culture, an apolitical mixture of good-humoured fatalism and brief escapism; and the populist appeal of the Tories, not only the masters of recreation, entertainment and imperial show, but also the guardians of domestic bliss and the family. Despite its voluntarist credentials and stronger links with the unions, Labour was by no means certain of overwhelming support beyond the organized working class. Hence, no doubt, the lack of pressure on its part for franchise reform.

According to some historians, the 'franchise factor', an artificial restriction that excluded the greater part of its likely support, was the main impediment to Labour's advance.[31] Until 1918 only about 60 per cent of adult males were entitled to vote. However, most non-voters were not a political class apart. Debarred by registration technicalities, they would appear on the roll from time to time, according to their circumstances and the efforts made by party agents. As for those who were permanently excluded, some 12 per cent of adult males, they were unlikely to benefit Labour. Vulnerable to charity, patronage and beer, the urban casual poor were susceptible to Tory blandishments. Among poor Irish immigrant communities a higher level of enfranchisement would have helped the Liberals, not Labour. The 'franchise factor', then, did not entirely operate to Labour's disadvantage.[32] The party, however, could not ignore the question of women's suffrage.

For the Women's Trade Union League (WTUL) and its offshoot, the National Federation of Women Workers, the priority was industrial, the struggle to organize and sustain female trade unions, but some of its full-time organizers, talented working-class women like Helen Silcock and Ada Nield Chew, were quick to recognize the importance of the vote. Less hindered by the male trade-union establishment, the Women's Co-operative Guild (WCG) took a more positive line on female suffrage. Founded in 1883, the Guild provided a forum for working-class women to discuss grievances beyond the confines of kitchen and home, training them to stand in local elections for School and Poor Law Boards, useful political experience to strengthen the claim for the parliamentary franchise. By the end of the century the ground was well prepared for a radical suffragist campaign led by working-class women from the WCG, WTUL, Clarion groups and textile unions. The new Labour Party, however, refused to elevate female suffrage above other issues. Most Labour members took an 'adultist' line, preferring to wait for a comprehensive measure of electoral reform embracing all men and women, tactics which infuriated suffragette militants, advocates of immediate remedial action for women. Although the cause of much dissension at party conferences, women's suffrage was finally to prove a unifying force, an issue which distinguished Labour from the Liberals. Having been somewhat alienated by the unhelpful attitude of the labour movement, suffragists were to concentrate their efforts on Labour in the last years of peacetime.

By Edwardian times there was considerable support at Westminster for female suffrage, but no room for the Liberal government to manoeuvre. Enfranchisement under existing arrangements would restrict the vote to wealthy women, an undue bonus for the Tories. Any comprehensive franchise reform, male and female, would be blocked by the Tories through the Lords' veto, unless accompanied by redistribution, which would include a drastic reduction in Irish seats unacceptable to the Liberal government and its nationalist allies. Anger at this impasse prompted the suffragettes, increasingly dominated by Mrs Pankhurst's autocratic daughter Christabel, into unprecedented militancy. The Women's Social and Political Union (WSPU) abandoned links with the ILP to mount a sensational but socially conservative campaign of middle-class womanhood to coerce the political establishment into conceding 'Votes for Ladies'. Alarmed by suffragette militancy, the various working-class groups fell in behind the adultist line, to which end the WTUL, WCG and the recently-formed Women's Labour League joined together as the People's Suffrage Federation. Behind the scenes, Arthur Henderson negotiated an accommodation with the National Union of Women's Suffrage Societies (NUWSS), a sedate middle-class organization (the Lancashire textile workers apart) which had previously followed a non-party, anti-adultist and anti-militant constitutional stance. By the terms of the agreement, the NUWSS offered to raise an Election Fighting Fund (EFF) to assist Labour candidates, finance which was particularly welcome after the Osborne judgement. A shrewd innovation by the suffragists, the EFF threatened to undermine the electoral cooperation on which the Asquith government relied: indeed, the logic of the EFF, as MacDonald (alone?) rued, ran counter to the Progressive Alliance. Aided by the organizational prowess of NUWSS women (who proved themselves experts in registration, an area of notable Labour deficiency), Labour was encouraged to squeeze the Liberals where they were most vulnerable, by fomenting revolt among working-class voters. Although intended as a tactical device to shift the log-jam, a temporary expedient to be abandoned as soon as the desired legislation was on the statute book, the EEF developed into a wider alliance. Disillusioned with the Liberals, radical and progressive women were among the first of the middle-class groups to switch to Labour. The First World War accelerated the trend, establishing Labour as the true guardian of the radical tradition, the heir to the progressive inheritance.[33]

CONCLUSION: THE FIRST WORLD WAR AND AFTER

Put to the test by war, progressivism failed to uphold radical values or to protect working-class interests. No longer the party of laissez-faire, the Liberals were untroubled by the interventionist demands of war until faced with compulsory conscription, an issue which challenged such fundamental values as the individual freedom of conscience. Lloyd George and the hawks triumphed, an ascendancy which Asquith, the deposed premier, chose not to contest. There was no attempt on his part to rally the radical forces against the illiberality of total war, no revival of Midlothian and pro-Boer traditions. He continued to support the war effort, but refused to join the new government, a policy which perplexed radicals, pacifists and other opposition Liberals. Disgusted by Lloyd George, disappointed in Asquith, Liberal activists withdrew their support and turned to Labour, seemingly the better guardian of the radical–pacifist tradition – Liberal and Labour candidates in 1918 often commented on the number of ex-Liberal constituency activists running Labour campaigns. Having lost the support of constituency workers, and perceived as a party of the right, Liberals were unable to sustain any electoral revival in the inter-war years.[1]

Labour emerged from the war considerably strengthened, a united independent force no longer constrained by the Progressive Alliance, abandoned in 1918. Admittedly, there were internal divisions over the war, more so than among the Liberals, but these did not prevent the party's advance. Labour gained access to the wartime machinery of state while penetrating deeper into working-class communities. Between the pacifist and the patriotic wings, the majority of the party reluctantly concluded that war was justified, upon which basis they participated in government. But Labour was by no means compromised by coalition politics and industrial truce. Working-class interests were protected by extra-parliamentary and 'unofficial' means. Particulary important here was the War Emergency Workers' National Committee (WEWNC), an amalgamation of various organizations – pro-war, anti-war, cooperative, trade-union and socialist – brought together under Labour auspices to defend working-class living standards on the home front. While progressive Liberals concerned themselves with military strategy and the war effort, the WEWNC attended to the more immediate problems of prices, housing, rent control, and pensions and benefits for soldiers and their families. Angered by the Military Service Act, the WEWNC took a more aggressive line after 1916, campaigning for the 'Conscription of Riches' through taxation, sequestration and nationalization. But this did not presage a forward thrust to socialism, an acceptance of Sidney Webb's collectivist prescriptions. Lacking a coherent ideology, 'Conscription of Riches' was an effective slogan for Labour, prefiguring the famous 'socialist' Clause Four of the party's post-war constitution, a rallying point around which the adherents of different ideologies and the representatives of different interests were able to assemble.[2]

The new party constitution was designed to consolidate this enlarged labour alliance in preparation for the Fourth Reform Act. Individual membership was a natural evolution, an important point of entry for disillusioned middle-class progressive liberals. Power, however, remained firmly in the hands of the trade unions, whose dominance of the National Executive, and hence of party policy, was specifically underwritten. Having exploded in the pre-war years, the rapid extension of trade unionism continued throughout the war and beyond, accompanied by a narrowing of differentials as wartime controls favoured the less skilled workers at the expense of the old craft elite. Under threat at the workplace, craft workers turned to unofficial militancy, direct action and syndicalism, while the general unions, now massive bureaucratic structures, consolidated their control of the official movement and party. This ironic reversal of previous roles enabled Labour to continue unchanged in ways and means while expanding beyond its former sociological limitations.

The shibboleth which distinguished Labour from the Liberals, the Clause Four commitment to 'secure for the producers by hand or by brain the full fruits of their industry, and the most equitable distribution thereof that may be possible upon the basis of common ownership of the means of production', carried no ideological or prescriptive force. Labour made steady electoral advance through moral rhetoric and practical proposals which, as Duncan Tanner has shown, varied pragmatically with local circumstance and need.[3] By such fragmented means, Labour established itself as the major (but not the only) anti-Tory party. This was not the final electoral triumph of radicalism. In 1929 the Labour share of the vote peaked at 37 per cent. Its electoral advance since 1918 notwithstanding, Labour had neither absorbed all the Progressive vote nor unified the working class as a Labour/socialist electoral bloc. Given the obstacles of the British electoral system, the way forward posed the familiar radical dilemma of how to reconcile and subsume the competing languages of class. To attract a wider working-class constituency required either a more ideological or a more populist radical projection, whereas the adhesion of the progressive middle class depended upon a moderate, rational and 'modernizing' register.

The history of radicalism, it has been argued here, was complex and contested, informed and complicated by con-

flicting class inflexion of its political rhetoric. The constitutionalist idiom served both to accentuate and to miti-
gate such tensions. In some contexts, constitutionalism
provoked 'class' division as radical audiences defined (and
polarized) themselves against rival interpretations, inclusive or exclusive, of its hallowed language and practice.
At other times, constitutionalism served to affirm a wider
national identity and superiority, a cross-class construction reinforced by the mid-Victorian dominance of respectability and the rise of Anglo-Saxon 'racism'. The sense of
national pride and providential destiny continued to inform political debate in the late nineteenth century, by
which time historicist constitutionalism was less evident
than notions of an 'organic' corporate identity and common citizenship. Despite the democratic implications of
the new mass political culture, class tensions were not eradicated. Gradual and uneven as it was, the rise of Labour
undermined the cross-class constituency of progressive
Liberalism. Labour acquired a distinct image and identity, linked in cultural and organizational style to the much-
expanded ranks of organized labour, to the 'traditional'
(but by no means inclusive) 'representation' of the working class which, having emerged in the late nineteenth
century, remained little altered until post-Second World
War 'affluence'. There was some socialist rhetoric in this
political–cultural alignment, but the continuities with
Chartist and earlier forms of popular radicalism were more
pronounced. As its name implied, Labour stood for
'labourism', for the due protection and reward of labour,
the traditional demand of popular radicalism. This 'working-class' image, however, was not necessarily advantageous
or empowering within the body politic, despite the belated advent of the democratic franchise. The image, indeed, was not entirely of Labour's own making. The
inter-war electoral hegemony of the Tories owed much
to their promotion of a crude class stereotype, depicting
the manual working class as indelibly greedy, unionized,
masculine and Labour. Defined against this (necessary)

threat, the Tories could unite a variety of otherwise conflicting economic, social and gender interests as the 'public', the responsible 'constitutional classes'.[4] In the competitive arena of political rhetoric, where populism and constitutionalism were still at a premium in the construction of image and identity, radicalism had yet to secure its definition of political inclusion.

NOTES

Notes to the Introduction

1. J. A. Epstein, 'The Constitutionalist Idiom', in his *Radical Expression: Political Language, Ritual and Symbol in England, 1790–1850* (New York, 1994), pp. 3–28.
2. D. Nicholls, 'The English Middle Class and the Ideological Significance of Radicalism, 1760–1886', *Journal of British Studies*, 24 (1985), pp. 415–33.
3. David Cannadine, 'The Past and the Present in the English Industrial Revolution', *Past and Present*, 103 (1984), pp. 131–72.
4. N. R. Crafts, *British Economic Growth during the Industrial Revolution* (Oxford, 1985), pp. 68–9.
5. R. Gray, 'Class, Politics and Historical "Revisionism"', *Social History*, 19 (1994), p. 211.
6. Neville Kirk, 'History, Language, Ideas and Post–modernism: a Materialist View', *Social History*, 19 (1994), pp. 221–40.
7. Jon Lawrence and Miles Taylor, 'The Poverty of Protest: Gareth Stedman Jones and the Politics of Language – a Reply', *Social History*, 18 (1993), p. 5.
8. Patrick Joyce, *Visions of the People: Industrial England and the Question of Class, 1840–1914* (Cambridge, 1991); James Vernon, *Politics and the People: A Study in English Political Culture, c. 1815–1867* (Cambridge, 1993); Richard Price, 'Historiography, Narrative and the Nineteenth Century', *Journal of British Studies*, forthcoming.
9. Gareth Stedman Jones, *Languages of class: Studies in English Working Class History 1832–1982* (Cambridge, 1983).
10. E. F. Biagini and A. J. Reid (eds), *Currents of Radicalism: Popular Radicalism, Organized Labour and Party Politics in Britain 1850–1914* (Cambridge, 1991).

189

11. Duncan Tanner, *Political Change and the Labour Party 1900–1918* (Cambridge, 1990).

12. Michael Savage, *The Dynamics of Working-Class Politics. The Labour Movement in Preston, 1880–1940* (Cambridge, 1987).

13. Frank O'Gorman, 'Campaign Rituals and Ceremonies: The Social Meaning of Elections in England 1780–1860', *Past and Present*, 135 (1992), pp. 79–115.

14. Paul Pickering, 'Class without Words: Symbolic Communication in the Chartist Movement', *Past and Present*, 112 (1986), pp. 144–62.

15. P. Mandler, *Aristocratic Government in the Age of Reform: Whigs and Liberals, 1830–1850* (Oxford, 1990); J. Parry, *The Rise and Fall of Liberal Government in Victorian Britain* (New Haven, 1993).

16. Paul Adelman, *Victorian Radicalism: The Middle-Class Experience 1830–1914* (London, 1984), p. 2.

17. Quoted in Lucy Brown, 'The Chartists and the Anti-Corn Law League', in Asa Briggs (ed.), *Chartist Studies* (London, 1959), p. 348.

18. John Vincent, *The Formation of the British Liberal Party* (London, 1972).

19. D. A. Hamer, *The Politics of Electoral Pressure: A Study in the History of Victorian Reform Agitations* (Brighton, 1977); and D. A. Homer, *Liberal Politics in the Age of Gladstone and Rosebery* (Oxford, 1972).

20. Jon Lawrence, 'Class and Gender in the Making of Urban Toryism, 1880–1914', *English Historical Review*, 108 (1993), pp. 629–52.

21. Biagini and Reid (eds), *op. cit.*, p. 243.

Notes to Chapter 1: The Eighteenth-Century Context

1. E. P. Thompson, 'Eighteenth-Century English Society: Class Struggle without Class?', *Social History*, 3 (1978), pp. 133–65.

2. Linda Colley, 'Eighteenth-Century Radicalism before Wilkes', *Transactions of the Royal Historical Society*, 5th series, 31 (1980), pp. 1–19.

3. E. P. Thompson, *The Making of the English Working Class* (London, 1968), pp. 74–6; J. Brewer, *Party Ideology and Popular Politics at the Accession of George III* (Cambridge,

1976), ch. 9; G. Rudé, 'Collusion and Convergence in 18th-Century Political Action', in his *Paris and London in the Eighteenth Century: Studies in Political Protest* (London, 1970), pp. 319–40.

4. G. Rudé, 'The Gordon Riots: A Study of the Rioters and their Victims', in *ibid.*, pp. 268–92.

5. G. Claeys, *Thomas Paine: Social and Political Thought* (Boston, 1989), pp. 6–19.

6. For a useful introduction to Habermas, see Geoff Eley, 'Rethinking the Political: Social History and Political Culture in 18th and 19th Century Britain', *Archiv für Sozialgeschichte*, 21 (1981), pp. 427–57.

7. A. Sheps, 'The American Revolution and the Transformation of English Republicanism', *Historical Reflections*, 2 (1975), pp. 3–28.

8. C. Hill, 'The Norman Yoke', in J. Saville (ed.), *Democracy and the Labour Movement* (London, 1954), pp. 11–66.

9. E. C. Black, *The Association. British Extra-Parliamentary Political Organization, 1769–1793* (Harvard, 1963); T. M. Parssinen, 'Association, Convention and Anti-parliament in British Radical Politics, 1771– 1848', *English Historical Review*, 88 (1973), pp. 504–33.

10. G. Newman, *The Rise of English Nationalism: A Cultural History 1740–1830* (London, 1987), ch. 7.

11. J. Seed, 'Gentleman Dissenters: The Social and Political Meanings of Rational Dissent in the 1770s and 1780s', *Historical Journal*, 28 (1985), pp. 299–325.

12. C. Berry, 'The Nature of Wealth and the Origins of Virtue: Recent Essays on the Scottish Enlightenment', *History of European Ideas*, 7 (1986), pp. 85–99.

Notes to Chapter 2: Radicalism, Revolution and War

1. Olivia Smith, *The Politics of Language 1791–1819* (Oxford, 1984), p. 36.

2. H. T. Dickinson, *British Radicals and the French Revolution 1789– 1815* (Oxford, 1985), pp. 25–36.

3. M. Philp, 'The Fragmented Ideology of Reform', in M. Philp (ed.), *The French Revolution and British Popular Politics* (Cambridge, 1991), pp. 50–77.

4. G. Claeys, 'The French Revolution Debate and British Political Thought', *History of Political Thought*, 11 (1990), pp. 59–80.

5. G. Claeys, *Thomas Paine: Social and Political Thought* (Boston, 1989), ch. 8.

6. I. Hampsher-Monk, 'John Thelwall and the Eighteenth-Century Radical Response to Political Economy', *Historical Journal*, 34 (1991), pp. 1–20.

7. J. Dinwiddy, 'Interpretations of Anti-Jacobinism', in Philp (ed.), *op. cit.*, pp. 38–49.

8. A. Goodwin, *The Friends of Liberty: The English Democratic Movement in the Age of the French Revolution* (London, 1979), chs 7 and 8.

9. *Memoir of Thomas Hardy*, in D. Vincent (ed.), *Testaments of Radicalism: Memoirs of Working-Class Politicians 1790–1835* (London, 1977), p. 51.

10. Linda Colley, 'Whose Nation? Class and National Consciousness in Britain 1750–1830', in *Past and Present*, 113 (1986), pp. 97–117.

11. C. Emsley, 'Repression, "Terror" and the Rule of Law in England during the Decade of the French Revolution', *English Historical Review*, 100 (1985), pp. 801–25.

12. Quoted in Goodwin, *op. cit.*, pp. 384–6.

13. Hampsher-Monk, *op. cit.*, pp. 1–3.

14. Malcolm Chase, *The People's Farm: English Radical Agrarianism 1775–1840* (Oxford, 1988), chs 2 and 3. See also H. T. Dickinson's introduction to his edition of *The Political Works of Thomas Spence* (Newcastle, 1982).

15. J. A. Hone, *For the Cause of Truth: Radicalism in London 1796–1821* (Oxford, 1982), pp. 117–35.

16. P. Mandler, *Aristocratic Government in the Age of Reform: Whigs and Liberals, 1830–1850*, pp. 17–22.

17. E. P. Thompson, *The Making of the English Working Class* (London, 1968) pp. 515–42.

18. C. Emsley, 'The Home Office and its Sources of Information and Investigation', *English Historical Review*, 94 (1979), pp. 532–61.

19. Roger Wells, *Insurrection. The British Experience 1795–1803* (Gloucester, 1983), chs 5–8.

20. John Foster, *Class Struggle and the Industrial Revolution. Early Industrial Capitalism in Three English Towns* (London, 1974), p. 38.

21. Alan Booth, 'Popular Loyalism and Public Violence in the North-west of England, 1790–1800', *Social History*, 8 (1983), pp. 295–314, and Alan Booth, 'Food Riots in the North-west of England 1790–1801', *Past and Present*, 78 (1977), pp. 84–107.
22. Marianne Elliott, 'The "Despard Conspiracy" Reconsidered', *Past and Present*, 75 (1977), pp. 46–61.
23. J. L. Baxter and F. K. Donnelly, 'Sheffield and the English Revolutionary Tradition 1791–1820', *International Review of Social History*, 20 (1975), pp. 398–423.
24. Peter Spence, 'The Rise and Fall of Romantic Radicalism: England 1800–1810', unpublished PhD thesis, University of Cambridge, 1993.
25. A. D. Harvey, *Britain in the Early Nineteenth Century* (London, 1978), pp. 245–6.
26. Dror Wahrman, 'National Society, Communal Culture: an Argument about the Recent Historiography of Eighteenth-century Britain', *Social History*, 17 (1992), pp. 43–72.
27. J. E. Cookson, *The Friends of Peace: Anti-war Liberalism in England 1793–1815* (Cambridge, 1982).
28. N. C. Miller, 'John Cartwright and Radical Parliamentary Reform, 1808–1819', *English Historical Review*, 83 (1968), pp. 705–28.
29. J. R. Dinwiddy, 'Sir Francis Burdett and Burdettite Radicalism, *History*, 65 (1980), pp. 17–31.
30. J. R. Dinwiddy, '"The Patriotic Linen-Draper": Robert Waithman and the Revival of Radicalism in the City of London, 1795–1818', *Bulletin of the Institute of Historical Research*, 46 (1973), pp. 72–94.
31. Hone, *op. cit.*, ch. 4.
32. George Spater, *William Cobbett: The Poor Man's Friend*, 2 vols (Cambridge, 1982), vol. ii, pp. 314–16.
33. G. Rudé, *Protest and Punishment* (Oxford, 1978), pp. 13–26, 52–8.
34. John Bohstedt, *Riots and Community Politics in England and Wales 1790–1810* (London, 1983), and John Bohstedt, 'Women in English Riots 1790–1810', *Past and Present*, 120 (1988), pp. 88–122.
35. A. J. Randall, 'The Shearmen and the Wiltshire Outrages of 1802: Trade Unionism and Industrial Violence', *Social History*, 7 (1982), pp. 283–304.
36. J. R. Dinwiddy, 'Luddism and Politics in the Northern Coun-

ties', *Social History*, 4 (1979), pp. 33–63.

37. John Rule, *The Labouring Classes in Early Industrial England 1750–1850* (London, 1986), pp. 278–9.

38. J. R. Dinwiddy, 'Bentham's Transition to Political Radicalism, 1809–10', *Journal of the History of Ideas*, 35 (1975), pp. 683–700.

Notes to Chapter 3: The Radical Mass Platform

1. John Belchem, *'Orator' Hunt: Henry Hunt and English Working-Class Radicalism* (Oxford, 1985), ch. 2.

2. H. Hunt, *Memoirs of Henry Hunt, Esq.*, 3 vols (London, 1820–2), vol. ii, p. 75.

3. Belchem, *op. cit.*, pp. 53–4.

4. T. M. Parssinen, 'The Revolutionary Party in London, 1816–20', *Bulletin of the Institute of Historical Research*, 45 (1972), pp. 266–82.

5. Iain McCalman, *Radical Underworld. Prophets, Revolutionaries and Pornographers in London, 1795–1840* (Cambridge, 1988), ch. 5.

6. Belchem, *op. cit.*, pp. 58–70.

7. John Belchem, 'Radical Language and Ideology in Early Nineteenth-century England: The Challenge of the Platform', *Albion*, 20 (1988), pp. 247–59.

8. Quoted in Belchem, *'Orator' Hunt*, p. 65.

9. J. Stevens, *England's last Revolution: Pentrich 1817* (Buxton, 1977); M. Thomis and P. Holt, *Threats of Revolution in Britain 1789–1848* (London, 1977), pp. 44–61.

10. *Journals of the House of Commons*, 73 (1818), Appendix, p. 778.

11. Belchem, *'Orator' Hunt*, pp. 84–90.

12. 'A Radical Reformer', *Manchester Observer*, 6 February 1819.

13. Quoted in Belchem, *'Orator' Hunt*, p. 94.

14. *Ibid.*, ch. 4.

15. J. Epstein, 'Understanding the Cap of Liberty: Symbolic Practice and Social Conflict in Early Nineteenth-Century England', *Past and Present*, 122 (1989), pp. 75–118; John Belchem, 'Republicanism, Popular Constitutionalism and the Radical Platform in Early Nineteenth-Century England', *Social History*, 6 (1981), pp. 1–32.

16. Belchem, *'Orator' Hunt*, pp. 98–112.

17. *Ibid.*, pp. 112–32. See also J. Stanhope, *The Cato Street Conspiracy* (London, 1962); and P. B. Ellis and S. M. A'Ghobhainn, *The Scottish Insurrection of 1820* (London, 1970).

18. T. W. Laquer, 'The Queen Caroline Affair: Politics as Art in the Reign of George IV', *Journal of Modern History*, 54 (1982), pp. 417–66; Anna Clark, 'Queen Caroline and the Sexual Politics of Popular Culture in London, 1820', *Representations*, 31 (1990), pp. 47–68; Craig Calhoun, *The Question of Class Struggle: Social Foundations of Popular Radicalism during the Industrial Revolution* (Oxford, 1982), pp. 105–15.

19. Quoted in Linda Colley, 'The Apotheosis of George III: Loyalty, Royalty and the British Nation, 1760–1820', *Past and Present*, 102 (1984), p. 124.

Notes to Chapter 4: Ideology, Public Opinion and Reform

1. John Belchem, *'Orator' Hunt: Henry Hunt and English Working-Class Radicalism* (Oxford, 1985), pp. 151–7. Joel Wiener, *Radicalism and Freethought in Nineteenth-Century Britain: The Life of Richard Carlile* (Westport, 1983), ch. 5; Iain McCalman, 'Unrespectable Radicalism: Infidels and Pornography in Early Nineteenth-Century London', *Past and Present*, 104 (1984), pp. 74–110; J. A. Epstein, 'Reason's Republic: Richard Carlile, Zetetic Culture and Infidel Stylistics', in his *Radical Expression: Political Language, Ritual and Symbol in England, 1760–1850* (New York, 1994), pp. 100–46.

2. Iain McCalman, 'Females, Feminism and Free Love in an Early Nineteenth-Century Radical Movement', *Labour History*, 38 (1980), pp. 1–25.

3. *Lion*, 24 July and 9–23 October 1829.

4. I. Prothero, *Artisans and Politics in Early Nineteenth-Century London: John Gast and his Times* (London, 1981), chs 9 and 10.

5. Noel Thompson, *The People's Science: The Popular Political Economy of Exploitation and Crisis 1816–34* (Cambridge, 1984), chs 4–8.

6. J. F. C. Harrison, *Robert Owen and the Owenites in Britain*

and America: The Quest for the New Moral World (London, 1969); Barbara Taylor, *Eve and the New Jerusalem: Socialism and Feminism in the Nineteenth Century* (London, 1983).

7. *Poor Man's Guardian* 21 June 1834.

8. Parry, *The Rise and Fall of Liberal Government in Victorian Britain* (New Haven, 1993) ch. 1.

9. J. R. Dinwiddy, *From Luddism to the Reform Bill in England 1810–1832* (Oxford, 1986), pp. 13–18.

10. A. Tyrell, *Joseph Sturge and the Moral Radical Party in Early Victorian Britain* (London, 1981), ch. 5.

11. Ian Dyck, 'William Cobbett and the Rural Radical Platform', *Social History*, 18 (1993), pp. 185–204.

12. John Cannon, *Parliamentary Reform 1640–1832* (Cambridge, 1973), ch. 9.

13. Mandler, *Aristocratic Government Age of Reform: Whigs and Liberals, 1830–1850* (Oxford, 1990), pp. 128–30.

14. J. Stevenson, *Popular Disturbances in England 1700–1870* (London, 1979), pp. 218–27; Thomis and Holt, *Threats of Revolution in Britain 1789–1848* (London, 1977), pp. 85–99.

15. Prothero, *op. cit.*, pp. 268–92.

16. D. J. Rowe (ed.), *London Radicalism 1830–1843: A Selection from the Papers of Francis Place* (London, 1970), pp. 48–64.

17. Clive Behagg, *Politics and Production in the Early Nineteenth Century* (London, 1990), ch. 4.

18. Belchem, *'Orator' Hunt*, ch. 8 and p. 276.

19. Prothero, *op. cit.*, pp. 293–6.

20. Quoted in Belchem, *'Orator' Hunt*, pp. 274–5.

21. R. Sykes, 'Trade Unionism and Class Consciousness: The "Revolutionary" Period of General Unionism', in J. Rule (ed.), *British Trade Unionism 1750–1850* (London, 1988), pp. 178–99. See also, Stewart Weaver, *John Fielden and the Politics of Popular Radicalism 1832–1847* (Oxford, 1987), pp. 81–112; and R. G. Kirby and A. E. Musson, *The Voice of the People: John Doherty, 1798–1854* (Manchester, 1975), pp. 274–302.

22. *Destructive*, 7 June 1834.

23. P. Hollis, *The Pauper Press: A Study in Working-class Radicalism of the 1830s* (Oxford, 1970); Joel Wiener, *The War of the Unstamped. The Movement to Repeal the British Newspaper Tax, 1830–1836* (Ithaca, 1969).

24. Frank O'Gorman, 'The Unreformed Electorate of Hanoverian England: The Mid-Eighteenth Century to the Re-

form Act of 1832', *Social History*, 11 (1986), pp. 44–7.

25. Parry, *op. cit.*, p. 99.
26. B. L. Kinzer, *The Ballot Question in Nineteenth-Century English Politics* (New York, 1982), pp. 16–50.
27. Tyrell, *op. cit.*, ch. 6.
28. Mandler, *op. cit.*, ch. 5.
29. Cobden to F. W. Cobden, 5 October 1838, in J. Morley (ed.), *The Life of Richard Cobden* (London, 1903), p. 126.
30. Gareth Stedman Jones, 'Rethinking Chartism' in his *Languages of Class: Studies in English Working Class History 1832–1982* (Cambridge, 1983), pp. 174–5.
31. *Northern Star*, 23 June 1838, quoted in James Epstein, *The Lion of Freedom: Feargus O'Connor and the Chartist Movement, 1832–1842* (London, 1982), p. 97.

Notes to Chapter 5: Radicalism and Class

1. Dorothy Thompson, *The Chartists* (London, 1984), pp. 57–64.
2. Carlos Flick, *The Birmingham Political Union and the Movement for Reform in Britain 1830–1839* (Folkestone, 1978), ch. 7.
3. R. Sykes, 'Early Chartism and Trade Unionism', in James Epstein and Dorothy Thompson (eds), *The Chartist Experience: Studies in Working-class Radicalism and Culture, 1830–1860* (London, 1982), pp. 159–62.
4. James Epstein, *The Lion of Freedom: Feargus O'Connor and the Chartist Movement, 1832–1842* (London, 1982), chs 3 and 4.
5. K. Judge, 'Early Chartist Organization and the Convention of 1839', *International Review of Social History*, 20 (1975), pp. 370–97. T. M. Kemnitz, 'The Chartist Convention of 1839', *Albion*, 10 (1978), pp. 152–70.
6. J. Bennett, 'The London Democratic Association', in Epstein and Thompson (eds), *op. cit.*, pp. 87–119.
7. T. M. Kemnitz, 'Approaches to the Chartist Movement: Feargus O'Connor and Chartist Strategy', *Albion*, 5 (1973), pp. 67–73.
8. Clive Behagg, *Politics and Production in the Early Nineteenth Century* (London, 1990), pp. 202–18.

9. R. Sykes, 'Physical Force Chartism: The Cotton District and the Chartist Crisis of 1839', *International Review of Social History*, 30 (1985), pp. 207–36.

10. David Jones, *The Last Rising: The Newport Insurrection of 1839* (Oxford, 1985); Ivor Wilks, *South Wales and the Rising of 1839: Class Struggle as Armed Struggle* (London, 1984).

11. A. J. Peacock, *Bradford Chartism 1838–1840* (York, 1969), pp. 34–53.

12. Eileen Yeo, 'Some Practices and Problems of Chartist Democracy', in Epstein and Thompson (eds), *op. cit.*, pp. 345–80.

13. Eileen Yeo, 'Christianity in Chartist Struggle 1838–1842', *Past and Present*, 91 (1981), pp. 109–39.

14. Quoted in Yeo, 'Some Practices and Problems', p. 351.

15. Epstein, *Lion of Freedom*, pp. 236–49.

16. D. A. Hamer, *The Politics of Electoral Pressure: A Study in the History of Victorian Reform Agitations* (Hassocks, 1977), ch. 5; Norman McCord, *The Anti-Corn Law League* (London, 1958).

17. R. Bellamy, 'Introduction', in R. Bellamy (ed.), *Victorian Liberalism: Nineteenth-Century Political Thought and Practice* (London, 1990), pp. 1–14.

18. B. Harrison and P. Hollis, 'Chartism, Liberalism and the Life of Robert Lowery', *English Historical Review*, 82 (1967), pp. 503–35; B. Harrison, 'Teetotal Chartism', *History*, 58 (1973), pp. 193–217.

19. W. Lovett, *Life and Struggles of William Lovett in his Pursuit of Bread, Knowledge and Freedom* (London, 1876), ch. 13.

20. Lucy Brown, '*The Chartists and the Anti-Corn Law League*', in Asa Briggs (ed.), *Chartist Studies* (London, 1959), pp. 342–71.

21. A. Tyrell, *Joseph Sturge and the Moral Radical Party in Early Victorian Britain* (London, 1981), ch. 10.

22. T. Cooper, *The Life of Thomas Cooper* (London, 1872), p. 222.

23. Epstein, *Lion of Freedom*, pp. 273–86.

24. See John Foster's 'Introduction', in Mick Jenkins, *The General Strike of 1842* (London, 1980).

25. G. S. Jones, 'Rethinking Chartism', in his *Languages of Class: Studies in English Working Class History 1832–1982* (Cambridge, 1983), pp. 174–8. See also, P. Mandler, *Aristocratic Government in the Age of Reform: Whigs and Liberals, 1830–1850* (Oxford, 1990), pp. 200–01.

26. Epstein, *Lion of Freedom*, pp. 249–57. See also Joy MacAskill, 'The Chartist Land Plan', in Briggs (ed.), *op. cit.*, pp. 304–41; and A. M. Hadfield, *The Chartist Land Company* (Newton Abbot, 1970).

27. E. J. Hobsbawm and G. Rudé, *Captain Swing* (London, 1973); R. Wells, 'Rural Rebels in Southern England in the 1830s', in Clive Emsley and J. Walvin (eds), *Artisans, Peasants and Proletarians 1760–1860* (London, 1985), pp. 131–7.

28. David Jones, 'Thomas Campbell Foster and the Rural Labourer: Incendiarism in East Anglia in the 1840s', *Social History*, 1 (1976), pp. 5–43.

29. Dorothy Thompson, *op. cit.*, pp. 129–51. For a less critical view, see David Jones, 'Women and Chartism', *History*, 68 (1983), pp. 1–21.

30. Anna Clark, 'The Rhetoric of Chartist Domesticity: Gender, Language and Class in the 1830s and 1840s', *Journal of British Studies*, 31 (1992), pp. 62–88.

31. Jutta Schwarzkopf, *Women in the Chartist Movement* (London, 1991), ch. 7.

32. Ernest Jones, 'A Song for May', *Labourer* (1847), p. 193.

33. John Belchem, '1848: Feargus O'Connor and the Collapse of the Mass Platform', in Epstein and Thompson (eds), *op. cit.*, pp. 269–310. See also, David Goodway, *London Chartism, 1838–1848* (Cambridge, 1982), pp. 80–5, 106–25; and John Saville, *1848. The British State and the Chartist Movement* (Cambridge, 1987).

34. John Belchem, 'English Working-class Radicalism and the Irish, 1815–50', in S. Gilley and R. Swift (eds), *The Irish in the Victorian City* (London, 1985), pp. 85–97.

35. 'L'Ami du Peuple', *Northern Star*, 23 December 1848.

36. Paul Adelman, *Victorian Radicalism: The Middle-Class Experience 1830–1914* (London, 1984), pp. 23–7.

37. Harney to Engels, 30 March 1846, in F. G. and R. M. Black, *The Harney Papers* (Assen, 1969), pp. 239–45.

38. H. Weisser, *British Working-class Movements and Europe 1815–1848* (Manchester, 1975), pp. 154–71.

39. Margot Finn, *After Chartism. Class and Nation in English Radical Politics, 1848–1874* (Cambridge, 1993), ch. 2.

40. F. B. Smith, *Radical Artisan. William James Linton 1812–97* (Manchester, 1973), ch. 5.

41. Tyrell, *op. cit.*, ch. 13.

42. John Belchem, '"Temperance in all things": Vegetarianism,

the Manx Press and the Alternative Radical Agenda of the 1840s', in M. Chase and I. Dyck (eds), *Living and Learning: Essays in Honour of J. F. C. Harrison* (forthcoming).

43. Cobden to Bright, 23 December 1848 and 1 October 1849, in J. Morley (ed.), *The Life of Richard Cobden* (London, 1903), pp. 502–04 and 515. *Manchester Examiner and Times,* 17 November 1849.

44. N. C. Edsall, 'A Failed National Movement: The Parliamentary and Financial Reform Association', *Bulletin of the Institute of Historical Research,* 49 (1976), pp. 108–31.

45. R. Quinault, '1848 and Parliamentary Reform', *Historical Journal,* 31 (1988), pp. 831–51.

46. G. Claeys, 'Mazzini, Kossuth and British Radicalism, 1848–1854', *Journal of British Studies,* 28 (1989), pp. 225–61.

47. Belchem, '1848', pp. 299–304.

48. G. Claeys, *Citizens and Saints. Politics and Anti-Politics in Early British Socialism* (Cambridge, 1989), ch. 7.

49. John Belchem, 'Chartism and the Trades, 1848–1850', *English Historical Review,* 98 (1983), pp. 558–87.

Notes to Chapter 6: Radicalism, Liberalism and Reformism

1. Quoted in Neville Kirk, *Labour and Society in Britain and the USA*, 2 vols (Aldershot, 1994), vol. ii. p. 181.

2. Trygve Tholfsen, *Working-Class Radicalism in Mid-Victorian England* (London, 1976), ch. 4.

3. M. Arnold, *Culture and Anarchy* (London, 1869), pp. 36–7.

4. J. Parry, *The Rise and Fall of Liberal Government in Victorian Britain* (New Haven, 1993), chs 8 and 9.

5. Miles Taylor, 'The Old Radicalism and the New: David Urquhart and the Politics of Opposition, 1832–1867', in E. F. Biagini and A. J. Reid (eds), *Currents of Radicalism: Popular Radicalism, Organized Labour and Party Politics in Britain 1850–1914* (Cambridge, 1991), pp. 23–48.

6. John Vincent, *The Formation of the British Liberal Party* (London, 1972).

7. D. A. Hamer, *The Politics of Electoral Pressure: A Study in the History of Victorian Reform Agitations* (Brighton, 1977), chs 8–13.

8. Quoted in Asa Briggs, *The Age of Improvement* (London,

1959), p. 492.

9. Vincent, *op. cit.*, pp. 195–244.

10. Patrick Joyce, *Visions of the People: Industrial England and the Question of Class, 1840–1914* (Cambridge, 1991), pp. 47–9.

11. Margot Finn, *After Chartism. Class and Nation in English Radical Politics, 1848–1874* (Cambridge, 1993), pp. 186–7.

12. Nigel Todd, *The Militant Democracy: Joseph Cowen and Victorian Radicalism* (Whitley Bay, 1991); Owen Ashton, *W. E. Adams: Chartist, Radical and Journalist* (Whitley Bay, 1991).

13. Royden Harrison, *Before the Socialists: Studies in Labour and Politics 1861–1881* (London, 1965), ch. 6.

14. F. M. Leventhal, *Respectable Radical. George Howell and Victorian Working-class Politics* (London, 1971), ch. 2.

15. Finn, *op. cit.*, chs 5 and 6; Stan Shipley, *Club Life and Socialism in Mid-Victorian London* (London, 1971).

16. H. Collins, 'The English Branches of the First International', in Asa Briggs and John Saville (eds), *Essays in Labour History* (London, 1960), pp. 242–75.

17. R. Harrison, 'Professor Beesly and the Working-class Movement', in *ibid.*, pp. 205–41. See also, M. E. Rose, 'Rochdale Man and the Stalybridge Riot: The Relief and Control of the Unemployed during the Lancashire Cotton Famine', in A. P. Donajgrodski, *Social Control in Nineteenth-Century Britain* (London, 1977), pp. 187–91.

18. Finn, *op. cit.*, pp. 238–9; E. F. Biagini, *Liberty, Retrenchment and Reform: Popular Liberalism in the Age of Gladstone 1860–1880* (Cambridge, 1992), pp. 268–75.

19. Leventhal, *op. cit.*, pp. 71–89.

20. Finn, *op. cit.*, pp. 239–54.

21. Paul Adelman, *Victorian Radicalism: The Middle-Class Experience 1830–1914* (London, 1984), ch. 3. John Gibbins, 'J. S. Mill, Liberalism and Progress', in R. Bellamy (ed.), *Victorian Liberalism: Nineteenth-Century Political Thought and Practice* (London, 1990), pp. 268–75.

22. S. Coltham, 'The *Bee-Hive* Newspaper: Its Origins and Early Struggles', in Briggs and Saville (eds), *op. cit.*, pp. 174–203.

23. R. Harrison, *Before the Socialists*, ch. 3.

24. Leventhal, *op. cit.*, ch. 5.

25. R. Harrison, *Before the Socialists*, pp. 290–302.

26. Jonathan Spain, 'Trade Unionists, Gladstonian Liberals,

and the Labour Law Reforms of 1875', in Biagini and Reid (eds), *op. cit.*, pp. 109–33.

27. F. A. D'Arcy, 'Charles Bradlaugh and the English Republican Movement, 1868–1878', *Historical Journal,* 25 (1982), pp. 367–83. See also, Jon Lawrence, 'Popular Radicalism and the Socialist Revival in Britain', *Journal of British Studies,* 31 (1992), pp. 169–70.

28. Dorothy Thompson, 'Queen Victoria, the Monarchy and Gender', in her *Outsiders: Class, Gender and Nation* (London, 1993), pp. 179–82.

29. D'Arcy, *op. cit.*, pp. 374–83. See also N. J. Gossman, 'Republicanism in Nineteenth–Century England', *International Review of Social History,* 7 (1962), pp. 51–60.

30. Todd, *op. cit.*, ch. 8.

31. Biagini, *op. cit.*, pp. 292–3.

32. *Ibid., passim.* See also the introduction in Biagini and Reid (eds), *op. cit.*, pp. 1–19.

33. Joyce, *op. cit.*, p. 68.

34. R. McWilliam, 'Radicalism and Popular Culture: The Tichborne Case and the Politics of "Fair Play"', in Biagini and Reid (eds), *op. cit.*, pp. 44–64.

35. Paul Johnson, 'Class Law in Victorian England', *Past and Present,* 141 (1993), pp. 147–69.

36. Patrick Joyce, *Work, Society and Politics: The Culture of the Factory in Later Victorian England* (London, 1982), pp. 189–91.

Notes to Chapter 7: Gladstone, Lib-Labism and New Liberalism

1. D. A. Hamer, *Liberal Politics in the Age of Gladstone and Rosebery* (Oxford, 1972) ch. 1.

2. J. R. Vincent, *Pollbooks: How Victorians Voted* (Cambridge, 1967), p. 45.

3. K. D. Brown, 'Nonconformity and Trade Unionism: The Sheffield Outrages of 1866'; and Reid, 'Old Unionism Reconsidered', in E. F. Biagini and A. J. Reid (eds), *Currents of Radicalism: Popular Radicalism, Organized Labour and Party Politics in Britain* 1850–1914 (Cambridge, 1991), pp. 86–105 and 214–43.

4. John Shepherd, 'Labour and Parliament: The Lib-Labs as the First Working-class MPs, 1885–1906', in *ibid.*, pp. 187–213.

5. E. F. Biagini, *Liberty, Retrenchment and Reform: Popular Liberalism in the Age of Gladstone 1860–1880* (Cambridge, 1992), pp. 357–8.

6. *Ibid.*, p. 50.

7. R. Gray, 'Class, Politics and Historical "Revisionism"', *Social History*, 19 (1994), p. 214.

8. Quoted in Biagini, *op. cit.*, p. 206.

9. Linda Walker, 'Party Political Women: A Comparative Study of Liberal Women and the Primrose League, 1890–1914', in Jane Rendall (ed.), *Equal or Different: Women's Politics 1800–1914* (Oxford, 1987), pp. 165–91.

10. Jon Lawrence, 'Popular Radicalism and the Socialist Revival in Britain', *Journal of British Studies*, 31 (1992), pp. 173–5.

11. Quoted in H. Pelling, *The Origins of the Labour Party* (Oxford, 1965), p. 224.

12. J. Parry, *The Rise and Fall of Liberal Government in Victorian Britain* (New Haven, 1993), p. 223.

13. D. A. Hamer, *The Politics of Electoral Pressure: A Study in the History of Victorian Reform Agitations* (Brighton, 1977), chs 8–13.

14. Parry, *op. cit.*, chs 10–12.

15. Paul Adelman, *Victorian Radicalism: The Middle-Class Experience 1830–1914* (London, 1984), ch. 5.

16. D. A. Hamer (ed.), *The Radical Programme, 1885* (Brighton, 1971).

17. *Ibid.*, p. xxxi.

18. W. D. Rubinstein, *Men of Property. The Very Wealthy in Britain since the Industrial Revolution* (London, 1981), pp. 62–3 and 106–7.

19. James Cornford, 'The Transformation of Conservatism in the Late Nineteenth Century', *Victorian Studies*, 7 (1968), pp. 35–66.

20. Quoted in J. P. Dunbabin, 'British Elections in the Nineteenth and Twentieth Centuries: a Regional Approach', *English Historical Review*, 95 (1980), p. 261.

21. D. Powell, 'The New Liberalism and the Rise of Labour, 1886–1906', *Historical Journal*, 29 (1986), pp. 369–93.

22. A. B. Cooke and J. Vincent, *The Governing Passion: Cabinet*

Government and Party Politics in Britain 1885–86 (Brighton, 1974), chs 2–6.

23. Parry, *op. cit.*, pp. 292–303.
24. M. Bentley, *The Climax of Liberal Politics. British Liberalism in Theory and Practice 1868–1918* (London, 1987), p. 137.
25. G. L. Bernstein, *Liberalism and the Liberal Politics in Edwardian England* (Boston, 1986), p. 10.
26. D. Brooks (ed.), *The Destruction of Lord Rosebery. From the Diary of Sir Edward Hamilton, 1894–1895* (London, 1986).
27. Quoted in H. V. Emy, *Liberals, Radicals and Social Politics 1892–1914* (Cambridge, 1973), p. 106.
28. John Gibbins, 'J. S. Mill, Liberalism and Progress', in R. Bellamy (ed.), *Victorian Liberalism: Nineteenth-Century Political Thought and Practice* (London, 1990), p. 107.
29. R. Bellamy, 'T. H. Green and the Morality of Victorian Liberalism', in Bellamy (ed.), *op. cit.*, pp. 141–2.
30. M. Freeden, 'The new Liberalism and its Aftermath', in *ibid.*, p. 177.
31. P. F. Clarke, *Liberals and Social Democrats* (Cambridge, 1978), ch. 2.
32. Freeden, *op. cit.*, pp. 182–3.

Notes to Chapter 8: Labour's Turning-point?

1. See the essays by Reid, Thane and Tanner in E. F. Biagini and A. J. Reid (eds), *Currents of Radicalism: Popular Radicalism, Organized Labour and Party Politics in Britain 1850–1914* (Cambridge, 1991).
2. Stanley Pierson, *Marxism and the Origins of British Socialism: The Struggle for a New Consciousness* (Ithaca, 1973).
3. Stephen Yeo, 'A New Life: The Religion of Socialism in Britain 1883–1896', *History Workshop Journal*, 4 (1977), pp. 5–56.
4. Paul Adelman, *Victorian Radicalism: The Middle-Class Experience 1830–1914* (London, 1984) p. 8.
5. H. J. Perkin, 'Land Reform and Class Conflict in Victorian Britain', in J. Butt and I. F. Clarke (eds), *The Victorians and Social Protest* (Newton Abbot, 1973), pp. 177–217.
6. Nigel Todd, *The Militant Democracy: Joseph Cowen and Victorian Radicalism* (Whitley Bay, 1991) ch. 10.

7. Owen Ashton, *W. E. Adams: Chartist, Radical and Journalist* (Whitley Bay, 1991).

8. Quoted in Jon Lawrence, 'Popular Radicalism and the Socialist Revival in Britain', *Journal of British Studies*, 31, (1992) p. 178.

9. D. C. Richter, *Riotous Victorians* (Ohio, 1981), ch. 8.

10. E. P. Thompson, *William Morris: Romantic to Revolutionary* (2nd edition, London, 1976), pp. 479–81.

11. Richter, *op. cit.*, ch. 9.

12. Lawrence, 'Popular Radicalism', pp. 175–9.

13. E. P. Thompson, *William Morris*, pp. 366–579. S. Coleman and P. O'Sullivan (eds), *William Morris and News from Nowhere* (Bideford, 1990).

14. Tony Brown (ed.), *Edward Carpenter and Late Victorian Radicalism* (London, 1990).

15. Quoted in D. Kynaston, *King Labour. The British Working Class 1850–1914* (London, 1976), p. 127.

16. Pierson, *op. cit.*, ch. 5.

17. Lawrence, 'Popular Radicalism', pp. 179–85.

18. H. Pelling, *The Origins of the Labour Party* (Oxford, 1965), pp. 59–69. F. Reid, 'Keir Hardie's Conversion to Socialism', in A. Briggs and J. Saville (eds), *Essays in Labour History 1886–1923* (London, 1971), pp. 17–46.

19. Lawrence, 'Popular Radicalism', p. 181.

20. Quoted in James Hinton, *Labour and Socialism. A History of the British Labour Movement 1867–1974* (Brighton, 1983), p. 52.

21. John Lovell, *British Trade Unions 1875–1933* (London, 1977), pp. 20–9.

22. E. P. Thompson, 'Homage to Tom Maguire', in Briggs and Saville (eds), *Essays in Labour History*, p. 311.

23. Pelling, *op. cit.*, ch. 6. David Howell, *British Workers and the Independent Labour Party 1888–1906* (Manchester, 1983), chs 12–17.

24. Pelling, *op. cit.*, pp. 132–9.

25. David Clark, *Colne Valley: Radicalism to Socialism* (London, 1981), pp. 2, 32–6, 50–2 and 125–6.

26. Neville Kirk, *Labour and Society in Britain and the USA: Challenge and Accommodation, 1850–1939* (Aldershot, 1994), ch. 2.

27. Richard Price, *Labour in British Society: An Interpretative History* (London, 1986), chs 5 and 6.

28. J. Saville, 'Trade Unions and Free Labour: The Background

to the Taff Vale Decision', in Briggs and Saville, *Essays in Labour History*, pp. 317–50.

29. H. Pelling, *Popular Politics and Society in Late Victorian Britain* (London, 1979), pp. 76–8.

Notes to Chapter 9: Liberals, Labour and the Progressive Alliance

1. Martin Pugh, *The Making of Modern British Politics 1867–1939* (Oxford, 1982), pp. 117–18

2. M. Bentley, *The Climax of Liberal Politics: British Liberalism in Theory and Practice 1868–1918* (London, 1987), p. 29.

3. P. F. Clarke, *Lancashire and the New Liberalism* (Cambridge, 1971).

4. A. W. Purdue, 'The Liberal and Labour Parties in North-East Politics 1900–1914: The Struggle for Supremacy', *International Review of Social History*, 26 (1981), pp. 1–24.

5. K. O. Morgan, 'The New Liberalism and the Challenge of Labour: The Welsh Experience, 1885–1929', in K. D. Brown (ed.), *Essays in Anti-Labour History* (London, 1974), pp. 159–82.

6. Avner Offer, *Property and Politics 1870–1914. Landownership, Law, Ideology and Urban Development in England* (Cambridge, 1981), ch. 22; B. B. Gilbert, 'David Lloyd George: Land, the Budget and Social Reform', *American History Review*, 81 (1976), pp. 1058–66.

7. Quoted in D. Powell, 'The New Liberalismn and the Rise of Labour, 1886–1906', *Historical Journal*, 29 (1986), p. 391.

8. Quoted in R. Barker, 'Socialism and Progressivism in the Political Thought of Ramsay MacDonald', in A. J. A. Morris (ed.), *Edwardian Radicalism 1900–1914* (London, 1974), p. 124.

9. Pat Thane, 'Labour and Local Politics: Radicalism, Democracy and Social Reform, 1890–1914', in E. F. Biagini and H. J. Reid (eds), *Currents of Radicalism: Popular Radicalism, Organized Labour and Party Politics in Britain 1850–1914* (Cambridge, 1991), pp. 261–70.

10. Quoted in David Martin, '"The Instruments of the People"?: the Parliamentary Labour Party in 1906', in D. Martin and D. Rubinstein (eds), *Ideology and the Labour Movement* (London, 1979), pp. 135–6.

11. Duncan Tanner, 'Ideological debate in Edwardian Labour Politics: Radicalism, Revisionism and Socialism', in Biagini and Reid (eds), *op. cit.*, pp. 271–93.

12. A. F. Reid, 'Old Unionism Reconsidered', in Biagini and Reid (eds), *op. cit.*, pp. 240–1.

13. P. Thane, 'The Labour Party and State "Welfare"', in K. D. Brown (ed.), *The First Labour Party 1906–1914* (Beckenham, 1985), pp. 183–216.

14. Chris Wrigley, 'Labour and the Trade Unions', in *ibid.*, pp. 129–57.

15. Quoted in Alun Howkins, 'Edwardian Liberalism and Industrial Unrest: A Class View of the Decline of Liberalism, *History Workshop Journal*, 4 (1977), p. 157.

16. Joseph White, 'A Panegyric on Edwardian Progressivism', *Journal of British Studies*, 16 (1977), pp. 145–52.

17. D. Clark, *Colne Valley: Radicalism to Socialism* (London, 1981) ch. 11.

18. James Hinton, *Labour and Socialism. A History of the British Labour Movement 1867–1974* (Brighton, 1983), p. 94.

19. Quoted in Wrigley, *op. cit.*, p. 150.

20. John Lovell, *British Trade Unions 1875–1933* (London, 1977) pp. 46–9.

21. Roy Douglas, 'Labour in Decline, 1910–14', in K. D. Brown (ed.), *Essays in Anti–Labour History*, pp. 105–25.

22. Patricia Hollis, 'Women in Council: Separate Spheres, Public Space', in Jane Rendall (ed.), *Equal or Different: Women's Politics 1800–1914* (Oxford, 1987), pp. 194–5, and 209.

23. J. Liddington and J. Norris, *One Hand Tied Behind Us: The Rise of the Women's Suffrage Movement* (London, 1978), pp. 120–37.

24. G. L. Bernstein, 'Liberalism and the Progressive Alliance in the Constituencies, 1900–1914: Three Case Studies', *Historical Journal*, 26 (1983), pp. 617–40.

25. Martin Petter, 'The Progressive Alliance', *History*, 58 (1973), p. 51.

26. Quoted in M. Freeden, *The New Liberalism: An Ideology of Social Reform* (Oxford, 1978), p. 149.

27. David Martin, *op. cit.*, p. 142.

28. W. H. Fraser, 'The Labour Party in Scotland', in K. D. Brown (ed.), *The First Labour Party*, p. 60.

29. Ross McKibbin, *The Evolution of the Labour Party 1910–1924* (Oxford, 1974), p. 245

30. Jon Lawrence, 'Class and gender in the Making of Urban Toryism, 1880–1914', *English Historical Review*, 108 (1993), pp. 629–52.
31. H. C. G. Matthew, R. I. McKibbin and J. A. Kay, 'The Franchise Factor in the Rise of the Labour Party', *English Historical Review*, 91 (1976), pp. 723–52.
32. Pugh, *op. cit.*, pp. 141–4.
33. Martin Pugh, 'Labour and Women's Suffrage', in K. D. Brown (ed.), *The First Labour Party*, pp. 233–53; Liddington and Norris, *op. cit.*, *passim*.

Notes to the Conclusion

1. M. Hart, 'The Liberals, the War and the Franchise', *English Historical Review*, 97 (1982), pp. 820–32.
2. R. Harrison, 'The War Emergency Workers' National Committee 1914–1920', in A. Briggs and J. Saville (eds), *Essays in Labour History 1886–1923* (London, 1971), pp. 211–59; J. Winter, *Socialism and the Challenge of War: Ideas and Politics in Britain, 1912–18* (London, 1974), ch. 7.
3. Duncan Tanner, 'Ideological Debate in Edwardian Labour Politics: Radicalism, Revisionism and Socialism', in E. F. Biagini and A. J. Reid (eds), *Currents of Radicalism: Popular Radicalism, Organized Labour and Party Politics in Britain 1850–1914* (Cambridge, 1991), ch. 13.
4. Ross McKibbin, 'Class and Conventional Wisdom: The Conservative Party and the "Public" in Inter–war Britain', in his *The Ideologies of Class* (Oxford, 1990), pp. 259–93.

FURTHER READING

Given the vast amount of material published on radicalism for the 'long' nineteenth century covered in this study, it is difficult to keep a guide to further reading within manageable proportions. What is offered here is neither a comprehensive bibliography nor a definitive selection, but a list of some of the more important and useful titles for those coming new or relatively new to the subject. Details of specialized texts are provided in the notes.

There are several introductory surveys, covering significant parts of the period, including E. Royle and J. Walvin, *English Radicals and Reformers 1760–1848* (Brighton, 1982); D. G. Wright, *Popular Radicalism: The Working-Class Experience 1780–1880* (London, 1988); Paul Adelman, *Victorian Radicalism: The Middle-Class Experience 1830–1914* (London, 1984); and Clive Behagg, *Labour and Reform: Working-Class Movements 1815–1914* (London, 1991), which includes study guides and some source material. Among the useful shorter-scale surveys are two Historical Association Studies: H. T. Dickinson, *British Radicalism and the French Revolution 1789–1815* (Oxford, 1985) and J. R. Dinwiddy, *From Luddism to the First Reform Bill* (Oxford, 1986). Following his untimely death, many of Dinwiddy's incisive articles on popular radicalism, moderate reform, Luddism, Benthamism and Chartism have been reprinted in *Radicalism and Reform in Britain, 1780–1850* (London, 1992), essential reading for all students of early nineteenth-century British history. For the later period, the essays edited by Richard Bellamy on *Victorian Liberalism: Nineteenth-Century Thought and Practice* (London, 1990) provide a useful starting-point for the intellectual and philosophical development of radicalism.

Unfortunately, collections of documents on radicalism tend to cover a short time-span, with the exception of S. MacCoby's outdated selection in *The English Radical Tradition, 1763–1914*

(London, 1952). One way to approach 'primary' material is through radical autobiographies, many of which can be found in secondhand bookshops. David Vincent has edited a useful anthology, *Testaments of Radicalism: Memoirs of Working-class Politicians 1790–1885* (London, 1977).

In terms of theory and method, E. P. Thompson's monumental *The Making of the English Working Class* (London, 1963) remains essential reading for its inspirational emphasis on agency and culture. Some students may find the post-Thompson 'linguistic turn' less accessible. The foundation text here is Gareth Stedman Jones's essay 'Rethinking Chartism', in his *Languages of Class* (Cambridge, 1983). Post-structuralism merges with postmodernism in the recent cultural studies of Patrick Joyce, *Visions of the People* (Cambridge, 1991), and James Vernon, *Politics and the People: A Study in English Political Culture c.1815–1867* (Cambridge, 1993), both of which stress the continuity of radicalism and its populist register. M. Savage, *The Dynamics of Working-class Politics* (Cambridge, 1987) offers an alternative sociological methodology which accounts for local variations.

To turn from general theoretical and methodological issues to the topics and themes explored in individual chapters, the political ideas and 'mental furniture' of eighteenth-century radicals and reformers are best approached through H. T. Dickinson, *Liberty and Property: Political Ideology in Eighteenth-Century Britain* (London, 1977); William Stafford, *Socialism, Radicalism and Nostalgia: Social Criticism in Britain, 1775–1830* (Cambridge, 1987); Gregory Claeys, *Thomas Paine: Social and Political Thought* (London, 1989); and, for a more 'cultural' reading, Dror Wahrman, 'National Society, Communal Culture: An Argument about the Recent Historiography of Eighteenth-Century Britain', *Social History*, 17 (1992). John Brewer, *Party Ideology and Popular Politics at the Accession of George III* (Cambridge, 1976) includes an excellent analysis of Wilkes's commercialization of politics, to be read in conjunction with George Rudé's essays on collusion, convergence and the crowd in his *Paris and London in the Eighteenth Century* (London, 1970). On the development of extra-parliamentary tactics, see E. C. Black, *The Association: British Extra-parliamentary Organization, 1769–1793* (Harvard, 1963); and T. M. Parssinen, 'Association, Convention and Anti-parliament in British Radical Politics', *English Historical Review*, 88 (1973).

For the 1790s, Albert Goodwin, *The Friends of Liberty: The English*

Democratic Movement in the Age of the French Revolution (London, 1979), remains the standard work, but some exciting new approaches, linguistic and otherwise, are illustrated in M. Philp (ed.), *The French Revolution and British Popular Politics* (Cambridge, 1991). For the domestic and international dimensions of underground activity during the war years, see Roger Wells, *Insurrection: The British Experience, 1795–1803* (London, 1982); and Marianne Elliott, *Partners in Revolution: The United Irishmen and France* (New Haven, 1982). The middle-class approach is examined most fully in J. E. Cookson, *The Friends of Peace: Anti-war Liberalism in England 1793–1815* (Cambridge, 1982).

There are a number of scholarly biographies of radicals prominent in the post-war movement (and beyond), including I. J. Prothero, *Artisans and Politics in Early Nineteenth-Century London: John Gast and his Times* (London, 1981); George Spater, *William Cobbett: The Poor Man's Friend*, 2 vols (Cambridge, 1982); John Belchem, *'Orator' Hunt: Henry Hunt and English Working-class Politics* (Oxford, 1985); Joel Wiener, *Radicalism and Freethought in Nineteenth-Century Britain: The Life of Richard Carlile* (Westport, 1983); and Dudley Miles, *Francis Place 1771–1854: The Life of a Remarkable Radical* (Brighton, 1988). For important reassessments of the Spenceans and tavern radicals of the period, see Iain McCalman's remarkable reconstruction of 'unrespectable radicalism' in his *Radical Underworld: Prophets, Revolutionaries and Pornographers in London, 1795–1840* (Cambridge, 1988); and Malcolm Chase, *The People's Farm: English Radical Agrarianism 1775–1840* (Oxford, 1988). Critical engagement with the new cultural approach is to the fore in James Epstein's important articles, now published as a collection of essays, *Radical Expression: Political Language, Ritual and Symbol in England, 1790–1850* (New York, 1994).

Various ideological developments are analysed in W. Thomas, *The Philosophic Radicals: Nine Studies in Theory and Practice 1817–1841* (Oxford, 1979); Noel Thompson, *The People's Science: The Popular Political Economy of Exploitation and Crisis 1816–34* (Cambridge, 1984); and Gregory Claeys, *Machinery, Money and the Millennium: From Moral Economy to Socialism, 1815–1860* (Princeton, 1987), and also in his *Citizens and Saints: Politics and Anti-politics in Early British Socialism* (Cambridge, 1989). Despite its title, Barbara Taylor, *Eve and the New Jerusalem: Socialism and Feminism in the Nineteenth Century* (London, 1983) is restricted to Owenism.

The concluding chapters of John Cannon, *Parliamentary Reform 1640–1832* (Cambridge, 1972) provide the best analysis of the 1832 Act. For the subsequent development of middle-class radicalism, see B. L. Kinzer, *The Ballot Question in Nineteenth Century English Politics* (New York, 1982); N. McCord, *The Anti-Corn Law League* (London, 1958); and Alex Tyrell's study of the leading 'anti-everythingarian', *Joseph Sturge and the Moral Radical Party in Early Victorian Britain* (London, 1987). Stewart Weaver's study of *John Fielden and the Politics of Popular Radicalism 1832–1847* (Oxford, 1987) shows how one radical industrialist was drawn towards protectionism.

Such is the continuing flood of literature on Chartism that a revised and updated edition of the standard bibliography – J. F. C. Harrison and Dorothy Thompson (eds), *Bibliography of the Chartist Movement, 1837–1976* (Hassocks, 1976) – is currently in preparation. Certain works deserve special mention: Dorothy Thompson, *The Chartists* (London, 1984), the best general study; James Epstein, *The Lion of Freedom: Feargus O'Connor and the Chartist Movement, 1832–1842* (London, 1982), an exemplary exercise in the rehabilitation of a radical 'demagogue'; and J. Schwarzkopf, *Women in the Chartist Movement* (London, 1991), the first full-length (if not entirely convincing) study of the subject.

The new stress on continuity, asserted most forcibly in E. F. Biagini and A. J. Reid (eds), *Currents of Radicalism: Popular Radicalism, Organized Labour and Party Politics in Britain 1850–1914* (Cambridge, 1991), has brought an end to the comparative neglect of the post-Chartist decades. The standard studies of mid-Victorian radicalism by F. E. Gillespie, *Labor and Politics in England 1850–67* (Durham, 1927), and by Royden Harrison, *Before the Socialists: Studies on Labour and Politics 1861–81* (London, 1965), have now been complemented (if not superseded) by Margot Finn, *After Chartism: Class and Nation in English Radical Politics, 1848–1874* (Cambridge, 1983); and by Neville Kirk's Lancashire-based study of *The Growth of Working-Class Reformism in Mid-Victorian Britain* (London, 1985). Similarly, there is a new look to the history of mid-Victorian liberalism, most stridently expressed in E. F. Biagini's revisionist study of *Liberty, Retrenchment and Reform: Popular Liberalism in the Age of Gladstone, 1860–1880* (Cambridge, 1992). Of the new biographies of mid-Victorian radicals, the most lively is Nigel Todd, *The Militant Democracy: Joseph Cowen and Victorian Radicalism* (Whitley Bay, 1991).

The emphasis on radical continuity and the popular appeal of Gladstonian Liberalism has called into question the significance of new Liberalism. Liberalism, it seems, already resonated with a working-class audience before the adjustment to 'class politics' charted in P. F. Clarke's pioneering study of *Lancashire and the New Liberalism* (Cambridge, 1971). Whatever the electoral consequences, the intellectual development of new Liberalism still merits study, for which the best starting-point is M. Freeden, *The New Liberalism: An Ideology of Social Reform* (Oxford, 1978).

On the impact of socialist ideology and its adaptation to British political culture, see S. Pierson, *Marxism and the Origins of British Socialism: The Struggle for a New Consciousness* (Ithaca, 1973); Stephen Yeo, 'A New Life: The Religion of Socialism in Britain 1883–1896', *History Workshop Journal*, 4 (1977); and, with fashionable emphasis on continuity, Jon Lawrence, 'Popular Radicalism and the Socialist Revival in Britain', *Journal of British Studies*, 31 (1992). For the emergence of 'green' issues in the socialist–radical agenda, see S. Coleman and P. O'Sullivan (eds), *William Morris and News from Nowhere* (Bideford, 1990).

Henry Pelling, *The Origins of the Labour Party* (2nd edition, Oxford, 1965) is still the best introduction when read in conjunction with his collection of essays, *Popular Politics and Society in Late Victorian Britain* (2nd edition, London, 1979), which includes his contribution to the controversial debate on Labour and the downfall of Liberalism. For a brief introduction to this long-running historiographical controversy, see John Belchem, *Class, Party and the Political System in Britain 1867–1914* (Oxford, 1990). Duncan Tanner, *Political Change and the Labour Party 1900–1918* (Cambridge, 1990) provides a more detailed and localized discussion. Students should also consult the two collections of essays edited by K. D. Brown: *Essays in Anti-Labour History* (London, 1974), and *The First Labour Party* (Beckenham, 1985).

On women, radicalism and the vote, see Patricia Hollis, *Ladies Elect: Women in English Local Government 1865–1914* (Oxford, 1987); Jill Liddington and Jill Norris, *One Hand Tied Behind Us: The Rise of the Women's Suffrage Movement* (London, 1978); Jane Rendall (ed.), *Equal or Different: Women's Politics 1800–1914* (Oxford, 1987); and Brian Harrison, 'Class and Gender in Modern British Labour History', *Past and Present*, 124 (1989).

INDEX